UNDERSTANDING RESEARCH METHODS

A perennial bestseller since 1997, this updated tenth edition of *Understanding Research Methods* provides a detailed overview of all the important concepts traditionally covered in a research methods class. It covers the principles of both qualitative and quantitative research, and how to interpret statistics without computations, so is suitable for all students regardless of their math background. The book is organized so that each concept is treated independently and can be used in any order without resulting in gaps in knowledge—allowing it to be easily and precisely adapted to any course.

It uses lively examples on contemporary topics to stimulate students' interest, and engages them by showing the relevance of research methods to their everyday lives. Numerous case studies and end-of-section exercises help students master the material and encourage classroom discussion.

The text is divided into short, independent topic sections, making it easy for you to adapt the material to your own teaching needs and customize assignments to the aspect of qualitative or quantitative methods under study—helping to improve students' comprehension and retention of difficult concepts. Additional online PowerPoint slides and test bank questions make this a complete resource for introducing students to research methods.

New to this edition:

- New topic section on design decisions in research
- Additional material on production of knowledge and research methods
- Significant development of material on ethical considerations in research
- Fresh and contemporary examples from a wide variety of real, published research
- Topic-specific exercises at the end of each section now include suggestions for further steps researchers can take as they build their research project.

Michelle Newhart teaches sociology as an adjunct professor and works as an instructional designer at Mt. San Antonio College, a large, two-year college in California. A contributor to more than a dozen nonfiction books as either an author or editor, she holds a BA in sociology from the University of Missouri and an MA and PhD in sociology from the University of Colorado Boulder.

UNDERSTANDING RESEARCH METHODS

An Overview of the Essentials

Tenth Edition

*Mildred L. Patten and
Michelle Newhart*

Routledge
Taylor & Francis Group

NEW YORK AND LONDON

Tenth edition published 2018
by Routledge
711 Third Avenue, New York, NY 10017

and by Routledge
2 Park Square, Milton Park, Abingdon, Oxon, OX14 4RN

Routledge is an imprint of the Taylor & Francis Group, an informa business

First edition published by Pyrczak 1997
Ninth edition published by Routledge 2013

Editorial assistance provided by William Dolphin

Library of Congress Cataloging-in-Publication Data
Names: Patten, Mildred L. | Newhart, Michelle.
Title: Understanding research methods : an overview of the essentials / Mildred L. Patten and Michelle Newhart.
Description: Tenth edition. | New York, NY : Routledge, 2017. | Includes index.
Identifiers: LCCN 2016058231 | ISBN 9780415790529 (pbk.) | ISBN 9780415790536 (hardback) | ISBN 9781315213033 (ebook)
Subjects: LCSH: Research—Methodology.
Classification: LCC Q180.55.M4 P38 2017 | DDC 001.4/2—dc23
LC record available at https://lccn.loc.gov/2016058231

ISBN: 978-0-415-79053-6 (hbk)
ISBN: 978-0-415-79052-9 (pbk)
ISBN: 978-1-315-21303-3 (ebk)

Typeset in Bembo
by Apex CoVantage, LLC

Visit the eResources: www.routledge.com/9780415790529

CONTENTS

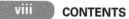

PART 8
Analyzing Data: Understanding Statistics   201

PREFACE

Understanding Research Methods provides an overview of basic research methods for use in courses offered in departments of sociology, psychology, education, criminal justice, social work, counseling, communications, and business, as well as closely related fields that would benefit from a survey of methods used in the social sciences.

WHY SHOULD STUDENTS HAVE AN OVERVIEW OF RESEARCH METHODS?

- Leaders in all fields rely on the results of research to make important decisions, such as how to adjust work environments to improve employee productivity and satisfaction, how to best address the problems of those who depend on social services, and which types of educational programs produce the best results. If students hope to become decision makers in their fields, they must understand research methods in order to effectively sort through conflicting claims found in the research literature and arrive at sound decisions.
- Many students will be expected to conduct simple but important research on the job. For instance, clinical psychologists are expected to track improvements made by their clients, teachers are expected to experiment with new methods in the classroom, social workers are expected to collect data on their clients, and many types of businesses use Internet or other data to track traffic and learn about their customers.
- All students will make lifestyle decisions that are at least in part based on research reported in the media. Should an individual take vitamin supplements? Which make of automobile is superior if the buyer's primary concern is safety? What are the best ways to promote healthy child development in one's children? Many types of answers are offered online, on television, or in print through social media, newspapers and newscasts, and in-depth articles. As a result of studying research methods, students can improve their ability to identify research-based claims and consume information crucially.
- Students may need to read and report on published research in other classes. They will be more skilled at doing this if they have a solid understanding of basic methods of research.

DISTINCTIVE FEATURES OF THE TEXT

In order to make this textbook meaningful, the following distinct features have been incorporated. Learning tools include the following:

- Material is divided into short "topics" instead of long chapters. These short topics help students take small steps through the exciting but highly technical field of research methods. Long chapters used in other research methods books prompt students to take big gulps, which often are not easily digested.

- Topics build on one another. When a topic relies on previously covered material, it begins with a reminder of what students should have mastered already. This helps students connect material, review appropriately, and make smooth transitions from one topic to the next.
- Technical jargon is defined in plain English and numerous examples make abstract research concepts concrete. In field tests, students agreed that this book is comprehensible.
- Exercises at the end of each topic encourage students to pause and make sure they have mastered the concepts before moving on. This is important because much of the material in this book is cumulative. Mastering an earlier topic is frequently a prerequisite for mastering a later topic.
- Three types of exercises are offered at the end of most topics to suit different teaching and learning needs. A set of questions tests comprehension of factual material. Discussion questions give students a chance to interpret and apply the material and work well to stimulate classroom discussions. Research planning questions provide direction and activities to help students plan a research project.
- Statistical material is presented at the conceptual level. It shows students how to interpret statistical reports but does not include computational details.

NEW TO THIS EDITION

In addition to its key hallmarks, the tenth edition incorporates new content and features:

- Several new topics have been added that help to contextualize research:
  - Topic 1: Knowledge and Research Methods
  - Topic 11: Ethical Principles in Research
  - Topic 15: Connecting the Literature to your Study
  - Topic 18: Why Academics Use Citation
  - Topic 20: Decisions in Quantitative Research Design
  - Topic 34: Sampling in the Modern World
  - Topic 45: Measurement in Qualitative Research
  - Topic 50: Designing Case Study Research
  - Topic 51: Mixed Methods Designs
  - Topic 65: Understanding Probability in Inferential Statistics
  - Topic 73: Regression Basics
- Several topics have been reordered and revised to create more coherence within the different parts of the book and to represent different dimensions of the research process.
- Qualitative aspects of design and analysis have been more consistently threaded throughout sections to ensure the topic is covered from start to finish.
- New examples from recently published research have been added throughout to keep this bestseller up to date.
- New figures and graphs have been added throughout to offer more visual aids to learning research methods.
- The appendices on electronic databases and electronic sources for statistics have been updated and citation guidance for psychology and sociology has been moved from the text to Appendices E and F.

ACKNOWLEDGMENTS

Dr. Anne Hafner and Dr. Robert Morman, both of California State University, Los Angeles, provided many helpful comments on the first draft of this book.

New material for subsequent editions was reviewed by Dr. Robert Rosenthal of Harvard University and the University of California, Riverside; Dr. Deborah M. Oh of California State University, Los Angeles; Dr. Richard Rasor of American River College; and Dr. George W. Burruss, Dr. Nicholas A. Corsaro, and Dr. Matthew Giblin, all of Southern Illinois University, Carbondale.

In preparation for the tenth edition, we received guidance from the following individuals: Daniel Choi, California State University, Fullerton; Richard C. Meyer, University of Nebraska at Kearney; Janice H. Laurence, College of Education, Temple University; and Julie A. Bardin, Florida State University. Special thanks to William Dolphin for his editorial assistance in preparing the tenth edition.

All of these individuals made important contributions to the development of this book. Errors and omissions, of course, remain the responsibility of the authors. The tenth edition welcomes new coauthor and sociologist Dr. Michelle R. Newhart. It is our hope that our combined disciplinary expertise and background across quantitative, qualitative, and mixed methods research will expand the usefulness of this book for beginning researchers.

Mildred L. Patten
Michelle R. Newhart

PART 1
Introduction to Research Methods

What is meant by research methods? Part 1 gives an overview of research methods and explains the types of research conducted in the social sciences and education. Topics 1 through 3 introduce research methods as a way of generating knowledge. Topics 4 through 9 describe common approaches to research, and Topics 10 and 11 introduce ethical considerations that underlie all types of research.

KNOWLEDGE AND RESEARCH METHODS

Research methods are the building blocks of the scientific enterprise. They are the "how" for building systematic knowledge. Let's take a moment to think about knowledge. How do you "know" things? One way you know things is through your own personal experiences. Even as personal experiences are rich in depth and detail, and create a lot of meaning in life, they are also quite limited in scope. If you try to generalize what is true for you, it is easy to *overgeneralize* and arrive at misleading conclusions for everyone.

Another fundamental way to gain knowledge is through the authority of others—your parents, teachers, books you have read, shows you have watched, news and articles from social media. This "second-hand" knowledge includes many diverse sources, and often this knowledge is more than one step removed from where it originated. Life is made simpler by inheriting knowledge from humanity's vast collection, instead of relying only on what you can discover for yourself. In fact, most people spend years attending school to acquire a basic set of knowledge that seems relevant for living and working in today's world. Even though it can still take a long time to learn even a small proportion of the knowledge that is available, the efficiency of being able to gain a lot of knowledge in this way benefits us and allows us to continue to build and further what is collectively known. However, not all information that is passed along is of equal value. While some of the things that we learn on the authority of others is based on scientific research, certainly there is much more information that is based simply on opinion, common sense, misinterpretation, or skewed information. It takes critical thinking skills to sort this out.

By learning about research, reading samples of research, and practicing research it is possible to expand your ability to think through knowledge and its acquisition in new ways. When you learn the rules on which research is based, you are learning to generate knowledge in the tradition and practice of science. Regardless of the method selected, social science research methods are designed to be systematic and to minimize **biases**. The goal is to produce findings that represent reality as closely as possible, overcoming some of the hidden biases that influence our conclusions when we are not systematic. As you will soon learn, research involves making many careful decisions and documenting both the decisions and their results. Decisions are important throughout the practice of research and are designed to help researchers collect evidence that includes the full spectrum of the phenomenon under study, to maintain logical rules, and to mitigate or account for possible sources of bias. In many ways, learning research methods is learning how to see and make these decisions.

These days, research is everywhere. Whether you pursue an academic career or enter an applied field, research skills are likely to have a valuable application. In academic research, the application is obvious. Academic writing nearly always describes research methods because academic work is judged first on the merits of its methods. Findings must be supported by how the information was collected, and whether it was thorough and unbiased, and addressed the research question appropriately. Outside of academia, more and more careers call on people to understand data, to design ways to solicit feedback or information, to actually collect the information, and to figure out through analysis what the responses mean. For instance, people in many fields and sectors of the job market want to understand who is using their products or services, how well they are carrying out internal or market objectives, how well their employees are performing, and who is interacting with their website or following them on social media. It is possible to specialize in research and become an expert in answering questions of this type, but even knowing some basic principles of research can help you to make intelligent and meaningful contributions. Knowing about research methods can also empower you in your personal life because it can make you a wiser, more critical consumer of all information. It can help you ask better questions about the information you encounter and ultimately act as a better informed citizen.

The accumulation of knowledge through research is by its nature a collective endeavor. Each well-designed study provides evidence that may support, amend, refute, or deepen the understanding of existing knowledge. However, individual studies, no matter how compelling, are rarely enough evidence to establish findings as "fact." It is through the ability to find similar findings across studies, and the variability that studies may find when they ask questions in different ways and of different groups, that theories (covered in Topic 3) grow to be established as our working knowledge. Much like language, scientific knowledge is a living conversation in which new studies and new inquiries allow what we know to grow and change over time.

■ TOPIC REVIEW

1. What are three ways we "know" things?
2. What makes scientific knowledge different from other types of knowledge?
3. What makes knowledge biased?
4. Why do research reports include a section describing research methods?
5. What is the goal of research in the social sciences?
6. What makes research a collective endeavor?

■ DISCUSSION QUESTIONS

1. Think about everything you know about schools. How much can you sort what you know from personal experience? From the authority of others? If you were to do research on schooling, what would you study?
2. Consider your chosen career path, or if you are not yet sure, bring to mind one career path you are considering. How do you think knowledge of research methods could help you in that career?

■ RESEARCH PLANNING

Think about a research interest that you have as you begin this book/course. Generate a list of questions that interest you about this topic. Are there any aspects of this research interest that seem especially prone to researcher bias?

TOPIC 2
EMPIRICAL RESEARCH

The **empirical approach** to knowledge simply means that it is based on observation, direct or indirect, or in other words, on experience.[1] In a casual sense, everyone uses the empirical approach in his or her daily life. For instance, a person may notice that the mail comes at the same time every day, and begin to expect the mail to arrive at that time, based on experience. Or a commute may typically take 30 minutes, so a worker decides to leave for work based on previous experiences of the commute length. As useful as observation and experience are, they can also be misleading, especially when they are not collected or reviewed systematically. In everyday thinking, we often make mental short-cuts that are helpful but not always accurate. We are all susceptible to biases in thinking that can cause us to overestimate the value of some information and underestimate the value of other evidence. For instance, **confirmation bias** is a tendency to recall or favor the information or interpretation that fits with one's existing beliefs. We give less con-sideration to information or interpretations that do not fit with what we already believe to be true. Not all biases are related to one's personal opinions. Take, for instance, **avail-ability bias**, in which we tend to rely on the most recent information we have or only consider the immediate examples that come to mind on a topic, which may not represent all the information very accurately.

It is also possible to misinterpret observations. A teacher might observe that students become restless during a particular lesson and interpret their response as boredom. The teacher may have misinterpreted the reason for the students' restlessness. The time of day may instead be the reason that students are restless, *not* the dullness of the lesson. Even if the lesson in question is boring to these particular students, the teacher might conclude that the lesson is boring to students *in general*. In fact, students who differ from the current students in ability level, background, or subject matter interests may find the lesson very engaging.

Researchers use the empirical approach as a way to avoid misleading results and poor interpretations. The key is carefully planning *why* they want to make observations, *how* to observe, *when* to observe, and *whom* they want to observe. Researchers create a plan or design, collect data in a systematic way, document their data collection, analyze data, and report the results. Empirical approaches to research encompass all research design approaches, including **experimental designs** and **nonexperimental designs** (see Topic 4). They include **qualitative** and **quantitative** approaches to research design and analysis. Research decisions about what methods to use comprise much of the rest of Part 1. Regardless of which method is used, researchers still need to answer these basic questions about their observations.

Let's consider a case in which researchers wish to determine which teaching approach will best help students acquire math skills. After considering their own personal experi-ences with learning math and reviewing literature on the topic, researchers learn that one effective approach uses "hands-on manipulatives." Manipulatives are concrete objects that can be viewed and physically handled by students to demonstrate or model abstract concepts. The researchers prepare a formal statement of research purpose, proposing to test "whether the use of hands-on manipulatives to teach Math Topic X will result in greater student achievement than teaching Math Topic X using a workbook-only approach."

Now that the researchers have defined their research question more concretely, they must decide how to carry out the research. Deciding *why* to make particular observations is connected to sufficiently narrowing one's research interest into a manageable project that has a clear research question. Approaches will vary depending on the question that is posed, the opportunities the researchers have to conduct research, and what information already exists to address the question.

Planning *how to observe* is also connected to matching approach and research question. As a part of the research design, researchers have to answer many "how" questions. This is because research involves translation between ideas and **measures**.[2] For instance, in the above example the researchers have to decide how to measure "greater student achievement." Figuring out *how* to measure something may be more or less challenging based on how abstract the concept that must be measured. Consider the first example of bored students in the classroom. Boredom sounds easy to identify but it can prove hard to measure. A person can "look bored," but how does the researcher know they are bored, and not simply sleepy? Perhaps the best method to measure boredom is to ask people to rate their boredom. This self-assessment approach might not work as well to measure differences in student achievement. Measures vary from established, standardized instruments such as psychological inventories, to interview questions that the researcher writes and adjusts to fit the goals of the specific study. Other examples of measures include surveys, scales, direct observation of behavior, and objective tests.

Researchers must also decide *when* they will use the measures to obtain the most relevant results. If you want to study student achievement, successful weight loss, criminal re-offending, or smoking cessation, your results may have a lot to do with when you ask. Measurement issues are explored in detail in Part 5 of this book.

When researchers plan *whom to observe*, they first decide whether to observe an entire population (such as all fifth-grade students in a school district) or just a sample of the population. If a sample is chosen, which is often the case, researchers decide how to select a sample that is not biased against any types of individuals or subgroups. For instance, asking students to volunteer to take a mathematics lesson might result in a sample of students who are more interested in, or better at, mathematics than students in the entire population. Such a sample might bias the results to look like better performance when compared against the population, which includes those who are less interested or more challenged by math. If a sample is biased and does not include all types of students who might be affected, the findings are less likely to align with reality. Methods of selecting unbiased samples are discussed in Part 4 of this book.

Once observations are made, the researcher has **data.** Data may be in the form of numbers, which are analyzed statistically. This is called quantitative research. Some data are not initially collected in numerical form but are translated into numbers. For instance, rating one's health may be in terms like "excellent, good, fair, or poor," which is then coded numerically and analyzed using statistics. Widely used statistical techniques are described in Part 8 of this book. Other scientific observations are *not* reduced to numbers but are expressed in words. For instance, interview data may be described in a narrative that points out themes and trends. Such research is referred to as *qualitative research*. The differences between qualitative and quantitative research are described throughout the book but are specifically addressed in Topics 7 and 8. Qualitative research design and methods are discussed in some detail in Part 6 of this book.

■ TOPIC REVIEW

1. On what is the empirical approach to knowledge based?
2. Is the empirical approach used in everyday living?
3. What does the question "how" establish?
4. According to the topic, do researchers usually observe a sample or a population?
5. Which type of research results are not reduced to numbers ("quantitative" or "qualitative")?

■ DISCUSSION QUESTIONS

1. Briefly describe a time when you were misled by an everyday observation (i.e., when you reached a conclusion on the basis of an everyday observation that you later decided was an incorrect conclusion).
2. You have probably encountered conflicting research reported in the mass media. For example, one study might indicate that drinking red wine improves health while another study indicates that it does not. Speculate on the reasons why various researchers might obtain different results when studying the same problem.

■ RESEARCH PLANNING

Return to your answers to the Research Planning activity in Topic 1. As you consider the general problem area in which you might conduct research, think about the "why," "how," "when," and "whom" questions posted in this topic. Take some preliminary notes on your answers to these questions.

Begin to think about the broad areas introduced in this topic, which will be covered in more detail as you work through the parts of this book. In your notes, consider creating headings for sections or pages to begin planning the following: "Research Question," "Design," "Measures," "Sample," "Timeline," and "Analysis." This will help you build a research plan. (Literature might also be a separate heading section; we will work on organizing literature separately.)

■ NOTES

1. Empirical approaches to knowledge are often contrasted with theoretical approaches, but they are not opposites and often work hand in hand. In a theoretical approach, researchers are often developing or testing a theory or idea about how the world operates. Examples of other approaches are (1) deduction, such as when one deduces a proof in mathematics on the basis of certain assumptions and definitions, and (2) reliance on authority, such as relying on a leader's pronouncements as a source of knowledge.
2. *Measures* are sometimes called *instruments*.

THE ROLE OF THEORY IN RESEARCH

Research and theory are interrelated. They form a cycle that is part of the collective dialogue of the scientific enterprise. A **theory** is a unified explanation of observations, some of which may otherwise appear contradictory. Typically, a theory will try to explain a relationship between two or more actions or things using rigorous criteria so that it aligns with logic and empirical evidence. Good theories are also designed to be generalizable to groups or situations beyond those immediately studied and to be testable, so that when they are applied to other situations there are clear ways to determine if they hold true, revealing their applications and limits. While theories often begin as ideas, they come to make up our working scientific knowledge when they are supported through the findings of repeated experiments or nonexperimental research.

Consider one of the most widely studied theories about learning: reinforcement theory. In this theory, positive reinforcement is defined as anything that increases the frequency of a response from an animal or individual. A common example of this is praising a dog as a reward for sitting on command. In reinforcement theory, the praise is the positive reinforcement, and it has increased the frequency of the sitting behavior in the dog, a part of learning. At first, reinforcement theory sounds obvious. If you reward a behavior, you increase the behavior that results in the reward. In a way, it is self-defining. Why would something that seems so obvious be so carefully studied? Because it explains many apparently contradictory observations. For instance, suppose an individual praises a dog regularly for sitting at first, but after a while, the person becomes lax and only offers praise for sitting every once in a while. What would you expect the result to be? Common sense might suggest that the dog's sitting behavior will decrease with the decrease in praise. However, we might actually observe an increase in the dog's sitting behavior because reinforcement theory indicates that intermittent reinforcement[1] is, under many circumstances, more effective than consistent reinforcement. Sometimes, answers that seem like common sense turn out to be right; sometimes the findings contradict the guess that common sense produces. Theories about behavior often start with common sense guesses, but research helps sort accurate guesses from inaccurate ones using empirical evidence and appropriate analysis of the data. Reinforcement theory offers an explanation for why certain behaviors increase in their frequency. Without this theory, it might be more confusing to understand behaviors that would appear inconsistent.

Sometimes, research is used to test hypotheses derived from existing theories. This is a **deductive** approach. It can also be considered a "top-down" approach because the theory precedes the data collection. Another way to think about the deductive approach is moving from a general principle to examining if it holds in a specific instance. **Hypotheses**

FIGURE 3.1 *"The Scientific Method as an Ongoing Process*"*

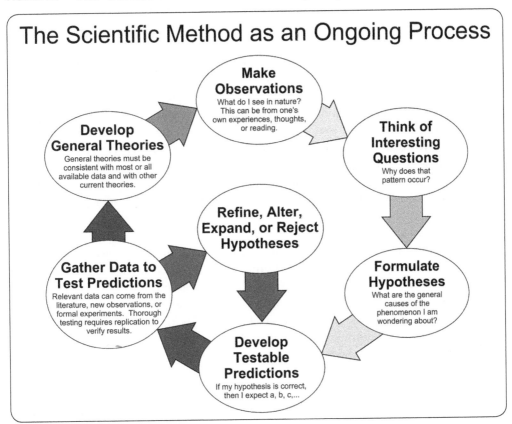

*this figure by Archon Magnus is licensed under CC BY-SA 2.0. It is loosely based on the wheel of science from the work of Walter Wallace (1971), *The Logic of Science in Sociology.*

are formulated to be consistent with the existing theory. For instance, self-regulated learning theory proposes that a student's level of cognitive engagement is determined by the goals they set. From this, a researcher might deduce that when students know they will be tested again on the same material, those who have lower goals (e.g., a goal of getting 70% right) should ask for less feedback about wrongly answered test items than those who have higher goals.[2] If this hypothesis is confirmed by the study, it lends support to the underlying theory. Assuming the study is methodologically strong, failure to confirm a hypothesis calls the theory (or parts of it) into question, causing theorists to consider reformulating it to account for the discrepancy. This is an approach that aligns with quantitative research approaches.

In an ***inductive* approach**, research provides a "ground-up" approach, using observations and conclusions to formulate a theory. It can also be thought of as moving from the specific to the general by adding up observations of specific events or people to notice patterns, and using those patterns to develop theories that explain the events or behaviors observed. *Qualitative researchers* often take an inductive approach to theory construction.

Consider the above example of the dog receiving intermittent positive reinforcement. It is the observations that reveal a pattern in which intermittent reinforcement produces more effective results.

Even though qualitative and quantitative research tend to start from different points, the process of science means that research often employs both approaches. Inductive observations of patterns may result in a theory that is then tested using hypothesis testing in a deductive manner. Deductive research may result in unexpected findings that the researcher then explores using inductive approaches. In truth, most types of research utilize both types of logic and benefit from going back and forth between data and theory. **Grounded theory** is a methodological approach that closely links theory development and research through an iterative approach[3] in which researchers alternate between theory development and research collection in an iterative fashion, so that each step influences the overall process. Both theory and data collection are regularly revised as new observations warrant. Figure 3.1 illustrates differences in the cyclical processes of the research method.

Students who are looking for a research topic for a thesis or term project would be well advised to consider a theory of interest. Testing some aspect of the theory can potentially make a contribution to the understanding of all aspects of behavior related to the theory. In addition, students will find it easier to defend their selection of a research topic and write the introduction to the research report if it can be shown that the study has implications for validating and refining an important theory.

When thinking about theory as a basis for research, keep in mind that no theory of human behavior is universal. There are almost always exceptions to every rule. This is why researchers usually examine *trends across groups* in order to test or develop theories. However, do not overlook the possibility of designing a study specifically to examine those individuals who do not perform as predicted by a theory. Understanding how the dynamics of their behavior differ from those of individuals who act in the way predicted by a theory may help in refining a theory to take account of exceptions.

■ TOPIC REVIEW

1. How is a *theory* defined in this topic?
2. Do researchers use "induction" *or* "deduction" to derive a hypothesis from a theory?
3. What are the two major functions of research mentioned in this topic?
4. If a hypothesis derived from a theory is not confirmed, what implications does this have for the theory?
5. Is grounded theory based on "induction" *or* on "deduction"?
6. Is the use of grounded theory more likely to be associated with "qualitative" *or* with "quantitative" research?

■ DISCUSSION QUESTION

1. Examine the discussion of a theory in a textbook in your field. Does the author of the textbook cite research that supports it? Does he or she suggest unresolved issues relating to the theory that might be explored in future research? Explain.

RESEARCH PLANNING

Is the purpose of your research to test a hypothesis deduced from a theory? (This is typically done by **quantitative** researchers; see Topics 7 and 8 for a brief explanation of the differences between qualitative and quantitative research.) Explain.

Is the purpose of your research to make observations on which a theory may be built? (This is typically done by **qualitative** researchers; see Topics 7 and 8 for a brief explanation of the differences between qualitative and quantitative research.) Explain.

NOTES

1. Technical terms for various schedules of reinforcement are not discussed here.
2. For more information on this theory and to see an example of research based on the theory, see van der Werf, G., Kuyper, H., & Minnaert, A. (2013). Emotions, self-regulated learning, and achievement in mathematics: A growth curve analysis. *Journal of Educational Psychology, 105,* 150–161.
3. For more information on the use of the grounded theory approach to research, see Part 6 of this book. Also see Zarif, T. (2012). Grounded theory research: An overview. *Interdisciplinary Journal of Contemporary Research in Business, 4*(5), 969–979.

EXPERIMENTAL AND NONEXPERIMENTAL STUDIES

Studies may have designs that are experimental, quasi-experimental, or nonexperimental. The fundamental difference between experimental and nonexperimental study designs rests in the use of a manipulation or treatment. Experimental designs introduce a specific treatment and then measure whether this treatment has an effect on some outcome. When used in medical studies, the "treatment" in the experiment is often a medicine, but in most social science disciplines, experimental treatments tend to be "manipulations." For instance, an educational researcher may wish to find out if students remember basic math skills better if they receive online math tutoring. Like the medicine in the pharmaceutical study, the online tutoring is a "treatment" that may or may not produce the desired effect.

Experimental and nonexperimental studies have different designs, which are covered in more detail in later topics within Parts 3, 4, and 7. To determine if a design is experimental or not, it helps to ask, "Will a treatment be introduced in the study?" However, introducing a treatment is not sufficient to make a study an experiment. Experiments must meet a few other criteria. Because experiments are trying to isolate the effect of the treatment, it is important to be able to rule out other factors. First, when possible, the researcher ideally measures how things were *before* the treatment was introduced. Consider the reasons for doing so. It would not mean much to give a group of volunteers a medicine that treats seasonal allergies if it was not known whether they were experiencing seasonal allergies *before* they took the medication. If the volunteers all felt perfectly fine after the medication, does it indicate that the medication is effective? Not if they all felt fine *before* the medication as well. For this reason, a pretest measure is highly desirable component of experimental designs.

If we continue with the allergy medicine example, we could find that a group had more allergies before taking the medication and fewer allergies after taking the medication. Is this sufficient to say that the medicine caused the relief from allergies? What if the pretest was taken at a time with a high pollen count, and the medicine was administered to the group on a day with a low pollen count? Everyone still reports fewer allergies, but there is another plausible explanation for the effect. Perhaps the difference resulted from the change in weather rather than the medicine. One way to help reduce the plausibility of other explanations is to have a **control group** that did not receive the treatment, in addition to the **experimental group** that received the treatment. A **true experiment** will divide participants into the control and experimental groups randomly (see more on random assignment in Part 5). Without random assignment to groups, a study does not meet the criteria of an experiment. In many medical studies, it is possible to make the study **blind**, which means that either the participant or the researcher does not know who received a treatment and who did not. In a study that is **double-blind**, neither the participant nor the researcher knows who is receiving the treatment. This element is not required to make a design an experiment, but it can reduce bias based on the expectations of an effect by either the participant or the researcher. Blinds are easier to introduce when the treatment is a pill instead of a manipulation, but it is still sometimes possible to use in the social sciences. One instance might be an education intervention in which those grading the assignments do not know which students received the experimental treatment and which were in the control group.

Experiments are generally considered a more definitive and rigorous form of evidence than nonexperimental studies because they answer more directly whether an intervention can help to explain an outcome, while controlling for other explanations. Some studies may be **quasi-experimental** by meeting some but not all of the criteria of an experiment. For instance, a study may include a treatment, before and after measures, and a control and experimental group, but no random assignment. This may still provide compelling evidence, especially if it can be argued that the control and experimental groups do not differ in substantial ways. At minimum, a treatment, random assignment, and a posttest measuring effects of the treatment can together comprise an acceptable experimental study. When few of the basic experimental conditions can be met, it is time to consider other possible quasi-experimental or nonexperimental designs because, as the allergy example above showed, each element that is missing or inadequate within an experimental design weakens confidence in the reported results. Sometimes, experimental conditions are not possible, practical, or ethical, and **nonexperimental study** is a better design.

In nonexperimental studies, researchers do not give treatments. Rather, they observe participants in order to describe them as they naturally exist, without introducing manipulations or treatments. Some common types of nonexperimental studies are **surveys, polls, interviews,** and **observation**. These methods may ask participants about their attitudes, beliefs, and behaviors instead of observing them. Nonexperimental studies come in many forms, which are explored in more detail in Topic 6. Generally, nonexperimental studies require a greater accumulation of evidence to support claims.

Let's consider some additional examples of experiments.

Example 1

Fifty students are divided into two groups at random. One group receives math instruction via a correspondence course on the Internet. The other group is given instruction on the same math skills using a traditional textbook. The purpose is to see if instruction via the Internet is more effective than traditional textbook instruction.

Example 2

A psychiatrist identified 100 clinically depressed clients who volunteered to take a new drug under her direction. She also identified 100 individuals with the same diagnosis and similar demographics (i.e., background characteristics such as age and gender) to serve as controls. The study was conducted to investigate the effectiveness of the new drug in treating depression.

Example 3

The students in one classroom were observed for an hour each day for a week, and their inappropriate out-of-seat behaviors were counted. During the next week, the teacher provided extra verbal praise when students were in their seats at appropriate times. During the third week, the teacher stopped providing the extra verbal praise. The results showed less inappropriate out-of-seat behavior during the second week of the experiment than in the other two weeks.

In Example 1, the group receiving the new type of instruction via the Internet is the experimental group, while the group receiving the instruction with a textbook is the control group. This experiment is a true experiment because all four conditions for an experiment are met: there is a treatment, participants are measured before and after instructions, there is a control and experimental group, and participants are randomly assigned using appropriate random assignment strategies.

Not all experiments are true experiments,[1] as illustrated by Examples 2 and 3. In Example 2, the experiment compared volunteers who were given the new drug with a group of individuals who were *not* given the new drug. In Example 3, the treatment consisted of "extra verbal praise." The classroom was observed before, during, and after the treatment, but there was no separate control group. This leaves open the possibility that another factor affecting the entire class could also help to explain the shifts in behavior over the weeks of the study.

Even though experiments 2 and 3 were quasi-experiments by design, they are still referred to as experiments because a treatment was administered. Consumers of research cannot distinguish between nonexperimental and experimental studies based on the type of measure used. Measures such as paper-and-pencil tests, interview schedules, and personality scales are used in both types of studies. The act of measurement itself is usually not considered to be a treatment. In fact, researchers try to measure in such a way that the act of measuring does not affect or change the participants. This is true in both experimental and nonexperimental studies.

By now, it should be clear that the purpose of an experiment is to explore cause-and-effect relationships (i.e., treatments are given to see how they affect the participants). The next topic describes how nonexperimental studies are also sometimes used for this purpose.

■ TOPIC REVIEW

1. Are treatments given in nonexperimental studies?
2. In an experiment, Group A was given verbal praise for being on time for appointments while Group B was given no special treatment. Which group is the control group?
3. Is it necessary to have at least two groups of participants in order to conduct an experiment?
4. What is the purpose of a nonexperimental study?
5. Is a survey an experiment?
6. Does knowing that a multiple-choice test was used in a study help a consumer of research determine whether the study was experimental *or* nonexperimental?
7. What is the purpose of an experiment?
8. A political scientist polled voters to determine their opinions on a decision by the Supreme Court. Is this an "experimental study" *or* a "nonexperimental study"?

9. A teacher compared the effectiveness of three methods of teaching handwriting by using different methods with different students. Did the teacher conduct an "experimental study" *or* a "nonexperimental study"?

■ DISCUSSION QUESTIONS

1. Suppose you read that an outbreak of intestinal disorders occurred in a town and the source was traced to contaminated chicken served in a popular restaurant. Is it likely the study that identified the source was "experimental" *or* "nonexperimental"? Why?
2. Have you ever conducted an informal experiment by giving a treatment to a person or a group and then observing the effects? If so, briefly describe it. Would you have obtained better information by including a control group? Explain.
3. Suppose you wanted to know whether having parents read to preschool children has a positive effect on the children's subsequent reading achievement. Do you think it would be better to conduct an "experimental study" *or* a "nonexperimental study"? Why?

■ RESEARCH PLANNING

Considering your area of research interest, what type of experimental study might reveal something of interest? What nonexperimental approaches might be fruitful?

■ NOTE

1. Types of experiments are explored more fully in Part 7, where the advantages of true experiments are discussed.

CAUSAL-COMPARATIVE STUDIES

As discussed in Topic 4, an **experiment** is a study in which treatments are given in order to observe their effects. When researchers conduct experiments, they ask, "Does the treatment given by the researcher *cause* changes in participants' behavior?"

When researchers want to investigate cause-and-effect relationships, they usually prefer experimental over nonexperimental studies. However, for physical, ethical, legal, or financial reasons, it may not be possible to conduct an experiment. For example, it would be unethical to learn about the effects of smoking by treating some participants with cigarette smoke by requiring them to smoke a pack of cigarettes a day for 15 years, and comparing this group to a nonsmoking control group, whose members are forbidden to smoke for 15 years. Clearly, the harm done to those forced to smoke would create ethical problems with such a research design. For this research problem, researchers cannot conduct an experiment. Even if it were ethical to conduct such an experiment, it might not be practical because researchers probably would not want to wait 15 years to determine the answer to such an important question.

When it is impossible or impractical to conduct an experiment to answer a causal question, a researcher must settle for information derived from nonexperimental studies. To continue with the above example, one way to learn about the relationship between smoking and cancer might be to identify a group with lung cancer. The researcher may then recruit a control group of individuals who do not have lung cancer but who are as similar to the experimental group as possible in **demographics** (basic statistical characteristics of humans that are used as identity markers, such as socioeconomic status, gender, or age) and compare them on prior cigarette smoking as well as other key characteristics, such as diet, exercise, alcohol use, prescription drug use, and other measures that may help determine exposure to environmental toxins. By choosing groups that are as similar to one another as possible *except* for having lung cancer, researchers can feel more confident in suggesting that the differences they do find between the groups may help to explain the difference in lung cancer status.

For instance, if the researchers find that smoking differentiates the two groups who are otherwise demographically similar, it suggests that smoking is a possible cause of lung cancer. However, there are several dangers in making a causal interpretation from a nonexperimental study. First, smoking and cancer might have a common cause. For example, perhaps stress causes cancer and causes individuals to smoke excessively. If this is the case, banning smoking will not prevent cancer, only reducing stress will. Another danger is that the researcher may have failed to match the correct demographics or other characteristics of the two groups. For instance, perhaps the researcher compared the group with lung cancer to a group without lung cancer based on age, race, gender, alcohol use, and activity level, but did not take into account whether the people in the study lived in urban or rural areas. If the group with lung cancer mainly resided in urban areas with heavy pollution, while those without lung cancer were all residents of rural areas, this weakens the argument that smoking was the key factor.

These types of problems would not arise in an experiment in which participants are divided by random assignment to form two groups. They would not exist because the random assignment would produce two groups that are equally likely to experience stress and equally likely to live in either rural or urban areas and, in fact, be roughly equal[1] in terms of all other potential causes of cancer.[2]

The above example of smoking and lung cancer illustrates a specific type of non-experimental study known as a **causal-comparative study** (sometimes called an *ex post facto* **study**).[3] The essential characteristics of this type of nonexperimental study are (1) researchers observe and describe some current condition (such as lung cancer) and (2) researchers look to the past to try to identify the possible cause(s) of the condition. Notice that researchers do *not give treatments* in causal-comparative studies. Instead, they only describe observations. Hence, they are conducting nonexperimental studies.

Although the causal-comparative method has more potential pitfalls than the experimental method, it is often the best researchers can do when attempting to explore causality among humans. Note that when it is used properly, and the comparison groups are selected carefully, the causal-comparative method is a powerful scientific tool that provides data on many important issues in all the sciences.

■ TOPIC REVIEW

1. According to the topic, do "experimental" *or* "causal-comparative" studies have more potential pitfalls when one is trying to identify cause-and-effect relationships?
2. Researchers look to the past for a cause in which type of study?
3. Is causal-comparative research a type of experiment?
4. Are treatments given by researchers in causal-comparative studies?
5. Random assignment to treatments is used in which type of study?
6. How is the term *demographics* defined in this topic?
7. A researcher compared the health of low-income adolescents who had received free lunches during their elementary school years with the health of a comparable group of low-income adolescents who had not received free lunches. The purpose was to determine the effects of free lunches on health. Did the researcher conduct an "experimental" *or* a "causal-comparative" study?
8. A researcher divided diabetes patients who were being released from the hospital into two groups. Upon their release, the researcher provided brief counseling for individuals with diabetes to one group while providing the other group with extended counseling. The purpose was to determine the effects of the two types of counseling on patients' compliance with physicians' directions during the first month after hospitalization. Did the researcher conduct an "experimental" *or* a "causal-comparative" study?
9. What is another name for a causal-comparative study?

■ DISCUSSION QUESTIONS

1. If you wanted to investigate the causes of child abuse, would you use the "experimental" *or* the "causal-comparative" method? Explain.
2. Suppose you read a causal-comparative study indicating that those who take vitamins A and E tend to be less overweight than the general population. What possible dangers are there in the interpretation that the vitamins *cause* individuals to maintain a healthy weight?

■ RESEARCH PLANNING

If you will be conducting a causal-comparative study, briefly explain why you chose this method. What are you comparing? What are the relevant characteristics that you would want to match in your two groups? What are some potential pitfalls that readers may want you to account for? How can you address these in your research plan?

■ NOTES

1. Because of the laws of probability, the larger the sample, the more likely that two groups formed at random will be equal in terms of their characteristics. Sample size is covered in Topics 31, 32, and 33.
2. The relationship between smoking and health has been examined in many hundreds of causal-comparative studies. On this basis, almost all experts agree that alternative interpretations are without merit. However, the results of some of the early studies on the health effects of smoking were disputed because the studies were not true experiments (i.e., they did not have random assignment to groups). Remember that most findings are based on multiple, sometimes hundreds of studies that support similar conclusions.
3. Other types of nonexperimental studies are covered in the next topic.

TYPES OF NONEXPERIMENTAL RESEARCH

As indicated in Topics 4 and 5, researchers only give treatments to participants in experimental studies. In nonexperimental studies, researchers observe or collect information from participants without trying to change them. Nonexperimental studies take many forms because they serve many purposes. The most common types of nonexperimental studies are briefly described here.

Causal-comparative research, described in the previous topic, is research in which researchers look to the past for the cause(s) of a current condition. It is used primarily when researchers are interested in causality but cannot conduct an experiment for ethical or other limiting reasons.

Surveys or **polls** describe the attitudes, beliefs, and behaviors of a population. To conduct a survey or poll, researchers draw a sample of a population, collect data from the sample, and then make inferences about the population. For instance, a researcher could survey a sample of individuals receiving SNAP benefits ("food stamps") to determine what types of food they purchase with this benefit. The results obtained from studying the sample could be generalized to the population (assuming that a good sample has been drawn).[1] If a researcher is able to interview everyone in a population (i.e., all individuals receiving SNAP benefits) instead of drawing a sample, the study is called a **census**. A census is a count (or study) of all members of a population. This is easy to remember if you consider that the United States Census, completed every 10 years, strives to include every single person in the United States. Unless a population size is small, completing a census study can be quite expensive. The anticipated cost of completing the 2020 census of all 300+ million United States residents is $12.5 billion!

While surveys usually include hundreds or even thousands of participants, a **case study** usually involves only one. For instance, some important theories in clinical psychology were developed from intensive one-on-one case studies of individuals. In a case study, the emphasis is on obtaining thorough knowledge of an individual, sometimes over a long period of time. Researchers do not confine themselves to asking a limited number of questions on a one-shot basis, as they would do in a survey.

In **correlational research**, researchers are interested in the degree of relationship among two or more *quantitative variables*. For instance, scores on a college admissions test and GPAs are quantitative (numerical), and because individuals *vary* or differ on both of them, they are variables.[2] If a researcher conducts a study in which he or she is asking, "Did those with high admissions scores tend to earn high GPAs?" the researcher is asking a correlational question. To the extent that the relationship between the two variables is positive—that is, the higher admission scores correspond to higher GPAs—the researcher can assert that the test successfully predicts GPAs.[3]

So far, studies are **cross-sectional**, meaning they are a snapshot of one moment in time. When researchers repeatedly measure traits of the same participants to capture similarity or change over a period of time, they are conducting **longitudinal research**. For instance, a researcher conducting longitudinal research could measure the visual acuity of a sample of infants each week for a year to trace visual development. Other examples include educational data, such as the Minnesota P-20, a statewide educational data system that collects student data from pre-kindergarten to completion of postsecondary education to gauge the effectiveness of various educational programs and initiatives.

Experiments and all the types of research mentioned so far in this topic belong to the class of research called **quantitative research**. A distinctive feature of quantitative research is that researchers gather data in such a way that the data are easy to quantify, allowing for statistical analysis. For instance, to measure attitudes toward Asian American immigrants, a quantitative researcher might use a questionnaire and count how many times respondents answer "yes" to statements about Asian Americans and then calculate the percentage who answered "yes" to each statement.

By contrast, in **qualitative research**, researchers gather data (such as responses to open-ended interview questions on attitudes toward Asian Americans) that must be analyzed through the use of informed judgment to identify major and minor themes expressed by participants. Most published qualitative research is collected through semi-structured interviews in which there is a core list of questions from which the interviewers may deviate as needed to obtain in-depth information. Other differences between qualitative and quantitative research are explored in Topics 7 and 8. In addition, Part 6 of this book describes qualitative research design in detail.

In **historical research**, information is examined in order to understand the past. Note that good historical research is not just a matter of developing a chronological list of so-called facts and dates. Rather, it is an attempt to understand the dynamics of human history. As such, it is driven by theories and hypotheses. In other words, by reviewing historical evidence, such as newspapers or other archival documents of the past, researchers are able to develop theories that may explain historical events and patterns. These theories lead to hypotheses, which are evaluated in terms of additional historical data that are collected. Historical researchers may use qualitative methods (e.g., examining historical documents, using insight and judgment to identify themes) or quantitative methods (e.g., counting certain types of statements made in historical documents). Historical research is typically taught in history departments and is not considered further in this book.

■ TOPIC REVIEW

1. Suppose a researcher administered an intelligence test to young children each year for five years in order to study changes in intelligence over time. The researcher was conducting what type of study?
2. Is the study in Question 1 experimental?
3. If a researcher conducts a poll to estimate public support for free childcare for mothers on welfare, the researcher is conducting what type of nonexperimental study?
4. A researcher determined the degree of relationship between vocabulary scores and reading comprehension scores. The researcher was conducting what type of nonexperimental study?
5. According to this topic, what is a distinctive feature of quantitative research?
6. How is most published qualitative research collected?

■ DISCUSSION QUESTIONS

1. Name a topic in your field of study that you might explore with a nonexperimental study. Which type of nonexperimental study would be most appropriate for your topic?
2. Think of a survey in which you were asked to serve as a participant. (You may have been sent a questionnaire in the mail, such as a consumer satisfaction survey, or you may have been contacted in person or by phone.) Did you cooperate and respond? Why? Why not?
3. Name two quantitative variables that might be studied through the use of correlational research.
4. Suppose someone prepared a list of educational events and their dates of occurrence in the past 100 years. Would the list be an example of good historical research? Explain.

■ RESEARCH PLANNING

Consider the differences in the types of nonexperimental research discussed in this topic. Which most fits with the study you would like to pursue and why? Does your research question clearly fit into one type? Explain the basis for your choice.

■ NOTES

1. Characteristics of good samples for quantitative research are explored in detail in Topics 25, 26, 31, and 32 in Part 4 of this book. Considerations in sampling for qualitative research are described in Topics 29 and 33 in Part 4 of this book.
2. Types of variables are described in Part 3, Topics 21, 22 and 23.
3. This relates to "validity," which is explored in Part 5 of this book. Correlational studies employ a statistic called a correlation coefficient, which is described in Topic 67.

QUANTITATIVE AND QUALITATIVE RESEARCH: KEY DIFFERENCES

Quantitative and qualitative research differ in many ways. The names derive from the key difference in how research results are presented. **Quantitative research** results are presented as "quantities" or numbers, which are usually but not always presented through statistical analysis. **Qualitative research** results are presented primarily through words, most commonly by interviewing people or observing settings and analyzing the data by reviewing interview transcripts and/or field notes. In qualitative studies, researchers often identify **themes** in the data. Researchers must identify concepts that are consistently raised, and the range of responses in relation to those themes, which are written about in the analysis of the phenomena under study. To arrive at different results, quantitative and qualitative studies begin with different plans and have different challenges in designing a study that will produce credible results.

Most research topics can be formulated into quantitative or qualitative research questions, but each approach has its strengths and weaknesses, and ultimately each type of research yields answers to different types of questions. Quantitative researchers emphasize studies that seek to generalize and approach methods with goals of objectivity and standardization. Qualitative researchers emphasize and study questions in which observation or interview responses are from participants who are involved in an interpretive process.

Qualitative researchers often approach planning *inductively,* and take an exploratory approach to questions that have not been adequately identified. They start by observing or formulating some well-designed questions to ask those involved in the area under study. From this initial data collection, the researcher may develop additional questions as themes emerge, allowing them to ask more refined questions about specific dimensions that turn out to be important. The strengths of qualitative research are in its ability to provide insights on interpretation, context, and meaning of events, phenomena or identities for those who experience them. Results from qualitative work are often expressed in a narrative format because respondents provide answers in their own words, or can be observed in real settings over a period of time, instead of being limited to specific choices in a survey, poll, or experiment. Qualitative research is good for research on topics or in settings where little is known, few theories exist, or the population is hard to reach.

Quantitative researchers often plan their research *deductively.* The most common approach is to evaluate existing theories on a topic and then try to apply those theories to a new or different scenario in order to see if the theories apply or require some adjustments when different conditions are considered. Quantitative research can help to extend the generalizability of information that was discovered through exploratory research. Most approaches to quantitative research aim for generalizability to a larger group but generally cannot reach all members of a group, and so the findings are based on a sample. The sample and measures have to follow procedures that improve the confidence with which results can be generalized to a larger group.

Qualitative and quantitative researchers examine previously published literature and include reviews of it in their research reports. However, quantitative researchers use literature as the basis for planning research, while qualitative researchers tend to deemphasize the literature at the outset of research, placing more emphasis on preliminary data.

When deciding on measures (sometimes called *instruments*) to use, quantitative researchers prefer those that produce data that can be easily reduced to numbers. This includes structured questionnaires or interviews with closed-answer or quantifiable questions, such as questions in a multiple-choice format. In contrast, qualitative researchers prefer measures that yield words or capture complex interactions and behaviors using rich description. This type of data collection is typically obtained through the use of measures such as unstructured interviews or direct, unstructured observations. It is always possible to reduce qualitative data to numerical data, but quantitative data cannot usually be expanded to provide qualitative data. Even though qualitative data can be reduced to numbers, this data may not be particularly useful because it may not meet the criteria used in statistical analysis of quantitative data.

Quantitative researchers often strive to select large samples to use as participants.[1] Quantitative researchers are able to work with large samples because objective measures such as anonymous, objective questionnaires usually are easy to administer to large numbers of participants in a short amount of time. Quantitative researchers tend to ask more targeted questions, and they hope to be able to generalize the results from the sample to some larger population, which may not be all people but may be a defined subgroup of people—for instance, all public school teachers in a specific district. **Statistics** can analyze a sample and estimate how well it represents a population. Because most quantitative research uses samples and statistical analysis, the sampling process is key to the credibility of the study.

In contrast, qualitative researchers tend to use smaller samples but spend more time with each participant in their study through extended, in-depth, unstructured one-on-one interviews and extensive observations over time. Qualitative researchers are more likely to select a *purposive sample* of individuals. The purpose of the study and the approach to analysis are different, and this means that the criteria for sample selection are also different. Researchers may select key informants and seek participants who represent the full range of those under study. If studying public school teachers, they might select several dimensions that matter for teachers' experiences, such as the district in which the person is teaching, the grade being taught, the subject taught, or how long the person has been teaching in the school system, and then ensure that each of these categories is adequately represented in the interviews or observations collected. Results often include verbatim responses from participants as evidence to back up analysis.

Because of the more intensive, sometimes participatory relationship to their research, qualitative researchers may choose to include relevant details about their personal backgrounds (such as having a mother who was a police officer) in order to explain their position in relation to their research and account for possible sources of bias in their point of view or how research participants responded to them.

While working with the participants, qualitative research designs may allow for the possibility of making adjustments in the measures, such as rewording questions or adding questions based on earlier responses by participants. Quantitative researchers seldom make such adjustments during the course of a research project. Instead, quantitative researchers plan their research in detail and follow the plan closely throughout the study because midstream deviations might be viewed as introducing subjectivity to the study. For data analysis, quantitative researchers tend to summarize all responses with statistics and seldom report on the responses of individual participants. Qualitative researchers, on the other hand, tend to cite individuals' responses (e.g., by quoting individual participants) in the Results section of a research report. Finally, quantitative researchers tend to generalize the results to one or more population(s), while qualitative researchers tend to limit their conclusions to only the individuals who were directly studied.

■ TOPIC REVIEW

1. Which method of research relies on the inductive approach?
2. Which method of research reports results using statistical analyses?
3. Do "qualitative" *or* "quantitative" researchers tend to rely more on published research literature in planning research?
4. In which method of research (qualitative or quantitative) would a researcher be more likely to make adjustments to the interview questions during the course of a research project?
5. Which method of research tends to have smaller samples?
6. Do "qualitative" or "quantitative" researchers prefer random sampling?
7. There are more likely to be quotations from participants in the Results sections of reports in which type of research?
8. In which type of research do researchers have more interest in generalizing the results to populations?

■ DISCUSSION QUESTIONS

1. In general, are you more likely to believe research results that are presented as themes and trends expressed in words *or* results described with statistics? Explain. (If you have not read academic research extensively, consider secondary reports of research such as those found in newspapers, magazines, and textbooks.)
2. Do you believe that both qualitative and quantitative research have valuable roles in advancing knowledge in your field of study? Why? Why not?

■ RESEARCH PLANNING

Consider your research question from both a "qualitative" and a "quantitative" approach, and think about what your final report would be able to discuss based on each approach. Which works best for your question, and why?

■ NOTE

1. Note that the term *participants* implies that the individuals being studied have voluntarily agreed to participate in a given research project. When individuals are being observed without their consent, they are more likely to be called *subjects*.

QUANTITATIVE AND QUALITATIVE RESEARCH DECISIONS

To understand some of the major differences in qualitative and quantitative research, consider this research problem: A metropolitan police force is demoralized, as indicated by high rates of absenteeism, failure to follow procedures, and so on. Furthermore, the press has raised questions about the effectiveness of the force and its leadership. In response, the police commission is planning to employ a researcher to identify possible causes and solutions.

Take a moment to think: If you were the researcher, what approach do you think would best suit the problem? A qualitative researcher would likely be interested in questions of "why," and might formulate some preliminary ideas or questions that can help to uncover how members of the police department are making meaning of these events or their reasons for participating in some of the reported behaviors. They might investigate by collecting preliminary observations and informal interviews. Questions would be exploratory and open-ended. The qualitative researcher would pay attention to topics that seem to come up with regularity—that is, the common themes that arise. Questions or observations might also attempt to learn more about specific behaviors such as absenteeism and the failure to follow procedures. Are these behaviors common or just a few people? Do they seem to cause or result in the police force being demoralized? The answers could help the researcher formulate additional questions and pursue those answers through more formal interviews or continued observations.

By contrast, a quantitative researcher would likely begin by reviewing the literature on topics related to organizational effectiveness, leadership, and demoralization in police forces or in other organizations. From this, the researcher might discover theories or combine ideas to hypothesize how leadership, police effectiveness, and morale are related. To see if the theories were relevant to the current case, the researcher would then formulate some hypotheses that could be tested by conducting research. For instance, maybe the researcher would read a theory about incentives that have been found to result in improved effectiveness in other studies of police behavior. The researcher could then carefully formulate hypotheses and create a plan to select a random sample that allows the results to be generalized to the department. The measure used might be a survey or an experiment that offers incentives to a randomly selected experimental group but not to a control group. In a quantitative study, the data will be used to either support or reject the hypotheses as potential explanations for the possible causes and solutions.

Each of these two research methods will need to carefully consider who is included in the study. Both qualitative and quantitative studies will have to decide how many people to include and how to account for meaningful diversity within the department. Diversity may be not only differences in race or gender, but also age, length of time on the force, people with or without a record of absenteeism, or people in different places in the department's hierarchy. Even though both studies must account for these factors, they will have very different criteria. As a method of analysis, statistics are evaluated on the correct selection and size of a sample, without which the results cannot be trusted to represent the larger population. The criteria in qualitative studies are not as reliant on the analytical requirements of the method, but the results will also be scrutinized for biases, and if it seems that groups were not included, it might limit the usefulness of the results.

Should the police commission select a researcher with a "quantitative" *or* a "qualitative" orientation? Clearly, the police commission faces complex decisions about how to improve the department. How would you answer the question in the first paragraph of this topic? What is the basis for your answer? Consider the discussion about qualitative and quantitative approaches in Topic 7, as well as the following points:

A. Some research questions inherently lend themselves more to a quantitative or qualitative approach. For instance, "What is the impact of terrorism on the U.S. economy?" lends itself to quantitative research because economic variables are generally numerical, and the question generalizes to a large group. "What is the emotional impact of terrorism on at-risk healthcare workers?" lends itself to a qualitative approach because it focuses on subjective effects, a more interpretive and harder to quantify issue. Note, however, that the second question could be examined with either qualitative or quantitative research.

B. When little is known about a topic, qualitative research should usually be favored. New topics are constantly emerging in all fields, such as new diseases (such as SARS), new criminal concerns (such as domestic terrorism), and new educational techniques (such as online adaptive quizzing). On new topics, there often is little, if any, previously published research. In its absence, quantitative researchers may find it difficult to employ the deductive approach or to formulate structured questions. How can a researcher decide exactly what to ask when little is known about a topic? In contrast, qualitative researchers can start with broad questions and refine them during the course of the interviews as themes emerge. Theories might be developed from qualitative results and lead to hypotheses that can be deduced and subsequently tested with quantitative research.

C. When the participants belong to a culture that is closed or secretive, qualitative research should usually be favored. A skilled qualitative researcher who is willing to spend considerable time breaking through the barriers that keep researchers out is more likely to be successful than a quantitative researcher who spends much less time interacting with participants and relies on honest answers to impersonal questions.

D. Consider a quantitative approach when potential participants are not available for extensive interactions or observation. For instance, it might be difficult to schedule extensive interviews with chief executives of major corporations. However, they might be willing to respond to a brief questionnaire, which would provide data that can be analyzed with statistics.

E. When time and funds are very limited, quantitative research might be favored. Although such limitations are arguable criteria for choosing between the two types of research, it is suggested because quantitative research can be used to provide quick, inexpensive snapshots of narrow aspects of research problems. Qualitative methods do not lend themselves to the more economical, snapshot approach. They can be, and often are, carried out by one person in an economical way when that person does the observation, interviews, and transcription of notes, but the work is intensive and likely to take more time than quantitative research.

F. When audiences require hard numbers (which legislators or funding agencies, for example, sometimes do), quantitative research should be favored or, at least, incorporated into qualitative research, possibly as a **mixed methods** project. When someone says, "Just the numbers, please," themes and trends illustrated with quotations are unlikely to impress. For such an audience, one should start by presenting statistics, when possible. This might open the door to consideration of more qualitative aspects of the findings. Notice that implicit in this criterion is the notion that both qualitative and quantitative approaches might be used in a given research project, with each approach contributing a different type of information. It is wise to remember that personal stories and narratives have a different power than statistics, but both have important contributions to make.

■ TOPIC REVIEW

1. Which of the following lends itself more to quantitative research?
   A. How do the social relations of adolescents who use illicit drugs differ from those who do not use them?
   B. How do school attendance and grades differ between adolescents who use illicit drugs and those who do not use them?
2. Which of the following lends itself more to qualitative research?
   A. What are the differences between the social interactions of students at commuter colleges and students who live on campus?
   B. To what extent does family income predict whether a student will choose to attend a commuter college or a college where most students live on campus?
3. Suppose a researcher wants to conduct research on members of a secretive fraternity. According to the information in this topic, which type of researcher is more likely to be successful in conducting the research?
4. If little is known about a new topic, which type of research is recommended for initial investigation?
5. For which type of research must participants usually be available for extensive interactions with researchers?
6. Which type of research is more suitable for getting a quick snapshot of a problem?

■ DISCUSSION QUESTIONS

1. Suppose a team of researchers wants to identify the characteristics of professors whom students perceive as being excellent. Would you advise them to conduct qualitative *or* quantitative research? Why?
2. Name a problem in your field of study that would probably lend itself more to the quantitative than the qualitative approach.

■ RESEARCH PLANNING

After reviewing this topic, do you have more insights on whether your research interest is better suited to qualitative or quantitative methods? Consider points A through F in the context of your topic of research interest. Do any of these points relate to your topic? If so, how might this advice influence your approach?

PROGRAM EVALUATION

Consider a school that receives a foundation grant for a new program that emphasizes parental involvement and shared decision making. In this program, decisions are made by an administrator with the advice and consent of both teachers and parents. The ultimate purpose is to help students improve on a variety of academic and social skills. As is typical of such grants, the granting agency requires a report on the implementation and effectiveness of the programs for which they provide funding. To prepare such a report, researchers conduct a **program evaluation** by engaging in **evaluation research.**

Evaluation research has much in common with other types of research, and it can take many forms and use many approaches including qualitative, quantitative, mixed methods, experimental, and quasi-experimental research designs. In fact, program evaluation is simply a research project in which much of the purpose is already defined by the program to be evaluated and the requirements of the granting agency. However, these elements of evaluation research create some major differences when compared with other types of research.

First, program evaluation is almost always **applied research** (i.e., research in which researchers wish to apply the findings directly to such practical decisions as whether to continue funding the program and whether to modify it). Experimental research, on the other hand, can be either **basic research** in which researchers are attempting to understand underlying theories that explain behavior without necessarily looking for direct, immediate applications, or applied research.

Second, new programs are, or should be, based on a **needs assessment.** A needs assessment is nonexperimental research in which researchers attempt to determine the practical needs of those who will be served by the program. For a school-based program, a researcher might ask such questions as, "What types of skills do the students need to acquire?" and "What types of program interventions to promote these skills will be most readily accepted by students, parents, and teachers?" Pure experimental research is seldom preceded by the formal needs assessment associated with program evaluation. A major goal of program evaluation is to estimate the extent to which a program has met the needs revealed in the assessment.

Third, the programs, which are analogous to treatments in an experiment, are usually subject to change during the course of the evaluation. For instance, perhaps a program is designed to give teachers a major role in decision making, with only a minor role for parents. If, in midstream, it is found that the parents are seeking more involvement, adjustments may be made in the program procedures to give parents a greater voice in decision making. Although it is almost unheard of for an experimental researcher to make changes in a treatment during the course of an experiment, skilled program evaluators are open to such modifications. In fact, program evaluators collect information during the course of a program that assists in modifying the program while it is being implemented. Collecting this information is called **formative evaluation.**

Formative evaluation has two prongs. First, information is collected on the *process* of implementing a program. For instance, when looking at the process, a researcher might ask, "Were the parents notified of the program in a timely manner?" and "Were the proposed meetings of parents and teachers conducted?" These questions clearly ask about the process, not the ultimate goals of student improvement. The second prong of formative evaluation involves collecting information on the progress toward the ultimate goals. For example, periodic achievement tests might be administered to determine if students are showing signs of improvement. If not, evaluators and program administrators might rethink the program they are implementing and make appropriate changes. By looking at progress, those responsible for the program can often prevent disappointment in the final results of a program evaluation.

When evaluators collect information about participants' attainment of the ultimate goals at the end of the program (e.g., at the end of a school year), the activity is called **summative evaluation**. A summative evaluation report contains information about the final or long-term benefits of the program for its ultimate clients (such as students). Summative evaluation often involves a comparison with a control group. For instance, students in a program might be compared with similar students in other schools who are not in the program. Note that while experimental researchers typically strive to use random assignment (like pulling names out of a hat) to form experimental and control groups, program evaluators usually have to find an external group (such as students at another school) to serve as the control group.

The final program evaluation research report should provide an overview of the needs assessment that led to the development of the program, the results of the formative evaluation (i.e., data on program implementation and client progress), and data from the summative evaluation (i.e., the extent to which clients reached the ultimate program goals). The report should also contain recommendations regarding extending the program in the future and for improving the program's implementation.

■ TOPIC REVIEW

1. Of "program evaluation" and "experimental research," which is almost always *applied research*?

2. Is a needs assessment associated with "experimental research" *or* with "program evaluation"?

3. Is it acceptable to modify the treatments (programs) during the course of a program evaluation?

4. Suppose that in a program evaluation, an evaluator asks, "How many children were reading at grade level by the end of the program?" Is this question relevant to "formative" *or* to "summative" evaluation?

5. Suppose that, in a program evaluation, an evaluator asks, "Are the clients in the job-placement program writing better résumés?" Is this question relevant to "formative" *or* to "summative" evaluation?

6. Suppose that, in a program evaluation, an evaluator asks, "Were key program personnel hired on time?" Is this question relevant to "formative" *or* to "summative" evaluation?

7. When a researcher looks at the process of implementing a program, is the researcher conducting "formative" *or* "summative" evaluation?

8. Is examining program participants' *progress* toward attaining the ultimate goals of the program part of "formative" *or* "summative" evaluation?
9. Is the attainment by participants of the final goals of a program a topic for "formative" *or* for "summative" evaluation?

■ DISCUSSION QUESTIONS

1. Suppose you were on the board of a foundation that was giving a grant to a social welfare agency's program. Would you obtain more useful information if you had the program evaluated by an employee of the program (such as the program director) *or* by an external, independent evaluator? Why?
2. Government agencies and organizations sometimes continue to fund certain programs despite prior negative summative evaluations. Speculate on some of the possible reasons that funding might be continued despite the evaluations. Are there reasons that would be justifiable?

■ RESEARCH PLANNING

Will you be evaluating a program in your research? If yes, name the program and indicate whether you will be conducting both "formative" *and* "summative" research.

THE DEVELOPMENT OF ETHICAL RESEARCH STANDARDS

Ethical considerations in research are associated with matters of right and wrong when research is being conducted on people (or animals). A formal set of ethics, and a review of research to ensure it meets these ethical principles, comes directly out of concerns in the scientific community and in society as a result of unethical research conducted during the 20th century. Some of the worst offenses were the nonconsensual medical experiments conducted by Nazi physicians during World War II on large groups of prisoners in Nazi concentration camps. They involved experimentation with medications, chemical warfare, and transplantation that routinely resulted in great harm to the subjects: trauma, disfigurement or disability, or death. Twenty-three of the doctors involved with the experiments faced trial for crimes committed under the guise of "research." In direct response to this trial, a set of 10 principles, called the **Nuremberg Code**, was formulated to define legitimate medical research.

It may not be hard to believe that the Nazis treated other human beings in unethical and inhumane ways that caused harm. However, it was not the only controversy that led to a more formal definition of ethics in research. Consider another notorious case from the United States. In the **Tuskegee Syphilis Study**, the U.S. Public Health Service followed a group of black men for 40 years, from 1932 until 1972, in order to learn about syphilis as a disease and understand its progression when untreated. At the time the study was started, there was no effective treatment available for syphilis. Researchers recruited as participants 600 black sharecroppers[1] from a poor rural southern community in Alabama. Participants were offered free medical care, meals, and life insurance to cover burial costs. Roughly one-third of the study participants did not have syphilis and served as the **control group**, while two-thirds had contracted syphilis prior to the start of the study. The men in the study were never informed of their disease, which the study simply referred to as "bad blood."

In the 1940s, it was learned that penicillin effectively treats syphilis. However, the researchers did not inform the Tuskegee study participants of this available treatment, nor did they treat subjects with penicillin. Instead, they allowed their research subjects to progress through the disease without treatment, even though doing so violated the Nuremberg Code. Outrage over the ethical breach of the Tuskegee study led directly to a report from the National Commission for the Protection of Human Subjects of Biomedical and Behavioral Research, released in 1978. Nicknamed the Belmont Report for the conference center on the Belmont estate in Maryland where it was produced, it summarizes guidelines for ethical research involving human subjects organized around three core principles of respect for persons, beneficence, and justice.

These are but two examples of research ethics violations in the 20th century that resulted in the formation of ethical codes for scientific research. Even though the Nuremberg Code and the Belmont Report are now historical documents, their basic principles continue to serve as the blueprint for the ethical rules that guide contemporary research on human subjects. These guidelines consist of rules to protect those who participate in research from harm. Topic 11 discusses this in more detail.

Most institutions where research is conducted have an ethics review process. At colleges and universities, the review committee is commonly called the **Institutional Review Board**, or IRB.[2] The IRB reviews proposals and monitors and approves research projects involving human subjects. This includes medical research and much of social science/behavioral research. Research that involves human subjects in the fields of medicine, health, psychology, sociology, anthropology, and education typically go through an IRB process of approval before the study is carried out. This includes work completed by graduate or undergraduate students, if it meets the definition of research and involves human subjects.

But what work counts as research that requires IRB review? Schools often use the definition of "research" provided by the "Common Rule," which was established in 1991 by the Federal Policy for the Protection of Human Subjects. According to the Common Rule, "research" is "a systematic investigation, including research development, testing, and evaluation, designed to develop or contribute to generalizable knowledge."[3] The key words here are "systematic" and "generalizable knowledge." Typically, this means that studies of a single story or case, oral histories, or other unstructured interviews may not count as research. If the goal is only to tell a single person's story or to report anecdotally rather than to draw broader conclusions from the data collection, it is likely not classified as research. Educational research may be considered exempt when it is conducted in an accepted educational setting and involves normal educational practices, such as instructional strategies or standardized tests. Likewise, observing public behavior without collecting information that allows the identity of those observed to be linked to specific people is likely not subject to review. However, it is best to inquire with your research adviser, professor, or your school's IRB office if there is any question about meeting the definition of research. The above types of research may still need to be submitted to an IRB to verify that the research plan allows the research to be exempted from further monitoring or review. For instance, research that only indirectly involves human subjects, such as working with a publicly available set of data, is still reviewed, but this may simply be to determine whether it is exempt or not.

To submit research for IRB review, documentation on the proposed research plan must account for the risks and benefits to those who participate in the research, as well as describe how subjects will be informed about the research and their right to withdraw from research at any time. It will also require a plan to protect the participants' privacy by keeping data safeguarded and stored securely. The ethical principles behind each of these considerations will be discussed in more detail in Topic 11.

■ TOPIC REVIEW

1. What examples of unethical research were presented in this topic?
2. What was the breach in ethics in the Tuskegee Syphilis Study?
3. What is the name of the ethics code formed after WWII in direct response to ethics breaches in research during the war?
4. What was the name of the ethics report after the Tuskegee Syphilis Study?

5. What goal did these ethics documents have related to human subjects research?
6. Who reviews and monitors research at colleges and universities?
7. What two qualities are required for a study to be considered "research" according to the Common Rule?
8. Is student work automatically exempt from research review?

DISCUSSION QUESTIONS

1. Review the Common Rule definition for "research" and discuss its implications for what counts as research, paying special attention to the key words. Try to formulate an example that shows the difference between a study that counts as research and one that does not.
2. The two cases outlined above were not the only cases of ethics violations leading to the formalization of ethical principles and ethics review processes for human subjects research. Bring additional examples of infamous ethics violation cases to class for discussion.

RESEARCH PLANNING

Consider the definition for "research" and the points made in the last paragraph about what you would need to report to an IRB committee. Generate ideas for how to incorporate these ethics requirements into your work.

NOTES

1. A "sharecropper" is a farmer who does not own his land, but rather rents it as a tenant and gives a part of each crop as rent to the landowner. It was a common practice during the period of Reconstruction, when the U.S. was attempting to re-establish the economic system in which blacks were afforded some opportunities in the labor force following the abolition of slavery. The sharecropping system was common in the South and in many ways substituted for slavery, creating exploitive conditions that resulted in poverty and debt.
2. Other professional organizations, including governmental agencies that complete research, have similar review processes, although the exact names and abbreviations of the review board vary.
3. "Federal Policy for the Protection of Human Subjects ('Common Rule')." 2016. Office for Human Research Protections. HHS. Gov.

ETHICAL PRINCIPLES IN RESEARCH

The principles in the Nuremberg Code and Belmont Report, on which much of modern IRB ethics reviews are based, revolve around a few important concepts. The first is that participants must be *protected from both physical and psychological harm.* The Belmont Report refers to this as the principle of **beneficence,** which means that research should strive to do no harm, to maximize possible benefits, and to use a research design that is best suited to minimize risks and maximize benefits. It is understood that not all harm can be anticipated in research planning, but it is the responsibility of the researcher to carefully create a research plan that minimizes the potential for harm and increases the potential for benefit. While harms should be minimized, the potential of the research to benefit society is also considered when weighing out a research plan.

Consider the following cases. A research psychologist might expose an experimental group to an anxiety-provoking stimulus in a study designed to advance a theory on the sources and effects of anxiety. Clearly, some participants might suffer mental anguish as a result of being exposed to the treatment. Participants also might be harmed in nonexperimental studies. For instance, the process of exploring sensitive topics (e.g., relationships with abusive parents) might cause participants to focus on them again, leading to renewed anxiety, sleeplessness, and so on. The research plan should minimize the possibility of harm and seek to mitigate any ill effects while maximizing the benefit to society. Risks in research should be proportional to the potential for their rewards to humanity. For instance, the above studies might improve understanding of anxiety, or increase an understanding of those who suffer abuse, leading to the development of more effective therapy or treatment options.

Another important principle within research ethics is that of **justice.** In essence, justice means that research subjects are all treated equitably, such that any burdens or benefits related to the research are shared fairly. It is especially important that vulnerable or conveniently accessible subjects are not exploited based on these characteristics. As an example, welfare subjects should not incur the risks of participation in a medical study that results in a treatment that only the wealthiest of society will benefit from.

In addition, those who participate in the research must be informed of the risks and the benefits of participating in the research and consent to participate, knowing that they also can refuse to answer specific questions or withdraw at any time. This represents the principle of **autonomy,** in which all individuals are free to make choices and participate in research voluntarily. A key to promoting ethical values is **informed consent.** To obtain informed consent, researchers tell the participants (1) the general purpose of the research, (2) what will be done to them during the research, (3) what the potential benefit(s) to them and others might be, (4) what the potential for harm to them might be, and (5) the fact that they may withdraw at any time without penalty, even midstream. This information is typically provided to participants in writing, and the participants (or their guardians) sign an informed consent form to indicate that they understand what they will be doing and freely agree to participate.

When those being researched have limited autonomy—including groups such as children, those with diminished mental capacity, or prisoners—additional safeguards are usually necessary to fully empower individuals in these populations to exercise autonomy in the context of their research participation. This may involve a higher standard of consent from multiple guardians or additional protocols that ensure the person is reminded of the voluntary nature of their participation.

Almost all researchers agree that participants have a right to *knowledge of the purpose* of the research before they participate. Having this knowledge, they are in a better position to determine whether they want to participate. Unfortunately, complete honesty with participants about the purpose of a study sometimes interferes with completing research on important topics. For instance, suppose researchers want to study the influence of lobbyists on a group of state legislators. The researchers might persuade some legislators to allow the researchers to shadow them (i.e., follow them around unobtrusively) if the purpose is only vaguely described as "to understand the state's political process." However, how many legislators (especially those who allow themselves to be unduly influenced by lobbyists) would agree to being shadowed if researchers revealed the true purpose of their research? Is it ethical to present only a vague general purpose that does not reveal specific goals? Do government employees have a right to privacy on the job? These types of questions illustrate the difficulties in balancing the need to protect participants with the need to collect information of benefit to society.[1] Providing the right context to obtain valuable data but satisfy the mandate of informed consent may require nuance and careful consideration to reach the right balance. Historical examples of research involving deception have become famous due to the controversy, but deception is still permitted in some rare instances when the value and importance of the study warrant such a design.

Certainly in instances of deception, but also in many other cases where any potential for harm was identified, participants are **debriefed** after participation in a study. Debriefing consists of reviewing the purpose(s) of the study and the procedure(s) used, with an offer to share the results with the participants when the results become available. The process of debriefing should also include reassurance that the data will remain confidential. In addition, participants should be allowed to ask for information about any aspect of the study in which they participated. During debriefing, researchers should try to identify participants who may need more help in overcoming unanticipated harm to them than a standard debriefing session provides. At the debriefing session, information should be provided on how participants can contact the researchers in the future, either for more information or to request assistance with any harmful effects that might be identified at a later date.

Another aspect of the principle of autonomy is participants' **right to privacy.** For instance, most individuals would probably agree that it would be a violation of parents' rights to privacy if researchers questioned children about discord between their parents without parental consent, even if the results might be very useful to educators, sociologists, psychologists, and other professionals. Related to this is the requirement to maintain confidentiality in how data is collected, stored, and reported. Even if participants freely and knowingly provide information to researchers, the researchers have an obligation to collect the information in such a way that confidentiality is protected. That may include conducting interviews in locations that allow for privacy, protecting the information collected by placing it behind password encryption, or separating the names of participants from their responses. In addition, the report itself should not discuss or describe individual characteristics of participants in such a way that the identities can be surmised. This is often accomplished in statistics by using aggregated numbers such as group averages.

■ TOPIC REVIEW

1. What is the principle of beneficence, and what steps should researchers take to support it?
2. What principle is involved when informing participants that they are free to withdraw from a study at any time without penalty?
3. Under the principle of informed consent, is it acceptable to hide the general purpose of a study from the participants?
4. Should informed consent be in writing?
5. Is debriefing done before *or* after a study is conducted?
6. What does debriefing cover?
7. Should information about participants be kept confidential even if the participants freely provided it to researchers?

■ DISCUSSION QUESTIONS

1. Is it ethical to present only a vague general purpose that does not reveal specific goals? Try to consider points both for and against this approach to research.
2. Suppose a researcher wants to keep a class of third-grade students in from recess to administer an attitude-toward-school scale. The purpose is to help teachers to understand their students' attitudes and how they might affect students' achievement in school. Is there potential for harm in this case? Would it be wise to seek informed consent from the parents? Why? Why not?
3. A researcher interviewed adolescents on their use of marijuana (with their informed consent). During the course of the interviews, some participants named other individuals who use marijuana but who have not provided informed consent to the researcher. Does this raise ethical concerns? What, if anything, can the researcher do to protect the other individuals?
4. Suppose one of your instructors asks you to be a participant in a research project but does not tell you the purpose of the research. Would you ask for information on the purpose before deciding whether to participate? Would you feel pressured to participate because the researcher is your instructor?

■ RESEARCH PLANNING

Consider the three principles of beneficence, justice, and autonomy. What potential issues would your study have in these three ethical areas?

Will you be obtaining informed consent? Will you have your consent form reviewed by your professor? By a university committee? By others? Explain.

■ NOTE

1. For more information on this topic, refer to *Ethical Principles in the Conduct of Research with Human Subjects*, published by the American Psychological Association. Visit www.apa.org for more information.

PART 2
Reviewing and Citing Literature

The first step in planning a new research project is often reviewing research conducted by others. This part of the book discusses the why and the how of reviewing literature, and explains how it can help new researchers identify a suitable research idea to undertake. Topic 12 explains the reasoning behind literature reviews, and Topic 13 describes how to approach the literature search, with an emphasis on how to use digital resources and electronic databases. Topic 14 helps familiarize researchers with the literature review by describing the common elements they contain, and Topics 15, 16, and 17 follow through on this by covering other good approaches to organizing and writing a synthesis of the relevant literature. Topics 18 and 19 cover some essentials on why and how to cite references based on different academic styles. Appendix E offers examples and technical advice for applying the American Psychological Association (APA) style and Appendix F covers the American Sociological Association (ASA) style when writing your literature review and research report.

WHY RESEARCHERS REVIEW LITERATURE

At the outset of a project, the researcher must translate the topic of interest into a researchable question. The process of taking an interesting topic and making it into a researchable question can be especially challenging for beginners, but the literature review can help. Remember the discussion in Topic 1 about research and knowledge. All research projects are part of a larger conversation and a larger set of evidence—the cumulative evidence produced over many studies across the research community that, when taken together, constitutes "science."

Literature reviews require the researcher to consider the important scholarly research, a process that serves to frame the research they are preparing to undertake. Framing research is another way of saying that the researcher is learning about the conversation around the topic of interest, and figuring out where in that conversation the new work will fit. It is coming to understand what is already known about the topic, what current theories are accepted, what competing theories there may be, and the conditions under which that knowledge was collected. In framing the research, a review of the literature also helps the researcher narrow the question by identifying overlaps, gaps, and ways questions have been framed already in the literature.

An examination of the theoretical as well as the research literature helps the researcher identify a specific research purpose, question, or testable hypothesis. In some cases, researchers may choose to replicate questions that have already been asked, and try to contribute more information to this conversation. In a **strict replication,** researchers try to mimic the original study in all important respects because the purpose of a strict replication is to see if the same types of results as those of the original study will be obtained. If the results of a study cannot be replicated by other researchers, the results of the original study may be viewed as invalid.

Another possibility is to locate an important study and conduct a **modified replication.** This is a replication with some major modification[s], such as examining a new population or using an improved measurement technique. For instance, in the case of studying the education of bilingual children, a researcher may examine interesting gaps in what previous research studied—say, in which languages the children are bilingual, or the ages of the children, or the educational outcomes being considered—and expand a question in that direction. For a question of this type, it can be useful to stick fairly closely, both conceptually and methodologically, to prior work in order to be able to more easily compare results and draw conclusions across studies.

Even when replication is not the goal, research questions often build upon or expand existing research. Published research studies typically make specific suggestions for future research in the last section of their research reports,[1] and those planning new research can draw from these suggestions to formulate a good question.

After examining the existing research in a problem area, a researcher may arrive at a creative idea that is *not* a direct extension of existing research. While there are important cases of this in the history of science, they are rare. Thus, it is extremely unlikely that a novice researcher will have such an insight at the beginning of a professional career. Put another way, new research almost always has its origins in existing research.

"New topics" that explore areas of new technology or trending issues are often still directly connected to existing research. Even when it seems there is no literature exactly on point, there will still be relevant literature that discusses the main theories or concepts being used, or that is at a slightly higher level of generality about phenomena of the same type. Take as an example the topic "How does social media affect the formation of friendships among children in grades 1 to 6?" Social media is new, and specific types of social media change in popularity fairly rapidly. What literature might you review? The literature on formation of friendships would be useful, as would any other literature that deals with technology and formation of friendships. Among the reasons for reviewing literature are identifying important studies that form natural neighbors to your idea, as well as learning about the theories they have used and findings they have reported. The questions that researchers explored in these studies can help you formulate a research question, as well as identify gaps and overlaps in who has been studied and who is absent from studies.

Because there are many topics on which the results of published research are conflicting, another possibility is to plan a study designed to resolve a conflict. Published reviews of research often point out such conflicts and offer possible explanations for them.

The literature review has many reasons. It frames the research, specifically by connecting the new work to existing research. It allows the researcher to show knowledge of influential work in the field to date, and to argue how the current study furthers prior work or is unique from it—in part answering the important question that every study must answer: so what, or why does this matter? In addition to framing research, literature reviews provide useful cues for writing a better researchable question. In addition to the content, literature reviews have three additional benefits. First, reviewing the literature helps researchers identify useful **measures** (also called **instruments)** that have been used successfully by other researchers. This may include identifying which standardized educational or psychological tests are commonly used in research on a specific topic, or reviewing the surveys that other studies have used to improve one's own questions or align them for more direct comparison with existing studies. It is also a way to identify seriously flawed measures, which can then be avoided. Second, a researcher may be able to identify and avoid dead end topics: ideas for research that may have already been thoroughly investigated and shown to be unsuccessful. An example is a treatment that was tried but failed to produce the desired effects in an experiment. Third, researchers can get ideas on report structure. Reviewing the literature offers many examples for how to organize and write research reports. By paying careful attention to the style and organization used by previous researchers, researchers can get ideas for how to best structure their own writing.

Literature reviews can stand alone as articles, and some types of journals or annual reviews are dedicated to publishing them. They help newcomers or non-specialists by offering detailed overviews on specific topics, summarizing the history of research on each topic, as well as its current status and controversies. In addition standalone literature review articles often provide specific details about how the literature was reviewed—for instance, such a review would describe what journals or databases were searched, for which years, and with what key terms. It would report the number of results returned and explain how those results were then sorted. These aspects of the standalone literature review serve a purpose similar to documenting how empirical research is carried out—they provide transparency in the methods used to allow the reader to assess the value, comprehensiveness, and limitations of the reported results.

Most often, literature reviews are a part of introducing empirical research. A well-crafted literature review will show the readers the context within which the research was conducted. For students conducting research, writing reviews of research allows them to demonstrate to instructors, thesis committee members, and others that they are aware of and conversant in the research that is relevant to their study. In the next topic, methods for searching for literature electronically are explored. Then, the remaining Part 2 topics explore specific techniques for writing literature reviews.

■ TOPIC REVIEW

1. When planning research, which should come first?
   A. Identify a broad problem area
   B. Develop a testable hypothesis or research problem
2. Suppose a researcher conducted a replication of a study but used a sample from a population different from the one used in the first study. What type of replication did the researcher conduct?
3. Should a researcher be surprised to find conflicting results in the research literature on a given topic?
4. According to this topic, students would be wise to try to find a creative, new research idea (not derived from the literature) to explore in their first research project. Is this statement true *or* false?
5. How can a researcher use a review of literature to help justify a study they have undertaken?

■ DISCUSSION QUESTION

1. What information in this topic most convinces you that reviewing published literature is an important part of the research-planning process? Explain.

■ RESEARCH PLANNING

Have you begun reading the literature on your problem area? If yes, which description best fits your research approach at present (strict replication, modified replication, newly combined area, resolving a conflict)? How might this shape your review of the literature? Explain.

Was your research purpose or hypothesis explicitly suggested in the literature you have read? Explain.

■ NOTE

1. The last section is usually labeled "Discussion." See Part 10 for more information on the typical structure of research reports.

LOCATING LITERATURE IN ELECTRONIC DATABASES

Most original reporting of empirical research appears as articles published in scholarly journals, and journals are most easily found in databases. This topic explores how to locate journal articles using online research databases. Most researchers and students access journal content through the databases to which their libraries subscribe. These databases are curated collections of published, scholarly, peer-reviewed work that can be easily sorted and filtered to find specific articles. Without a database subscription, the content is behind a paywall, although there are exceptions. (The educational database *ERIC* is an example. For more information on electronic databases, see Appendix A.) Limited content such as abstracts or excerpts of content are often available for free online.

Database searches work a bit differently than searching the web. Web searches are more flexible, but because they are not limited to scholarly work (unless you select to search from a site that aggregates only scholarly work, such as Google Scholar), finding research articles among the search results can be challenging. Even if searches in web browsers pull a list of scholarly articles, clicking on a link often leads to a paywall instead of an article, unless the person holds a subscription or is logged into a library that subscribes to that resource.

Databases are curated to a specific set of sources, such as a group of journals, but sometimes contain other items such as newspaper articles, book abstracts, or government documents. Four of the most commonly used databases in the social and behavioral sciences are: (1) *Sociological Abstracts*, which covers journal articles published in more than 1,800 journals; (2) *PsycINFO*, which contains more than 2.6 million citations; (3) *PsycARTICLES*, which includes over 25,000 searchable full-text journal articles dating as far back as 1894; and (4) the already mentioned *ERIC*, which contains abstracts of articles in education found in more than 1,165 journals dating from 1966 to the present. Not all databases are limited to peer-reviewed, scholarly journals. For instance, Sociological Abstracts includes dissertations, *PsycINFO* includes books, and *ERIC* includes unpublished documents, such as conference papers.

These are just a few of the many additional databases out there. College libraries usually list their collection on a webpage and often group databases by subject area to help students identify the most relevant listings. Some important electronic databases are described in Appendix A. Whichever database is used, it is important to first read carefully the instructions for using the particular database being accessed. All databases allow searches based on publication information and keywords, but the entry of search information differs, and databases offer different special features to assist users.

Locating literature electronically requires both technique and technical knowledge. First, technique. The main technique to develop is the ability to identify the right databases and search terms or combinations of terms in order to find the most relevant literature. To generate a useful list of terms, think through the specific parameters of your research, paying special attention to the specific terminology associated with the topic you are studying and the concepts important to your research questions. For instance, if you are studying bilingual education, you may not only want to look up "bilingual," but also the specific aspect you are interested in. What outcomes are you reviewing? Are they related to specific theories of development or intelligence? Identify words or phrases that relate to the research. Consider synonyms for the words or phrases that you have identified. These terms and combinations can help you expand or narrow your search.

Now, the technical. Searching databases works best when you know some basic rules. Databases are designed to help you find what you are looking for. For instance, articles are tagged with standardized subject terms or keywords in order to help searches pull the most relevant results, even when articles use different terminology. For example, if you look up "adaptive learning," you may find that the subject listed is actually "adaptive testing." After verifying that the two concepts are discussing the same thing, you may find that using this standardized subject term yields much better results. Subject words are usually listed along the side of the results, in the preview, or in the article record, which you see when you click on the article title. You can also narrow results by using advanced search options to limit dates or language.

Databases (and Google searches) understand **Boolean operators**, also known as **logical operators,** so you can use the words AND, OR, and NOT (usually they must be capitalized) to string together a set of conditions that will help to expand or narrow a search. Using AND narrows a search because it imposes two conditions for an entry to qualify. For instance, searching "adaptive AND learning" creates a smaller pool of returned results because the entry has to contain both words to come back in the results. Using OR expands the search because entries need only contain one of the terms listed to be returned in the search. "Adaptive OR learning" means that entries with either word would be returned, so there are many more results. Figure 13.1 A and B illustrates the use of the Boolean searches.

A search can also be made more precise by using *NOT*. Using the instruction *"alcohol abuse NOT college"* will identify all articles relating to alcohol abuse but exclude those that relate to alcohol abuse at the college level. This is helpful if a word can be interpreted in more than one way (e.g., "ball" can be a round object used in sports, or a dance that Cinderella attends) by identifying an association with the unintended meaning and excluding it from the search.

While databases are ultimately needed, a literature search can be started using a search engine such as Google Scholar. While complete versions of articles may not be accessible, **abstracts** can be viewed. Abstracts appear at the beginning of articles and offer a very short, 50- to 300-word summary of the article's contents: the research question, what information was collected, and the key findings. Abstracts provide enough information to determine if an article is relevant, and can also help to identify good search terms. To use an article in a literature review, more than the abstract is needed, but relevant articles can be identified and the information can be used to look them up in the library's databases.

Another helpful way to identify relevant articles is to locate annual review journals, sometimes called "annals," within your discipline. Annual review articles provide a comprehensive review of the primary research done on specific themes and topics. These articles present an overarching frame, identifying trends from specific eras and presenting the camps of differing opinion on an issue. Their bibliographies can become a list of

FIGURE 13.1A Boolean results: adaptive AND testing AND college.

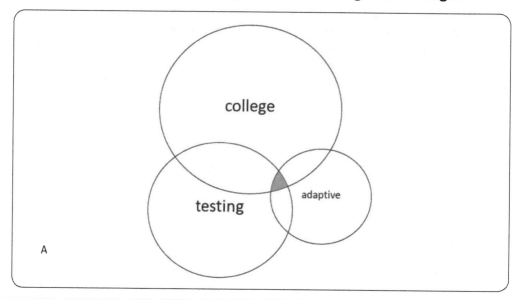

FIGURE 13.1B Boolean results: adaptive AND testing NOT college.

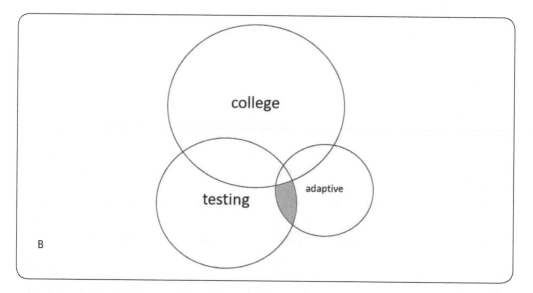

To visualize Boolean logic, imagine a search for adaptive AND testing AND college. This would return the part that includes the space where all three overlap, which is the gray area in Figure 13.1A. You can see how requiring all three terms reduces the results of the search. In Figure 13.1B, notice how the gray area for the results changes when the request is adaptive AND testing NOT college.

suggested sources to investigate. In addition to the bibliography, many databases also let you see who has cited the current article since it was published. Sometimes, the papers that cite articles you are interested in also become good items to include in your own review.

As with all things in research methods, it is best to document the literature search, especially searches in online databases when you have reached a set of useful search parameters. Record what databases were searched, and the exact parameters you used to complete the search, including exact words and dates. Record the number of results that were returned. When you write up your research, it will be useful to be able to report exactly what you searched where and the results you got. Decisions on which database and which search terms to use should be logical. If a large number of results were returned, you may want to remember the themes that appeared across your search results so you can explain why you skipped over some results. For instance, if you documented that you searched for "depression" and "college" in *PsycInfo*, limiting to peer-reviewed, scholarly articles, you may want to say that some articles were about clinical education for treatment, and these results were not relevant. If several well-designed searches revealed very few studies, it may be worth discussion when you report on your research, especially if you are making a case that your topic has not been explored. However, to make this case, your search must be diligent and well crafted; otherwise, readers may question whether the results were instead due to poor search techniques. For more information on accessing electronic databases or searching for articles to include in a literature review, consult a college reference librarian. Seriously. They are there to help you, and they are experts in searches. You can learn a lot and save yourself the time and uncertainty about the quality of your search. Once you find relevant literature, what do you do with it? That is the subject of the next four topics.

■ TOPIC REVIEW

1. What is a database?
2. What are some differences between web searches and database searches?
3. What are some benefits for using database searches instead of searching for articles at home on the Internet?
4. What is a technique for preparing to search a database?
5. What is a "subject" within a database?
6. Which of the following will yield a larger number of references?
   A. A search using "alcohol abuse *AND* treatment."
   B. A search using "alcohol abuse *OR* treatment."
7. If a researcher wanted to search for journal articles on Term A but wanted to exclude articles that also include Term B, which logical operator should the researcher use?
8. What are two techniques for locating useful literature for the review in addition to searching databases?

■ DISCUSSION QUESTIONS

1. When you next search for journal articles, what advice from this topic will you put to use to approach your search?

2. If you have searched for journal articles in the past, briefly describe your experience(s). Was it easy to do? What suggestions do you have for others who will be doing it for the first time?

■ RESEARCH PLANNING

Name some keywords you might use in an electronic search of the literature. Try referring to a thesaurus, specialized encyclopedia, or the standardized database terms for your keywords. Now locate at least three databases you plan to access, and find the contact info of the research librarian you can call or email with questions.

STRUCTURING THE LITERATURE REVIEW

A literature review's main purpose is to summarize the existing scholarship. It is a standard part of a research report whose role is to introduce themes and topics in previously published articles and books that orient the reader to the conversation about the topic. Often, it presents persuasive information to help make a case about the importance of the topic and research.

Literature reviews start most writing that reports original research, including journal articles, theses, dissertations, and sometimes student papers. When the literature review is a part of a larger work, it comprises about 20% of that piece of work. It may be only a few paragraphs in a shorter length article or consist of a chapter in most dissertations. As mentioned in Topic 12, literature reviews can be published as standalone articles, but the most common type of literature review is the one found at the outset of an empirical article. We will focus on this example in this topic.

In empirical articles, the literature review often appears at the beginning, and may flow directly from the introductory paragraph or follow directly after an introduction. It may or may not be labeled with a heading, depending on journal style and length of article. It provides context for the presentation of original research, followed by sections about the study's hypotheses, methods, and findings, and a concluding section that discusses the broader implications of the findings, as well as their limitations.

A straightforward recipe for starting a literature review is to define key terms and establish the importance of the research topic. There are a few tried and true ways to establish a topic's importance. One is to provide a compelling key statistic. Example 1 is the first paragraph of an original research article on fear of cancer recurrence among breast cancer survivors, taken from the journal *Health Psychology*.

Example 1

Breast cancer affects 1 in 8 women in North America (American Cancer Society, 2011; Canadian Cancer Society, 2011). The majority of breast cancer patients successfully complete treatment and become survivors. Studies show that survivors have unmet needs (i.e., supportive care needs that, according to the survivor, have not yet been appropriately addressed; Harrison, Young, Price, Butow & Solomon, 2009), the most frequently cited one being fear of cancer recurrence (FCR; Baker, Denniston, Smith, & West, 2005; Herschbach et al., 2004; Lebel, Rosberger, Edgar, & Devins, 2007). FCR has been described as the sword of Damocles that hangs over patients for the rest of their lives (Baker et al., 2005). FCR is defined as "the fear or worry that the cancer will return or progress in the same organ or in another part of the body" (Simard & Savard, 2009; Vickberg, 2003). The current literature suggests that moderate to high levels of FCR affect 33% to 56% of cancer patients (Llewellyn, Weinman,

McGurk, & Humphris, 2008; Vickberg, 2003). FCR is associated with impairment in functioning, psychological distress, stress-response symptoms, and lower quality of life (Dow, Ferrell, Leigh, Ly, & Gulasekaram, 96; Mellon, Northouse, & Weiss, 2006; Vickberg, 2003).[1]

The authors begin with a compelling statistic. Note that each claim made in this paragraph is supported by citations. The language is careful. This is an important aspect of the literature review portion of academic work (discussed more in Topic 18). It is critical that the premises on which the article is based are not simply the author's opinion but reflect the findings of existing research, and that claims do not overstate the conclusions in the original source[s]. For instance, when the authors state, "Studies show" that survivors have unmet needs, the citation includes more than one study. Overstating the findings of prior research or sloppiness in describing them will undermine the credibility of not just the literature review but the report as a whole.

Statistics are not the only evidence that is connected to sources; the author is careful to define the major terms related to the study that will follow. Key terms should be clearly defined. Definitions may also include concrete information on what is included within a term, or how it is measured. For instance, the main term, fear of cancer recurrence, or FCR, is both defined and linked to important outcomes. When the authors discuss "unmet needs," they begin to clarify what needs are included (supportive care needs).

Literature reviews often start with a combination of definitions and statements of supporting evidence (with statistics, if any) indicating the importance of the problem area.[2] Note that definitions are not invented by the authors. It is acceptable to quote a published conceptual definition, as long as the source is properly cited. Definitions and statistics are central elements to establish a topic that will be presented in the research. Other strategies for making a persuasive argument include establishing that a trend is increasing or decreasing, arguing for the importance of the trend, making a case that a particular topic has not been adequately covered in other studies, or providing facts that may surprise the reader about something familiar to them. All three strategies help to make a case for the importance of the contribution the new research can make.

Example 2 comes from the literature review in a peer-reviewed article on cyberbullying. This article had a separate introduction and literature review. The introduction included definitions of bullying and cyberbullying in making the claim (with citations) that bullying is not new, but cyberbullying is on the rise. This excerpt shows the first sentences from the Literature Review section:

Example 2

Prior to 2002, no research existed on the topic of cyber-bullying (Hinduja & Patchin, 2012). However, researchers have found that two-thirds of students reported that cyber-bullying is just as serious as traditional bullying, if not worse, as people often feel shielded from the ramifications of their actions and, therefore, may state things they would not ordinarily say in person (Strom et al., 2012). Further research conducted on 124 middle school students found that 32% of its participants felt that cyber-bullying was a problem in their school (Accordino & Accordino, 2011). Interestingly, research suggests that the highest frequency of cyber-bullying is found in public schools, followed by all-girl private schools, with the least cyber-bullying incidents occurring at private charter schools (Mark & Ratliffe, 2011).[3]

In this example, you can see some commonly used elements of the literature review in action. The report claims that there was little research prior to 2002. Statistics claim that many students are affected, and establish that the issue is important to students. There is also a fact of interest (where bullying most frequently occurs) that might surprise or contradict what someone expects about the trend in cyberbullying. All claims presented are tied to sources, and all relate directly to the specific areas that the research in the report will cover.

■ TOPIC REVIEW

1. What is the purpose of the literature review?
2. What are different types of articles or reports that include literature reviews?
3. What portion of research reports typically consists of the literature review?
4. This topic suggests two elements that writers almost always use to begin a literature review. What are these two elements?
5. What are some additional strategies to begin a literature review?
6. Review the examples. Can you find an illustration where the citations match the language used in the claims? Are there examples where they do not match?

■ DISCUSSION QUESTIONS

1. Why is careful language important to making claims in the literature review? What are some examples of how to use language carefully when making claims in a literature review?
2. Consider the literature review excerpts in Appendix C. Each excerpt shows the beginning paragraph(s) of a literature review in a research article. In your opinion, do they each convince you of the importance of the respective problem areas? Explain.

■ RESEARCH PLANNING

What statistics might open your literature review? What terms might be important to define at the outset? How might you use some of the other suggested strategies to persuade your readers that your research topic is important?

■ NOTES

1. Lebel, S., Beattie, S., Arès, I., & Bielajew, C. (2013). Young and worried: Age and fear of recurrence in breast cancer survivors. *Health Psychology, 32*, 695–705. doi:10.1037/a0030186
2. See Appendix C for examples of beginnings of reviews.
3. Herrera, J., Kupczynski, L., & Mundy, M. (2015). The impact of training on faculty and student perceptions of cyberbullying in an urban south central Texas middle school. *Research in Higher Education Journal, 27*, 29 pages.

CONNECTING THE LITERATURE TO YOUR STUDY

Topic 13 discussed how to locate relevant literature for your study and Topic 14 discussed ways to begin a literature review. This topic continues to build the literature review by considering how to structure the literature review and connect it to your research.

Author and researcher Gary Klein[1] conducted many research projects on differences between novices and experts across many settings. He found that experts and novices differ in knowing what to pay attention to. Because novices do not yet know what information is most useful, they often try to pay attention to too many things, and do not give more weight to the cues that are most important. Experts—whether in nursing, firefighting, or playing chess—know what information to pay close attention to *and* just as importantly, what information to ignore. This ability to filter the environment for important cues makes their performances superior to beginners. What does this have to do with the literature review? Reading academic literature to prepare a literature review involves filtering through many sources. A part of the job is knowing how to filter articles for relevant information to your topic.

Connecting the literature to your study involves two tasks, and researchers are likely to jump back and forth between them as they learn more from the literature and develop a more targeted research question. The first task is to come up with an outline of topics that the literature review should include. Depending on the length of the article, these may form the headings and subheadings in the final literature review. Even if there are no headings, these may define the focus of each paragraph. Let's say your research is on cyberbullying prevention among middle school children. As suggested in Topic 14 the introduction or the start of the literature review is likely to begin with a definition of cyberbullying and a presentation of compelling statistics to establish the importance of studying it. Now that these are established, what else should the literature review cover?

It can be very helpful to review the major and minor subheadings in original research articles and literature reviews to see what topics others have treated as important. For instance, a standalone literature review by Notar and colleagues (2013) divided their paper into the topics shown in Example 1.

Example 1

Definition [of Cyberbullying]
Nuances of Electronic Communication
Reasons for Cyberbullying
Roles in Cyberbullying
Victims
Gender Differences in Response to Cyberbullying

> *Is cyberbullying largely a problem for girls?*
> *Traditional v. cyber[bullying]*[2]

The second task is to scrutinize elements of the research question and the research plan that is taking shape. What will the reader need to know about the state of research on your project in order to grasp your research and its findings? For instance, in the case of cyberbullying prevention among middle school children, the literature review would likely want to include information on what is currently known about preventing cyberbullying. What prevention strategies have been tried? Has research studied their success? If so, were they successful? It is important to stay on the topic at hand. If there are two types of prevention strategies that are common, and the current research only deals with one, it is worth noting that there are two types, but the literature review need not discuss research on the second strategy in any depth.

Let's look at another example. In a research article on maternal depression and childhood health inequalities, the literature review covers the topics in Example 2.

Example 2

Importance of Understanding Children's Health
Maternal Depression and Children's Health
Potential Mechanisms Linking Maternal Depression to Children's Health

Socioeconomic status
Family instability and change
Maternal health and health behaviors

Additional Correlates of Maternal Depression and Children's Health[3]

After establishing the topic's overall importance, the next three headings in Example 2 really set the stage for discussing the relationship between the two main topics from the article's title: maternal depression and childhood health. They do so by summarizing what the literature has said thus far about this relationship, narrowing the focus to the specific topics that are most relevant to the research.

Good literature reviews do not go over articles one at a time. Instead, they group the literature together by topic. For instance, in the article on maternal depression and children's health, the author explains that the article is concerned with children's physical health outcomes. Example 3 provides an excerpt of the author's discussion under the second heading, "Maternal Depression and Children's Health," which summarizes findings from studies that used these variables:

Example 3

There are several examinations linking maternal depression and child health. Angel and Worobey (1988), in their cross-sectional study of Mexican children in the Hispanic Health and Nutrition Examination Survey (Hispanic HANES), find that maternal depression is one of the largest predictors of poor health among children ages six months to 11 years. Regional studies come to similar conclusions. One study finds that maternal depression is associated with fair or poor health among children under the age of three, though this study uses a cross-sectional, convenience sample of children visiting hospital clinics or emergency departments (Casey et al. 2004). Evidence from a sample of 150 mostly white, middle- to upper-class children with a family history of asthma shows that asthma diagnoses by age eight are higher in children of depressed mothers (Klinnert et al. 2001). Greater depressive symptoms in mothers are associated with more visits to hospital emergency departments (Bartlett et al. 2004; Minkovitz et al. 2005), more hospitalizations (Casey et al. 2004), and fewer well-child visits (Minkovitz et al. 2005). Thus, though there is evidence that maternal depression may lead to health problems in children, the existing literature is often based on small, cross-sectional, or homogenous samples of children and does not examine the mechanisms linking maternal depression and children's health.[4]

Instead of writing a series of abstracts (i.e., writing a summary of one article, then a summary of another article), the author lumps together findings on the theme "examinations linking maternal depression and child health." She succinctly describes methods and findings, specifically pointing out what the research, taken together, does and does not tell us about the relationship. She has expertly filtered the information for the audience around one of the two research questions her research investigates: "What is the relationship between maternal depression over time and 5-year-old children's health?" The second question, "To what extent do socioeconomic status, family instability and change, and maternal health and health behaviors explain the association between maternal depression and children's health?" is clearly represented in the literature review under the subsection heading "Maternal health and health behaviors."

■ TOPIC REVIEW

1. What two tasks are necessary to connect the literature to your study?
2. Are these two tasks completed in a specific order?
3. What is the first useful thing to review in research articles and literature reviews to see what topics are important?
4. What is the second useful thing to review in research articles and literature reviews to see what topics are important?
5. Instead of writing a series of abstracts, what should the writer do?

■ DISCUSSION QUESTION

1. Consider ways to take notes from articles in your literature review that will help you accomplish the two tasks above. What information about each article would you need in your notes in order to be able to combine findings and summarize them by topic or theme? What details might you want to have on hand about the design of each study to compare or critique the research design?

■ RESEARCH PLANNING

Name some of the headings and subheadings you anticipate using to organize your literature review.

■ NOTES

1. See Klein, G. (1999). *Sources of Power: How People Make Decisions.* Cambridge, MA: The MIT Press.

2. Notar, C.E., Padgett, S., & Roden, J. (2013). Cyberbullying: A review of the literature. *Universal Journal of Educational Research, 1*(1), 1–9.

3. Turney, K. (2011). Maternal depression and childhood health inequalities. *Journal of Health and Social Behavior, 52*(3), 314–332.

4. Ibid.

PREPARING TO WRITE A CRITICAL REVIEW

A literature review should be a *critical* assessment of the literature on a topic. Novice writers often make two common mistakes that lead to *uncritical* reviews. First, they often take the results of each study to be "facts" that have been proven. As indicated below, all studies should be presumed flawed and, therefore, to offer only degrees of evidence, not "truths" to be accepted uncritically. Second, novice writers often discuss all studies as though they were equal in quality when some studies are methodologically superior to others.

To prepare to write a critical review, the writer should assess the quality of each research article that will be cited. The first important area that requires critical assessment is sampling. More often than not, researchers work with samples that are less than ideal (such as volunteers instead of random samples of the populations of interest). Weaknesses in sampling limit the generalizability of the results. For instance, the results of a study on learning theory using a sample of psychology students who volunteered to serve as participants would have limited generalizability to nonvolunteers.

The second important area that requires critical assessment is measurement (sometimes referred to as *instrumentation*). It is safe to presume that all measures are flawed to some extent. Furthermore, it is safe to presume that various methods of measuring a given variable might lead to somewhat different results. For instance, one researcher on nutrition might measure by asking overweight adolescents to keep diaries of what they eat throughout a day. Fearing that participants might not be completely truthful in diaries, another researcher on nutrition might observe the food choices of overweight adolescents in the school cafeteria. The second method has the limitation of being conducted in a highly structured environment, where the food choices might be limited. Neither method is right or wrong. Instead, both methods have limitations, which should be considered when critically assessing the results of the studies.

The third important area to consider when critically assessing studies to cite in a literature review relates to issues with validity, which, as discussed, applies especially to experiments (i.e., studies in which treatments are administered to participants so that one can estimate the effects of the treatments on the participants' subsequent behaviors). Experiments are often flawed by having inappropriate control conditions (such as comparing a treatment group consisting of volunteers with a control group from the general population). Also, laboratory experiments (e.g., receiving rewards for making appropriate food choices in a laboratory setting) may have limited generalizability to receiving rewards in a natural environment (i.e., the rewards may have effects in the natural environment different from those in the laboratory setting).

Issues in sampling are discussed in detail in Part 4 of this book, while issues in measurement are covered in Part 5, and considerations in the evaluation of experiments are covered in Part 7. Careful attention to these parts of the book will help in making informed assessments of the results of published studies.

Fortunately, researchers often discuss the limitations of their studies, usually in the last section of their research reports. Examining researchers' self-assessments of the limitations of their research can help writers of literature reviews when citing the studies. Example 1 shows a portion of such a discussion of limitations.

Example 1

However, this study does have limitations, including the small sample size and the nonrandomized controlled design. Consequently, observed changes in study end points may be explained by the natural course of postoperative recovery. Also, no biochemical verification was used to confirm self-report of smoking status (p. 185).[1]

Because flaws are widespread in research, it is important to assess the seriousness of the flaws and use appropriate terms when describing the results. For instance, Example 2 shows some terms that might be used to describe the results of research with serious weaknesses.

Example 2

Doe's (2013) study provides some evidence that. . .
Recent research by Doe (2013) raises the possibility that. . .
Preliminary evidence suggests that. . . (Doe, 2013).

Of course, some studies provide strong evidence, such as a national survey using a large, representative sample. Sometimes, there is a series of studies on the same topic, all of which have similar results, making the overall findings of the series highly reliable. Terms that might be used to refer to strong evidence are shown in Example 3.

Example 3

Overall, this set of studies clearly indicates that. . .
In summary, the five studies described provide nearly conclusive evidence that. . .
Doe's (2013) national survey demonstrates that. . .

It is not necessary to use terms such as those in Examples 2 and 3 to qualify every comment about each study cited in a literature review. However, keep in mind that when a writer presents a finding or statement from the literature without qualification, readers are likely to assume that the writer believes that the underlying methodology and logic are reasonably sound.

■ TOPIC REVIEW

1. According to the topic, novice writers often make two common mistakes. What is the first one that is mentioned in this topic?
2. According to the topic, novice writers often make two common mistakes. What is the second one that is mentioned in this topic?

3. "More often than not, researchers work with samples that are less than ideal." According to this topic, is this statement true *or* false?

4. "It is safe to assume that flawed measures are rare in research." According to this topic, is this statement true *or* false?

5. Do researchers often discuss the limitations of their own studies?

6. When a writer presents a finding or statement from the literature without qualification, readers are likely to assume what?

■ DISCUSSION QUESTION

1. Suppose this statement appeared in a literature review: "The results of Doe's (2011) study clearly prove that A is higher than B." In light of the information in this topic, is such a statement justified? Explain.

■ RESEARCH PLANNING

What steps can you take to write a critical review in your current research project? Explain, and be specific to your topic.

■ NOTE

1. Hoffman, A.J., Brintnall, R.A., Brown, J.K., von Eye, V., Johnes, L.W., Alderink, G., & VanOtteren, G.M. (2013). Too sick not to exercise: Using a 6–233k, home based exercise intervention for cancer-related fatigue self-management for postsurgical non-small cell lung cancer patients. *Cancer Nursing, 36*, 175–188.

TOPIC 17

CREATING A SYNTHESIS

As indicated in the previous topic, a literature review should be based on a critical assessment of the previously published work on a topic. However, it should consist of more than just critical summaries of individual studies. Instead, a literature review should be a **synthesis**—providing a whole picture of what is known and what is not known, as well as an attempt to show how diverse pieces of information fit together and make sense.

A key to creating a synthesis is to write a review that moves from subtopic to subtopic (not from one study to another), while citing whatever studies are relevant for each topic. See Examples 1 and 2 in Topic 15 for examples of a topic outline for writing a literature review.

To further the creation of a synthesis, the writer of a review should explicitly point out major trends and commonalities in the results of previous research. Let's return to the article used to consider literature review subjects in Topic 15. Example 1 illustrates how this article summarized studies in one paragraph of the literature review under the heading "Maternal Depression and Children's Health."

Example 1

There are several examinations linking maternal depression and child health. Angel and Worobey (1988), in their cross-sectional study of Mexican children in the Hispanic Health and Nutrition Examination Survey (Hispanic HANES), find that maternal depression is one of the largest predictors of poor health among children ages six months to 11 years. Regional studies come to similar conclusions. One study finds that maternal depression is associated with fair or poor health among children under the age of three, though this study uses a cross-sectional, convenience sample of children visiting hospital clinics or emergency departments (Casey et al. 2004). Evidence from a sample of 150 mostly white, middle- to upper-class children with a family history of asthma shows that asthma diagnoses by age eight are higher in children of depressed mothers (Klinnert et al. 2001). Greater depressive symptoms in mothers are associated with more visits to hospital emergency departments (Bartlett et al. 2004; Minkovitz et al. 2005), more hospitalizations (Casey et al. 2004), and fewer well-child visits (Minkovitz et al. 2005).[1]

In addition, when there are major discrepancies in results, they should be pointed out, and possible explanations for the discrepancies should be noted. Example 2 points out an important difference in the samples used in the studies.

Example 2

While the studies described previously support the prediction that X is greater than Y in samples of college students, a recent study of young adolescents found no difference in X and Y. It may be that X and Y operate differently within different age groups.

A whole picture of the literature on a research topic should also explicitly point out gaps in what is known, as illustrated in Example 3. Note that the purpose of research is often to fill a gap found in the literature. Example 3 completes the paragraph started in Example 1, pointing out a limitation of the research:

Example 3

Thus, though there is evidence that maternal depression may lead to health problems in children, the existing literature is often based on small, cross-sectional, or homogenous samples of children and does not examine the mechanisms linking maternal depression and children's health.[2]

To facilitate providing readers with an overview, writers of reviews should avoid giving extensive, detailed descriptions of the research methodology used in each study. Notice how, in few words, the writer in Example 1 was able to provide detail on findings and methods within the review of literature to arrive at the point made in Example 3. It is usually not necessary to provide in-depth details on how studies were conducted. The main exceptions are when the writer of the review wants to document a particular weakness in a study being cited (e.g., use of a small, unrepresentative sample) or when the details of the methodology might help to explain why two studies on the same topic arrived at substantially different results.

In addition, one or more paragraphs (or even whole sections) might be devoted to describing a particular author's written work when the work is central to one or more points being made in the literature review.

It can be very useful to keep a spreadsheet of studies with main topics, sample sizes, methodological details, and main findings in order to capture and compare the literature and ensure that the notes from original research articles have concentrated on the right information to collect in order to compose a literature review. It can also be useful to collect or paraphrase the points you may like to include in your own work from the findings of the article, along with the page number.

Because direct quotations break the flow of a presentation, they should be used very sparingly. Quotations normally should be used only for (1) presenting especially well-crafted definitions of key terms, (2) presenting concepts that are explained especially well with a particular set of words, and (3) clarifying differences of opinion in the literature when seeing that differences in wording (such as how theories are presented) might help readers to understand the issues involved.

The flow of presentation can be facilitated through the use of appropriate transitional terms and phrases (e.g., *however, as a consequence,* and *indeed*) both within and at the beginning of paragraphs. Finally, a brief summary placed at the end of a review can help readers to grasp the whole of the literature review.

■ TOPIC REVIEW

1. "An effective literature review should consist solely of a set of critical summaries of individual studies." Is this statement true *or* false?
2. "A key to creating a synthesis is to write a review that moves from subtopic to subtopic." Is this statement true *or* false?
3. Is it desirable to point out major trends and commonalities in the results of previous research?
4. Is it desirable to point out gaps in the literature?
5. Should the methodology employed in each of the studies cited in a review be described in detail?
6. When would it be appropriate to devote one or more paragraphs to describing a particular author's written work?
7. What is one way to collect research notes from articles to ensure that you have captured the right information and can compare it when composing a literature review?
8. Why should direct quotations be used sparingly?
9. What can be placed at the end of a review to help readers grasp the whole of the literature review?

■ DISCUSSION QUESTIONS

1. When you wrote term papers in the past, did you include many direct quotations from the authors you cited? Are you surprised by the suggestion made in this topic regarding quotations? Explain.
2. Before you read this topic, would you have been likely to write a series of summaries of previous research in the belief that the series would produce an effective literature review? Explain.

■ RESEARCH PLANNING

Have you started writing a literature review on your topic? If yes, what types of changes will you make to it based on what you learned in this topic? If not, how do you plan to approach it after reading this topic?

■ NOTES

1. Turney, K. (2011). Maternal depression and childhood health inequalities. *Journal of Health and Social Behavior, 52*, 314–332.
2. Ibid.

WHY ACADEMICS USE CITATION

Academic writing is a conversation in progress, where scientific theories and knowledge are being built, corroborated, debated, and debunked, often based on new empirical evidence or fresh analysis that has been added to the conversation. All claims that are made in an academic article must be backed up with evidence, and that evidence comes in two types: from the literature, or from your own data. The literature review is made up of the first type. It relies on things other people have said in the literature before turning to the data as evidence for claims. In both cases, the writer must connect the claims made to the evidence that supports it. The primary way this is done when claims are based on other sources is to acknowledge the source through citation.

Citation is the system that academic writing uses to acknowledge sources. It typically consists of two parts. First, the author provides a shorthand version of the source information within the flow of the writing. This may be incorporated into the sentence itself by referring to the author or study directly, or more commonly, it appears in parentheses or as a footnote following the information from the source. Second, the bibliography, which appears at the end, allows any reader to connect the shorthand information in the citation to the complete source information. For this reason, entries in the bibliography must include complete, specific information about a source, including its author names, year, title, publication name, and publisher information. Both steps are required for nearly all types of citation. Placing a source in the bibliography is rarely enough—the citation also indicates where ideas from a specific work appear in the text. Each citation in the text should match to a corresponding entry in the bibliography. Occasionally, and depending on the style used, authors list works in the bibliography that are not directly cited in the text because the work informed or influenced the overall discussion but no specific concept or quote from the work was incorporated into the text.

Sources are cited when information from them is used. This is true regardless of whether the source information is quoted directly or paraphrased. To not attribute the idea to the source from which it was borrowed is **plagiarism.** This is a form of theft. Not giving credit where it is due is the same as claiming the ideas are original to the author. If sources are not identified, how can readers distinguish between ideas that are the author's and ideas the author borrowed from others? Citation is also an essential ingredient in intellectual integrity and academic honesty because it distinguishes the author's original ideas and contributions from those that he or she is including, responding to, or building upon.

Different academic disciplines use different styles of citation, and each has a style guide that serves as a rule book for the style. You will need to learn the rules for the style that is used for your discipline. These technical differences are discussed in more detail in Topic 19. Regardless of which citation style is used, the important general rules of when to cite apply across all disciplines.

When you take the exact words from a source, even just a phrase, the words are to be placed in quotation marks. Direct quotes typically require more precise identification of the source; for instance, some styles require a page number. When quotations take up more than four lines (Chicago) or 40 words (APA and ASA style), they are set off from the text in an indented block, and no quotation marks are used. It is best to use long quotations only sparingly and only when there is a clear benefit or aesthetic reason for keeping the complete original wording of a passage. If there is not, it may be better to paraphrase as much as possible and only keep what is unique to the source and necessary to quote. Sometimes, even a single word, if it is key and unique to the text, should be quoted, but typically a quote is a full phrase. Check the rules in your discipline for any specific guidelines on handling quotations.

Paraphrasing is when you restate the idea or information from a source in your own words. These also must be attributed to the source from which the idea was borrowed. The important thing for a citation is that the idea was someone else's intellectual contribution. The use of paraphrase allows the writer to recombine ideas from multiple sources into paragraphs that emphasize or synthesize specific points in a way that extensive quoting does not allow. Paraphrasing also allows the author to maintain a consistent tone or style of presentation while presenting information from sources that sound quite different. Sometimes, paraphrasing can also restate an idea in shorter or simpler terms, or it can unpack an idea to elaborate further on the meaning. For these reasons, good writers paraphrase when possible. Paraphrasing absolutely requires acknowledgment of the source through citation. Suggestions from Topics 16 and 17 can help with how to incorporate the ideas of others into one's writing.

Let's look at an example. In the first passage, an assertion is made without attributing sources. In the second, attribution is added. Look for the key differences in how the information is presented.

Example 1

People who live in poor neighborhoods with disorderly or degraded physical environments are more likely to show signs and symptoms of depression, and their children are more likely to exhibit problem behavior. When families in high poverty neighborhoods move to better neighborhoods, these symptoms improve.

Example 1 is not a quote, but takes ideas from a 2007 article that is directly quoted in Example 2. This is from the literature review of an empirical article on depression and the urban built environment.

Example 2

Recent studies have shown that neighborhood social disorganization is associated with depressive symptoms and that living in socioeconomically deprived areas is associated with depression, with higher levels of child problem behavior, and with a higher incidence of non-psychotic disorders (Latkin and Curry 2003; Walters et al. 2004; Kaliff et al. 2001; Diesssen, Gunther, and Van Os 1998; Silver, Mulvey, and Swanson 2002). A randomized controlled trial that moved families from high poverty neighborhoods to non-poor neighborhoods showed that both parents and children who moved reported fewer psychological distress symptoms than did control families who did not move (Leventhal and Brooks-Gunn 2003).[1]

Example 1 makes the statements seem like the author's claims to fact, whereas Example 2 makes it clear that the authors are summarizing ideas from the work of others. Facts and data also require that a source be acknowledged, unless the information is so general and well known that is it considered common knowledge and need not be verified through a source. Examples of common knowledge include dictionary definitions and statements such as "The United States is in North America" and "Barack Obama was President of the United States." However, in many statements of fact, there is a gray area because some knowledge that is "common" for one group is not commonly known by others. If there is doubt, it is better to cite a source that corroborates your information than to assume everyone knows it. Most statistical information, while often commonly available, is tied to a specific time and population. To determine if a statistic needs citation, it can help to ask if the fact would still be true in 25 or 50 years. If something corresponds to a specific time period (how many people graduated from college in 2016), it probably needs a source.

Sometimes, citations are a judgment call. The best rule of thumb is: when in doubt, cite. It creates fewer potential problems to cite when you do not need to than to fail to cite when you should have acknowledged the source.

■ TOPIC REVIEW

1. What is citation?
2. What are the two parts to citing a source?
3. "When paraphrasing, it is acceptable to simply list the source in the bibliography." True or false?
4. What is plagiarism?
5. What are the two ways that claims are anchored to evidence in academic writing?
6. Is there one style for academic citation?
7. What types of information need to be cited?
8. Do facts and data need to have sources listed?
9. What is the best rule of thumb for citation when you are unsure?

■ DISCUSSION QUESTION

1. How is citation an integral part of the formation of scientific knowledge? Why does citation matter for academic honesty or integrity?

■ RESEARCH PLANNING

Consider what you have learned in this topic, paying particular attention to the examples above. Consider incorporating a review of your own writing to be sure the presentation is more like Example 2 than Example 1.

■ NOTE

1. Galea, S., Ahern, J., Rudenstine, S., Wallace, Z., & Vlahov, D. (2005). Urban built environment and depression: A multilevel analysis. *Journal of Epidemiology and Community Health, 59,* 822.

INTRODUCTION TO STYLE GUIDES

Organizations as diverse as the American Medical Association (AMA), International Business Machines Corporation (IBM), the Associated Press (AP), and the American Sociological Association (ASA) have published style guides to assist their authors and editors. Most academic nonfiction books follow the *Chicago Manual of Style*, so named because it was developed at the University of Chicago. Individual publishers, journals, and magazines also typically have in-house style guides.

Style guides differ from grammar handbooks. While grammar deals with the rules of a specific language, a style guide helps to create consistency in how certain elements and special words, terms, numbers, and abbreviations will be treated. For instance, consider this question: Should academic degrees be capitalized? The *AMA Manual of Style* provides this answer: "Capitalize academic degrees when abbreviated but not when written out" (AMA 2007:378).[1] Thus, when writing for the AMA, an author should write the following two sentences as shown here:

> Jane Doe earned her master's degree at Stanford University.
> Jane Doe, MA, will be the keynote speaker at this year's senior seminar.

The two sentences immediately above raise another problematic question: Should periods be used in abbreviations for academic degrees? As you can see, the answer is "no" if you are writing for the AMA. However, the answer is "yes" if you are writing for a newspaper using *The Associated Press Stylebook* (2004:5). Neither style guide is right or wrong, but rather each of the two guides has a different style on this issue. In fact, the *Chicago Manual* recently made a change to its style, moving from using periods to no periods in academic degrees.[2] What matters is consistency.

A second important function of style guides is to specify the contents and organization of manuscripts. For example, the American Sociological Association's *ASA Style Guide* describes the contents of title pages for articles submitted for publication. If you guessed that the title page should contain the names of the authors and their institutions, you would be correct. However, relying just on your intuition, you might fail to include other required elements: the word count of the document including footnotes and references and a footnote with contact information for the author who will respond to any correspondence, plus any acknowledgments, credits, or ID numbers for grants or funds used to support a study (although for student papers, these are typically not needed).

Third, style guides address issues of citation. They describe the exact format in which the citations should be listed within the text as well as how they should appear in the bibliography. There are two common citation styles. The first uses a superscript number at the reference point in the text that is connected to the same number at the foot of the page or in the endnotes where the source information appears. The second uses author last name and date of publication in parentheses at the end of the sentence that refers to the source's information. Either approach will also include a page number when the information is directly quoted from the original source.

The ***American Sociological Association's ASA Style Guide*** and the ***Publication Manual of the American Psychological Association (APA Manual)*** are two styles that are commonly found in social science disciplines. Each is published by the major association for professionals and academics working in those fields in the United States. The *APA Manual* covers the same general topics as the *ASA Style Guide*, but in greater detail. There are important similarities between the two styles. Both styles use the parenthetical citation style, meaning that sources are identified by author last name and date of publication at the end of a sentence, and include a page number if there is a direct quote. The styles do differ in small ways. For instance, ASA style puts no comma after the author names but APA style does. When a page number is used, ASA puts a colon, then the page number with no space, but APA style uses a comma. ASA style lists the page number with no abbreviation to indicate the word "pages," but APA does include an abbreviation ("p." or "pp.") when a page number is included. Example 1 shows the same citation used in APA or ASA style with these small differences.

Example 1

APA Style

According to multiple sources, students often experience difficulty remembering small differences between styles (Jones, 2015; Mason & Dixon, 2010). The top recommendation is "acquiring a style manual" (Jones, 2015, p. 29).

ASA Style

According to multiple sources, students often experience difficulty remembering small differences between styles (Jones 2015; Mason and Dixon 2010). The top recommendation is "acquiring a style manual" (Jones 2015:29).

While these differences in style are sometimes slight and do not greatly interfere with readers understanding citation information, consistency of style, including its use of punctuation, can be meaningful across the span of the document, including its relationship to the bibliography. For this reason, it is important to be consistent in adhering to the style you use. Basic rules and resources for using APA and ASA styles are described in Appendices E and F, respectively.

There are now many programs called "reference managers" or "citation managers" that automate much of the tedious citation and bibliography formatting that academic writing requires. Examples include Zotero, Endnote, RefWorks, and Mendeley. Some of these programs are web-based; some are installed as software on a computer. Some are free, and others cost money. University libraries may have an institutional license that allows students an account with a specific reference management solution. Most electronic research resources now allow users to download article citation information directly into these programs, and some support PDF attachment, sorting and filtering, and notes fields where article notes can be organized. These programs typically integrate with standard word processing programs to format citations and bibliographic entries properly. Using a reference citation manager can help writers implement style guides appropriately when it comes to citations and bibliography entries, but they will not implement the capitalization or abbreviation rules for a specific style.

■ TOPIC REVIEW

1. How is a style guide different than a grammar handbook?
2. Do all major style guides agree on punctuation for academic degrees?
3. Do style guides specify the contents and organization of manuscripts?
4. What are the two most common style guides in the social sciences?
5. Are there similarities between APA and ASA styles?
6. What is a "reference manager" or "citation manager"?
7. What elements does a reference manager format for you? What does it not format for you?

■ DISCUSSION QUESTION

1. Do you think it is more valuable to track your citations manually to learn your discipline's style, or are you more inclined to rely on a reference citation management program?

■ RESEARCH PLANNING

Which style guide should you use while you write your research proposal and research report? If it is APA or ASA, consider reviewing Appendices E and F for basic information. If not, look up and review the basic requirements of the style you are expected to use. Does it affect the type of information you might need to track in your notes about sources?

Consider how you might use a reference citation manager. If you are a student or affiliated with a college or university, check with your library to see if they have an institutional membership with a specific program that you can use. Look up some options and see whether a citation manager works for you. Whether you use a citation manager or not, make a plan for how to track citation information to make it easy to cite when you write from your notes and quotes.

■ NOTES

1. (AMA 2007:378) is a "reference citation" written in the style described by the *ASA Style Guide*. In the citation, the year 2007 is the year of publication, and the number 378 is the page number on which the quotation appears. An issue covered by academic style guides concerns the preparation of citations and reference lists.
2. The *ASA Style Guide* is based on the *Chicago Manual of Style*, which is a comprehensive and detailed style guide that is commonly used for academic books.

PART 3
Basic Concepts in Quantitative Research

Quantitative research collects data that will be analyzed as numbers. This section discusses concepts that are basic to designing the quantitative research question, with special attention to understanding variables and hypotheses. Topic 20 discusses basic decisions that are made in quantitative research. Topics 21 to 23 explain what variables are and how they are used in different research designs. Topic 24 puts this information together and shows how to form quantitative research questions in their typical form: the research hypothesis. The research hypothesis has a specific structure that is not necessarily intuitive but understanding its structure is important when reading and conducting scientific research.

DECISIONS IN QUANTITATIVE RESEARCH DESIGN

The design of a research study creates the framework for *how* to answer a research question. Many of the specifics for each decision point in devising and answering a research question are covered in other parts of the book. This topic focuses on designing a quantitative research question. In quantitative research, designs focus on collecting data that will be represented numerically and collected through surveys, polls, or by using existing datasets.

Quantitative research questions include information on the target population, the attributes or variables to be studied and what the researcher wants to know about them, and the type of analysis that will be used by the researcher to answer the question. A good research question will clearly explain the variables and their relationship. While your research interest may begin as a fairly abstract conceptual problem, the research question must anchor concepts in concrete, measurable elements and be limited to what can be answered through the data that will be collected. Finally, a good research question will pass the "so what?" test: it addresses an issue or question that contributes something tangible. With a good question, the researcher will be able to provide a persuasive argument about why the audience should care about the answer. This will entail connecting all of the elements of the research question together and providing a clear statement of who is being studied, well-defined concepts and variables that are being used, and the relationship between them that is being tested.

Quantitative research designs typically fall into one of two types: experimental or nonexperimental. Part 7 covers experimental designs. In this part, the focus is on nonexperimental quantitative studies, which can also be referred to as **descriptive** or **observational** studies because the researcher observes or describes what the subjects report and does not intervene with a treatment.

At the design phase, a researcher must decide the **unit of analysis** and ensure that it is appropriate to the question being asked. The unit of analysis is simply who or what constitutes one "unit" from which data has been collected in the study. In many studies, the unit of analysis is the individual person. This means that the data collected will represent individuals, and the analysis will discuss the findings in terms of individuals. Even when the data is grouped to show patterns among groups, the groups will consist of individuals. For instance, in a study that looks at teaching effectiveness, the unit of analysis might be individual teachers, but some research questions may require comparing larger units such as units within an organization, entire organizations, neighborhoods, states, or countries. For a teaching effectiveness study, the unit of analysis might be individual teachers and students, or it might be classrooms, schools, or even countries. Selecting a unit of analysis relates to the **target population.** This is the population to which the researcher wants to be able to generalize the results.

Most quantitative research designs use **samples** of a population because trying to include every member of the entire population is impractical unless the population is very small.[1] Analyzing quantitative data of a sample typically uses **statistics**.[2] Statistics allow the researcher to find patterns in data and to generalize findings from a sample to a population.

Once a topic is selected, it is usually the case that a broad interest must be narrowed in order to be researchable. The quantitative researcher also needs to define concepts clearly. Research requires precision, and this includes creating well-defined boundaries around not only the unit of analysis and sample, but also the concepts being used and how they will be measured. In the example above on "teacher effectiveness," it may be important to clarify, for instance, who counts as a teacher and who does not. Another concept to define is "effectiveness." What does effectiveness mean?

Getting clear on the concepts and their boundaries often leads to progress on how to **operationalize** the concepts being used. In operationalization, concepts are translated into constructs that are directly observable. Clarifying concepts is important in all types of studies, but operationalization is especially important to quantitative research because the quality of its results will be judged in part on how well concepts were translated into the variables that were measured. Defining measures in a study is also key to creating good research questions. Topics in this section will cover in more detail the role of variables and their operationalization, leading up to the creation of hypotheses, the typical form into which research questions are translated in most quantitative designs.

Lastly, an important part of developing any research design involves answering the question "so what?" A researcher should not only be able to state a question but explain to others why they should care about the question and its answers. Quite often, researchers will present this in a **research proposal**. Students might write a proposal to get instructor approval, or scientists might submit one to obtain funding for a study. Institutional Review Boards (IRBs) also require a researcher to permit a version of the research proposal to be vetted by this committee before it is carried out. Research proposals lay out how studies will be conducted and often make the case for their relevance. Research proposals typically have a statement of the problem or objective followed by an account that begins to make a case for the study in all the ways that have been described thus far: it includes a short literature review that shows where the study fits and why it is needed, followed by a detailed description that explains the decisions that have been made about the research design. This includes who will be studied, what the variables are, how data will be collected and how items will be measured, and how the data will be analyzed. Research proposals may include requirements for the schedule, budget, and how ethical issues such as confidentiality will be managed.

■ TOPIC REVIEW

1. What are the two types of quantitative research design?
2. Most quantitative research uses what to study a population?
3. What is a target population?
4. What is a unit of analysis?
5. Why is defining a sample important to developing a quantitative research question?
6. What quality does a concept need to have when it is defined in a research question?
7. What are some of the uses of a research proposal?

■ DISCUSSION QUESTION

1. Consider the research topic of teaching effectiveness used in the topic above. Consider some of the different choices that could be made based on the suggestions made in this topic. Notice the variation within the responses that you and your fellow students generate. What are some of the strengths and weaknesses in the research questions that were developed?

■ RESEARCH PLANNING

Now consider your own research interest. Begin the process of narrowing the target population, defining the unit of analysis, and thinking through the concepts that you will need to define. Record these so you can refine them as you work through topics that cover each area in more detail.

■ NOTES

1. More on the specifics of sampling can be found in Part 4.
2. When an analysis is conducted on population data, it is called a **parameter**. Statistics are covered in detail in Part 8.

VARIABLES IN NONEXPERIMENTAL STUDIES

A **variable** is a trait or characteristic that can *vary* within a population. It is a variable, then, if it has at least two categories or values that will apply to participants or units in the study. The opposite of a variable is a constant—a value or category that stays the same for everyone or for all units included in a study.

Research includes different types of variables that are generally grouped into **categorical variables** and **continuous variables.** Categorical variables have mutually exclusive categories. There are two types. When variables have at least two categories, but the categories have no inherent order, they are called **nominal variables** or name variables. Nominal variables do not have a numerical value, but consist of words or "names" instead. Example 1 below has two nominal variables. Can you identify them?

Example 1

A sample of registered voters was surveyed. Each voter was asked first to name his or her gender (male or female), then to name the candidate for whom he or she planned to vote (Doe, Jones, or Smith). The purpose was to explore gender differences in voting preferences.

The two variables in Example 1 are (1) gender, with two categories (male and female); and (2) preferred candidate, with three categories (the three candidates: Doe, Jones, and Smith). Gender is an example of a nominal variable. Each respondent to the survey in Example 1 belongs to one—and *only one*—category, and there is no intrinsic value that determines the order of the categories.

The terminology is important. Be careful not to confuse a variable with its categories. For instance, "male" is not a variable, gender is. "Male" is one of the two *categories* of the *variable* called "gender." Here is how to visualize it:

Variable	*Gender*	
Nominal Categories	Male	Female

Researchers define variables in such a way that the categories within them are **exhaustive**, meaning all possible categories are accounted for. Another nominal category is "state in which you were born." States are a nominal category because there is no built-in order for which state is first, and which is last. Also, the choices are mutually exclusive because each person can only be born in one state. There are 50 options to make the choices exhaustive; however, a 51st option of "not born in the United States" might need to be offered to make the selections complete.

Nominal variables are not the only type of categorical variable. **Ordinal variables** are categories that have a rank order. Ordinal variables can be placed in an order, but the categories do not have a specific, measurable distance between them. An example would be asking someone to report on their overall health, and offer the choices: excellent, very good, good, fair, and poor. It is not possible to say that "excellent" has a specific and definite distance from "very good." It is also not possible to say that the gap between "excellent" and "very good" is the same gap as the distance between "very good" and "good."

Variable	*Overall Health*				
Ordinal Categories	Excellent	Very Good	Good	Fair	Poor

By contrast, **continuous variables** can be quantified. They have a numerical value, allowing them to be placed in order and the distance between each item to be exactly described. There are two types of continuous variables. The first type is called an **interval variable.** Interval variables have a numeric value, so they can be measured along a continuum with clearly defined intervals between values. Intervals are also sometimes referred to as **scaled variables.** A classic example is temperature. It is a good example because in addition to showing that it is numerical, temperature also distinguishes the unique qualities of an interval variable: it does not have a zero value that indicates the complete lack of something. Because these values are scaled to intervals, they do not necessarily compound in the same way. For instance, we cannot say that 80 degrees feels exactly twice as hot as 40 degrees, but we can say how far apart they are on the scale. In research on people, we are unlikely to use temperature. Interval variables are most commonly used when a test or measure is scaled to evaluate participants. We are familiar with a few scales of this type, such as SAT exams or IQ tests. These tests are scaled. Technically, there may be a zero value, but it is unlikely to suggest that the person lacks any intelligence. The scale has definitive intervals, but they do not necessarily indicate specific quantities so that someone with an IQ of 240 is twice as smart as someone with an IQ of 120.

The second type of continuous variable is called a **ratio variable.** Just like interval variables, ratio variables are numerical and can be measured along a continuous number line. The difference is that the number line for a ratio variable has a zero value, and zero means that none of that variable is present. Grade point average (GPA) is tied to a numerical measurement that has a zero value indicating a lack of any grade points, for instance. GPA can be considered a ratio variable. Height, mass, and distance are other examples of ratio variables, where a zero value means that it has no height, no mass, or no distance.

One method for remembering the four types of variables is the acronym NOIR, which may help you remember both the names and the order. With each variable type, the criteria have greater specificity. Continuous variables can always be reduced to categorical variables. A common instance in the research of reducing a continuous variable to a categorical one is age. Age is a ratio variable. It is numerical, and it is tied to a timeline in which the zero value means none of the age variable is present. However, it can be treated as a categorical variable if the researcher groups age into categories. For research on adults, this might look something like: 18 to 24, 25 to 34, 35 to 44, 45 to 54, 55 to 64, and 65 or over. Note that the categories must include all possible values, and the categories must not overlap.

Another way that variables are classified is as either **independent** or **dependent**. When researchers conduct a causal-comparative study (see Topic 5 to review), the presumed cause of an effect (such as smoking) is called the *independent* variable, and the response or outcome (such as lung cancer) is called the *dependent* variable. One way to remember the difference is to keep in mind that variables vary. Those that are *dependent* are being examined for how much their variation *depends* upon the influence of another variable that is being measured. *Independent* means that you are not trying to determine what influences that variable—it varies, but the factors are independent of those being measured in this study. Figure 21.1 provides a visual representation of the relationship between these two variable types.

In nonexperimental studies, some researchers refer to any variable that comes first (whether or not it is presumed to be a cause) as *independent* and to the one that comes later as *dependent*. For instance, *SAT* scores (the predictor variable) are usually determined before students earn their college GPAs. Thus, some researchers would call the *SAT* the independent variable and the GPA the dependent variable. It is also common to call the independent variable the **predictor** and the outcome variable (such as GPA) the **criterion**. The term *criterion* means *standard*. Hence, GPA is the standard by which the predictive accuracy of the *SAT* is often judged. If the SAT works as intended, high scores on the *SAT* should be associated with high GPAs, while low *SAT* scores should be associated with low GPAs. To the extent that this is true, the *SAT* is judged to be valid. To the extent that it is not true, the *SAT* is judged to be invalid. Procedures for determining the validity of a test are described in Part 5 of this book.

FIGURE 21.1 The *independent variable* (stimulus or input) causes changes in the *dependent variable* (response or output).

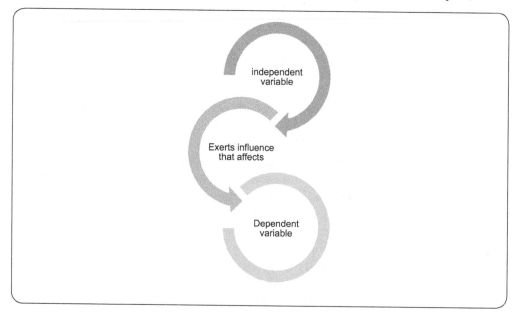

■ TOPIC REVIEW

1. What is the minimum number of categories that any variable must have?
2. Adults who were taking a course to learn English as a second language were asked to name their country of birth and their number of years of formal education. In this example, how many variables were being studied?
3. In Question 2, which variable is a categorical variable? Which type of categorical variable is it?
4. In Question 2, which variable is a continuous variable? Which type of continuous variable is it?
5. A sample of adults was asked their level of agreement with the statement, "The President of the United States is doing a good job of handling foreign relations." They were permitted to respond with either "strongly agree," "agree," "disagree," or "strongly disagree." How many variables were being studied?
6. What is a good way to remember the four types of variables?
7. Studies try to explain the variation in which type of variable—the dependent variable or the independent variable?
8. A researcher looked for the causes of social unrest by examining economic variables including poverty and income. Is social unrest an independent or a dependent variable?
9. If a researcher administers a basic math test to middle school children to see if its scores predict grades in high school algebra, what is the criterion variable?

■ DISCUSSION QUESTIONS

1. Suppose you want to measure income on a self-report questionnaire that asks each participant to check off his or her income category. Name the categories you would use. Are they exhaustive and mutually exclusive? Explain.
2. Name a quantitative variable of interest to you, and name its categories. Which type of variable is it? Are the categories mutually exclusive and exhaustive? Explain.

■ RESEARCH PLANNING

Name the major variables you will be studying. Consider the ways you can measure each variable in terms of the categories used, the number of categories, and any options on which type of variable it is. Keep in mind that variables can often be measured in different ways. Review the literature that uses variables that are similar to yours. How have they treated each variable? Are there advantages or disadvantages to adopting a similar way to measure the variable?

VARIABLES IN EXPERIMENTAL STUDIES

All experimental studies have at least one **independent variable** and one **dependent variable**. The purpose of the experiments is to estimate the extent to which independent variables cause changes in dependent variables.

As indicated in the previous section, an independent variable is a stimulus or input variable. Note that in experiments, researchers *physically manipulate* independent variables. Examples of physical manipulation are (1) giving a new drug to some participants while giving a placebo to others, (2) providing some students with computers while denying computers to others, and (3) using group counseling with some clients while using individual counseling with others. Thus, studies that claim to *physically manipulate* have administered a treatment that creates a tangible difference between those receiving and not receiving treatment through some real-world action or environmental change.

In *nonexperimental* studies, researchers do *not* physically manipulate independent variables. Instead, they observe independent variables as they occur (or have occurred) naturally. For instance, researchers observe the health of individuals who report drinking alcohol in nonexperimental studies—researchers do not provide participants with alcohol, and then monitor the results of ingesting it (see Topic 4 to review other differences between experimental and nonexperimental studies of causation).

In a simple experiment, as in Example 1 below, there is only one independent variable and only one dependent variable.

Example 1

On alternate weeks, a disruptive first-grade student is given extra praise for being in her seat when appropriate. The purpose of the study is to see if the extra praise will increase the amount of appropriate in-seat behavior.

In Example 1, the physical manipulation is giving or not giving extra praise, which is the independent variable (i.e., the stimulus or input variable). The dependent variable (i.e., the response or outcome variable) is the change in the student's in-seat behavior.

Often, experiments have more than one dependent variable. For instance, in Example 1, a researcher could observe not only if the treatment causes (1) more in-seat behavior, but also (2) improvement in the student's achievement and (3) improvement in the student's attitude toward school during the weeks in which the extra praise is given. If a researcher did this, the researcher would have three dependent variables.

Many experiments also have more than one independent variable. Often, these experiments are more interesting than those with only one independent variable because they provide insights into the causal effects of combinations of variables. Consider Example 2, which has two independent variables (childcare and transportation money).

Example 2

Voluntary, free job training was offered to all mothers on welfare in a small city. Four groups of the mothers were formed at random to explore the effects of these two independent variables: (1) providing or not providing free childcare while in training and (2) providing or not providing transportation money to get to the job-training site. Each group was assigned at random to one of the four treatment conditions shown here:

GROUP 1	GROUP 3
childcare *and*	*no* childcare *and*
transportation money	transportation money
GROUP 2	GROUP 4
childcare *and*	*no* childcare *and*
no transportation money	*no* transportation money

It was predicted that those in Group 1 (the group that was given *both* childcare and transportation money) would have the highest attendance rates in the job-training program, those in Group 2 would have the next highest, those in Group 3 would have the next highest, and those in Group 4 would have the lowest.

Notice that in Example 2, a researcher can determine (1) how effective childcare is, (2) how effective transportation money is, and (3) the effectiveness of both childcare *and* transportation money *in combination*. Thus, a researcher would get more information by looking at two independent variables in one study than by looking at each independent variable in a separate experiment (in which case a researcher could determine only points 1 and 2).

■ TOPIC REVIEW

1. All experiments have at least how many dependent variables?
2. In an experiment, what is the name of a stimulus or input variable?
3. What does *physically manipulate* mean in an experimental context?
4. Are dependent variables physically manipulated?
5. Can an experiment have more than one independent variable?
6. Every other customer entering a shoe store was given one of two different coupons. One coupon offered a second pair of shoes for 50% off. The other coupon offered to reduce the total price by 25% if two pairs of shoes were purchased. The purpose was to determine which coupon was more effective in getting individuals to buy two pairs of shoes. In this experiment, what is the independent variable?
7. In Question 6, what is the dependent variable?
8. A teacher showed an educational film on daily nutritional needs to one group of students and gave a handout on the same material to another group. The purpose was to determine which method of instruction was more effective in increasing students' knowledge of daily nutritional needs. In this experiment, what is the dependent variable?
9. In Question 8, what is the independent variable?

■ DISCUSSION QUESTIONS

1. In an experiment involving which books children select at the library, name a variable that would be easy for a researcher to physically manipulate in an experiment. Then, name a variable that might be affected by the manipulation.
2. Name a variable that you would be unwilling to physically manipulate due to ethical or legal concerns.

■ RESEARCH PLANNING

If you will be conducting an experiment, name the independent and dependent variables you will be studying. Is there an opportunity to look at more than one independent or dependent variable? Evaluate the reasons to pursue a study with additional variables, or the reasons to maintain single variables.

TOPIC 23

OPERATIONAL DEFINITIONS OF VARIABLES

Researchers must clearly define the variables in an experiment so that others may replicate the experiment or accurately analyze it. Topic 20 introduced the necessity of defining variables conceptually and operationally and this topic offers a more in-depth explanation of how this is accomplished.

Dictionaries provide **conceptual definitions** of variables. For instance, a researcher in speech communication might be interested in students' ability to *recite*, which has a dictionary definition along these lines: "to repeat or speak aloud from or as from memory, especially in a formal way." This definition is perfectly adequate if a researcher merely wants to communicate the general topic of his or her research to other individuals.

Suppose, however, that the researcher wants to conduct an experiment on the effectiveness of two memory aids on the ability to recite. As the researcher plans the research, it will become clear that a conceptual definition is not adequate because it does not indicate the precise steps the researcher will take in order to identify the variable. Redefining a variable in terms of concrete or physical steps is called *operationalizing* a variable. When a researcher operationalizes a variable, he or she is creating an **operational definition** that limits or constrains it. Example 1 shows the first attempt at creating an operational definition of students' ability to recite.

Example 1

For the research project, the ability to recite is defined as the number of words mispronounced, missing, or misplaced when students repeat aloud from memory Christian Abzab's poem *The Road Taken* in front of a panel of three teachers.

Notice that the definition in Example 1 is not fully operational because there might still be questions about the *physical arrangements*, such as "Will the students stand while reciting?" "In what type of room will the recitation take place (a classroom or auditorium)?" "Will the teachers be male or female?" and "Will the teachers already know the students?"

It is important to note that no attempt at operationalizing a variable will result in a completely operational definition because there are an infinite number of physical characteristics that might be addressed in any definition (e.g., the humidity in the room, the level of lighting, the type of flooring, the color of the walls). Thus, instead of striving for completely operational definitions, researchers try to produce definitions that are adequate to permit a **replication** in all important respects by another researcher. A replication is an attempt to confirm the results of a study by conducting it again in the same way. Deciding if a variable has been sufficiently operationalized to meet this criterion of adequacy (i.e., other researchers can replicate the study) involves subjective judgment, and all researchers may not agree on when it has been met.[1]

Note that a highly operational definition is not necessarily meaningful or relevant. For example, clients' self-esteem could be operationalized with the definition in Example 2.

Example 2

Positive self-esteem is defined as answering "yes" to the written question "Do you feel good about yourself?"

The definition in Example 2 is adequately operational because it indicates what specific question to ask in writing and what response to anticipate. However, the definition is quite narrow. For instance, it does not tap self-esteem in the various dimensions of clients' lives, such as self-esteem in the workplace or social settings. Thus, Example 2 illustrates that a definition can be operational without being adequate in other respects, such as being fully multidimensional.

Treatments given in experiments also should be operationalized. For instance, "verbal praise" given in an experiment could be operationalized in terms of the types of words used when giving praise, the frequency of the praise, the conditions under which the praise will be given, and so on.

If a researcher fails to provide operational definitions of all key variables in a research report, the report is vague at best, and the results are often of limited usefulness. For instance, if research shows that a certain program is helpful in reducing spousal abuse but the researcher fails to provide an adequate operational definition of the variables that were used, including how abuse was measured, the important dimensions of the interventions use, and how success was measured, consumers of research will not know how to conduct the program in applied settings.

■ TOPIC REVIEW

1. Which type of definition indicates physical steps?
2. In practice, are operational definitions ever fully operationalized?
3. Which of the following definitions of *gregarious* is more operational?
   A. Talking on the phone with friends for at least two hours each week.
   B. Being open and friendly when in social gatherings with others.
4. Which of the following definitions of being *computer literate* is more operational?
   A. Having taken at least two formal courses of instruction in an accredited school on the use of computers.
   B. Having knowledge of the origins and uses of computers in modern society and their implications.
5. Which of the following definitions of administering *nonverbal praise* (in an experiment) is more operational?
   A. Using various positive gestures involving various body parts without speaking.
   B. Nodding the head slightly in an up-down direction while smiling lightly with the lips closed.

6. To replicate the research of others, do researchers need "operational" *or* "conceptual" definitions?

7. Is it possible for a definition to be highly operational, yet inadequate in other respects?

■ DISCUSSION QUESTIONS

1. Suppose you read a research report claiming that low-socioeconomic-status (SES) children have lower self-concepts than high-SES children do. In the report, the only definition of self-concept is "feeling good about oneself." How much credence would you give the results in light of the definition? What additional information, if any, would you want about the definition if you were planning to replicate the study?

2. In a research report, job satisfaction is defined as "the number of times each participant said 'yes' to a set of questions such as 'Do you look forward to going to work most mornings?'" Is this definition completely operational? If not, what is missing from the definition?

3. Is the definition in Question 2 too narrow in terms of how you normally think about job satisfaction? Why? Why not?

4. Write a highly operational definition of "success in college."

5. Write a highly operational definition of "motivation to succeed on the job."

■ RESEARCH PLANNING

Name the major variables you will be studying. Define each variable, trying to be as operational as possible. (Note: After you have read published research on your topic, you may want to come back here and redefine some of your definitions in light of how other researchers have defined them.)

■ NOTE

1. When the results of a study are independently replicated by other researchers, it increases confidence in the results. This is the case because a given researcher may have blind spots, unconscious biases, and so on. Also, a given researcher may have been unlucky and have results that were influenced by large random errors. Independent replications by others reduce the odds that these factors are the cause of a particular finding. These are some of the reasons that replication is important.

RESEARCH HYPOTHESES, PURPOSES, AND QUESTIONS

A **research hypothesis** is a prediction of the outcome of a study. The prediction may be based on an educated guess or a formal theory. Example 1 is a hypothesis for a nonexperimental study.

Example 1

Hypothesis 1: First-grade girls have better reading comprehension than first-grade boys.

In Example 1, the researcher predicts that he or she will find higher reading comprehension among girls than boys. To test the prediction, a nonexperimental study is appropriate because the hypothesis does not suggest that treatments will reveal meaningful information. A simple research hypothesis predicts a relationship between two variables. The two variables in Example 1 are (1) gender and (2) reading comprehension. The hypothesis states that reading comprehension is related to gender. The hypothesis in Example 2 is for an experimental study.

Example 2

Hypothesis 2: Children who are shown a video that depicts mild violence will be more aggressive on the playground than those who are shown a similar video without violence.

In Example 2, the independent variable is violence (mild vs. no violence), and the dependent variable is aggressiveness on the playground. The hypotheses in Examples 1 and 2 are both examples of **directional hypotheses** because researchers predict the direction of the outcome (better scores or more aggression). Sometimes, researchers have a **nondirectional hypothesis**. Consider Example 3.

Example 3

Hypothesis 3: The child-rearing practices of blue-collar parents are different from those of white-collar parents.

The author of Example 3 states that there will be a difference, but the author does not predict the direction of the difference. This is perfectly acceptable when there is no basis for making an educated guess as to the outcome of a study. Instead of a nondirectional hypothesis, a researcher might state a **research purpose**. Example 4 shows a research purpose that corresponds to the nondirectional hypothesis in Example 3.

Example 4

The research purpose is to explore differences in child-rearing practices between blue-collar and white-collar parents.

A **research question** may also be substituted for a nondirectional hypothesis. Example 5 shows a research question that corresponds to the nondirectional hypothesis in Example 3 and the research purpose in Example 4.

Example 5

The research question is "How do the child-rearing practices differ between blue-collar and white-collar parents?"

When using a research question as the basis for research, researchers usually do *not* state it as a question that can be answered with a simple "yes" or "no," as is the case in Example 6.

Example 6

The research question is "Do the child-rearing practices of blue-collar and white-collar parents differ?"

Example 6 merely asks, "Do they differ?" This is not a very interesting research question because it implies that the results of the research will be only a simple "yes" or "no." Example 5 is superior because it asks, "*How* do they differ?"—a question that implies that the results will be complex and, thus, more interesting and informative.

The choice between organizing research using a nondirectional hypothesis, a research purpose, or a research question is purely a matter of personal taste—all are acceptable in the scientific community. When researchers are willing and able to predict the outcome of a study, they state a directional hypothesis—not a research purpose or question. In other words, a research purpose or a research question is a suitable substitute for a nondirectional hypothesis. It is inappropriate to use these as substitutes for a directional hypothesis.

Those who have read research reports in journals may have encountered references to another type of hypothesis: the **null hypothesis**. The null hypothesis is one that the researcher tries to disprove. "Null" is the default position that no relationship exists between two or more variables. This is a *statistical hypothesis* that needs to be considered when analyzing results obtained from samples in quantitative research studies. The null hypothesis will be explored in detail in Topic 66.

■ TOPIC REVIEW

1. Which type of statement (hypothesis, purpose, or question) predicts the outcome of a study?

2. "It is hypothesized that college students who have firm career goals achieve higher GPAs than those who do not have firm career goals." Is this a "directional" *or* a "nondirectional" hypothesis?

3. "It is hypothesized that children of immigrants and children of native-born citizens differ in their attitudes toward school." Is this a "directional" *or* a "nondirectional" hypothesis?

4. "Are children of alcoholics different from children of nonalcoholics in their social adjustment?" Is this research question stated appropriately? Why? Why not?

5. When researchers are willing to predict the outcome of a study, should they state a "directional" *or* a "nondirectional" hypothesis?

6. What are the two alternatives to stating a nondirectional hypothesis?

7. Consider nondirectional hypotheses, research purposes, and research questions. Are all three acceptable in the scientific community *or* is one type preferred over the others?

■ DISCUSSION QUESTIONS

1. Restate this hypothesis as a research purpose: "It is hypothesized that there is a difference in job satisfaction between those who receive regular feedback on their job performance and those who receive irregular feedback."

2. Is the hypothesis in Question 1 "directional" *or* "nondirectional"? Explain.

3. Could an experiment be conducted to test the hypothesis in Question 1? Explain.

4. Restate the following hypothesis as a research question: "It is hypothesized that those who exercise regularly and those who do not exercise regularly differ in other behaviors that affect health."

■ RESEARCH PLANNING

State a research hypothesis, purpose, or question for the research you are planning. (Note: You may have more than one of each.)

PART 4
Sampling

It is usually impractical to study an entire population, so researchers draw a sample, study it, and infer that what is true of the sample is probably also true of the population. Because an inference to a population is only as good as the method used to draw the sample, the advantages and disadvantages of various methods of sampling are explored in detail in this part of the book. Topic 25 discusses bias as a primary consideration in sampling approaches. Topics 26, 27, and 28 describe the probability-based sampling procedures common to studies that will analyze the data using statistical methods. Topic 29 segues to nonprobability methods of sampling used for qualitative research. Topic 30 discusses the need in all types of research to collect basic demographic information about the participants. Sample size is introduced in Topic 31, and then explained for quantitative approaches in Topic 32 and qualitative approaches in Topic 33. Finally, the issue of sampling in the modern world is discussed in Topic 34. In this last topic on sampling, the advantages and disadvantages of new communication technologies such as the Internet and cell phones are considered.

BIASED AND UNBIASED SAMPLING

For most research projects, it is impractical to try to reach every member of the population. A **population** may be large, such as all social workers in the United States, or small, such as all social workers employed by a specific hospital. If a researcher studies every member of a population, the researcher is conducting a **census**. For large populations, however, it is more efficient to study a sample instead of conducting a census.

Researchers frequently draw a **sample** from the population that they are ultimately interested in explaining or describing. Sampling has been developed so that researchers can study a subset of the population of interest and use analytical methods that allow them to make inferences about the population. That is, researchers infer that the characteristics of the sample are probably the characteristics of the population.[1]

The quality of a sample affects the quality of the inferences made from that sample to the population. Thus, a poor sample is likely to lead to incorrect inferences. The two questions researchers most commonly ask when evaluating a sample are "Is the size adequate?" (a question that is discussed in Topics 32 and 33) and "Is the sample biased?"

One of the methods for selecting an **unbiased** sample is to give every member of a population an equal chance of being included in the sample. This is called a **simple random sample**.[2] This method of **probability** sampling reduces bias by giving every member of the population an equal chance of being selected. A simple random sample can be drawn by putting the names of all individuals in the population on slips of paper, mixing them up, and drawing as many as needed for the sample. While the procedure sounds simple, in practice, it is rarely feasible to identify and include information to give every member of a population one and only one chance of being included.

For starters, researchers cannot always identify all members of the population of interest, and the failure to do so is a major source of bias in sampling. For instance, if the population of interest consists of all homeless individuals in a city, but researchers can identify only those who seek public assistance, researchers can sample only from those members of the population. This creates a bias against the less-visible homeless, who may be less resourceful, more destitute (or less destitute), and differ in other important characteristics from those who have been identified. To the extent that a sample is biased against less-visible homeless individuals, the inferences about all homeless individuals will be incorrect to an unknown extent (i.e., it is not possible to estimate how much error a bias of this type has caused because researchers do not have information on less-visible homeless individuals).

Second, it may be difficult to give every member one and only one chance of being included. Take for instance researchers who will be conducting interviews by phone and wish to include everyone in a specific neighborhood. Now some people have home phones, some have cell phones, and some have both, complicating the ability to include each person once and only once by simply using a telephone list.

Researchers who use **samples of convenience** (also known as *accidental samples*) also obtain biased samples. For instance, if a psychology professor wants to study a principle of learning theory as it applies to all college sophomores but only uses those students who happen to be enrolled in his or her introductory psychology class, the sample is biased against all other college sophomores. This introduces many possibilities for error. For instance, only some sophomores will elect to take a psychology course. The professor may have a reputation for requiring participation and presentations, and thus may attract students with learning styles that are different from those of the general population of college sophomores. Also, of course, different colleges attract different types of students, and this professor has sampled only from students enrolled at the college where he or she teaches.

A third major source of bias is **volunteerism**. Volunteerism takes two forms. First, sometimes researchers simply issue a call for volunteers. This is often done in medical research in which researchers advertise for potential participants, such as those with chronic heart conditions, in order to test new methods of treatment. What is wrong with this? The possibilities are almost endless. For instance, some individuals may volunteer because they are becoming desperate as their condition worsens, whereas those who are doing better may be less inclined to expose themselves to experimental treatment, *or* those who volunteer may be more persistent and resourceful (and thus in better health) than the general population of those with heart conditions. These two opposing possibilities illustrate why researchers strive to eliminate bias—because they often cannot even speculate accurately on the direction in which a given bias might affect the results of a study.

Second, volunteerism might bias a sample even if a researcher begins by identifying a random sample from an entire population. For instance, a researcher might draw a random sample of all freshmen at a college and contact them to take part in a study of attitudes toward the use of instructional technology in higher education. For a variety of reasons, many of those in the random sample the researcher has selected may refuse to participate. Those who do participate, in effect, are volunteers and may be fundamentally different from nonvolunteers—for instance, by being more interested in technology and more concerned about being successful in their educational pursuits.

Most large quantitative studies use some form of probability sampling, and the next three topics cover the most common methods. However, it is possible to create a valid study and minimize bias using a nonprobability sample. This is more common in qualitative research, and is discussed in Topics 29 and 30.

■ TOPIC REVIEW

1. In this topic, how is *population* defined?
2. If a researcher studies every member of a population, what type of study is he or she conducting?
3. How can a researcher draw an unbiased sample?
4. Suppose a researcher drew a random sample from a population of college students, but some of those selected refused to take part in the study. Are the students who participated in the study a "biased" *or* an "unbiased" sample of the population?
5. If a researcher mails questionnaires to all clients of a social worker and 50% of them are completed and returned, is the sample "biased" *or* "unbiased"?

6. Suppose a psychologist has his or her clients participate in an experiment simply because they are readily accessible (not drawn at random from the population of interest). What type of sample is being used?

7. Briefly describe one way a researcher can draw a simple random sample.

■ DISCUSSION QUESTIONS

1. Individuals who receive questionnaires in the mail often fail to return them, creating a bias because those who do return them are volunteers. Speculate on some things that a researcher can do to get more individuals to respond. (Consider mailed questionnaires you have received in the past and your reasons for responding or not responding.)

2. Are you convinced by the text that researchers should go to great lengths to avoid bias in their samples? Why? Why not?

3. Suppose you drew a random sample of all licensed clinical psychologists in your community to interview by phone. On the days you made the phone calls, some of the psychologists were not available to be interviewed, so you drew replacements for them at random from the population of licensed clinical psychologists. Speculate on whether the sample is "biased" or "unbiased" in light of the fact that replacements were drawn at random.

■ RESEARCH PLANNING

Do you anticipate that you will be drawing a sample for your study, or will you be conducting a census?

If you will be sampling, do you anticipate that you will be using a biased sample? If yes, what do you anticipate will be the source of the bias? Is there anything you can do to reduce the bias? Explain.

■ NOTES

1. The process of *inferring* from a sample to a population is also called *generalizing*. Inferential statistics, which are described in Part 8 of this book, assist in determining the reliability of inferences made from samples to populations.

2. Another method for drawing a simple random sample is described in the next topic.

TOPIC 26

SIMPLE RANDOM AND SYSTEMATIC SAMPLING

As indicated in the previous topic, **a simple random sample** is one in which every member of a population is given an equal chance of being included in a sample. A random sample can be as simple and low-tech as putting names on slips of paper, and then drawing them from a hat. Another way to select a simple random sample is to use a random numbers table (for an example, see Table 26.1 at the end of this topic). Websites such as Research Randomizer (https://www.randomizer.org), Stat Trek (http://stattrek.com/statistics/random-number-generator.aspx), and the Random Integer Generator (https://www.random.org/integers/) include tools that allow researchers to generate a random numbers table based on how many numbers are needed and their minimum and maximum values.

Random numbers tables are literally tables of numbers that are unrelated to each other or to anything else. Until computerized tools became available, researchers relied on published books of random numbers tables. Such books can still be used. Whether random numbers tables are generated online or referenced in books, the researcher starts by assigning each member of the population a number. It should become attached to that person's identifying information as a column in a spreadsheet of names or as a designated number-name for each member of the population. Each number should contain the same number of digits. For instance, if there are 70 members of a population, 70 has two digits so any numbers that are only one digit will add a zero in front of them. The researcher should name one of the individuals 00, another one 01, a third 02, and so on. It does not matter who the first individual is because the researcher is not selecting individuals. The number associated with each name only prepares individuals for random selection.

The researcher then uses the random numbers generated or the table of random numbers to make a selection. For instance, when an online random number generator is used, the researcher can set parameters such that the randomizer will make a random selection of numbers from the total number in the population. These numbers can be downloaded in various formats to make it easy to connect with entries that are already in an electronic format. Numbers can also be manually assigned and a printed random table can be used to make the selection. In this case, the researcher simply points to a number on the table without looking and reads the number of digits that are needed to form the first number of the individual selected. That is, the first number pointed to becomes the first digit in the number. If Row #1 of the sample table is selected, the first digit of the first number is 2. The digit to the right of it is 1; together, they constitute the number 21. Based on the 70 individuals above, all numbers should be two-digit numbers. Thus, 21 has been selected. Now, look at the next two digits to the right, 0 and 4. (Ignore the space between number columns; it is there only to help guide your eye.) Thus, individual number 04 has been selected. The next two digits are 9 and 8. Because there are only 70 individuals in the population, no one is named 98. Thus, this number does not select anyone, so

TABLE 26.1 **Sample Table of Random Numbers**

Row #						
1	210	498	088	806	924	826
2	073	029	482	789	892	971
3	449	002	862	677	731	251
4	732	112	077	603	834	781
5	332	583	170	140	789	377
6	612	057	244	006	302	807
7	709	333	740	488	935	805
8	751	909	152	650	903	588
9	356	965	019	466	756	831
10	850	394	340	651	744	627

the researcher continues right to the next two numbers in the first row in the table. The researcher should continue in this manner until he or she has the number of participants that will be included in the sample.[1]

Random samples are subject to error. For instance, quite by chance a random sample might contain a disproportionately large number of males, high achievers, and so on. Error created by random sampling is simply called **sampling error** by statisticians. Fortunately, if researchers use samples of adequate size (discussed in Topics 32 and 33), sampling errors are minimized. In addition, researchers can evaluate the effects of sampling errors by using inferential statistics, which are discussed in detail in Part 8 of this book.

Notice that bias also creates errors when sampling (see Topic 25). However, errors due to bias are nonchance errors, which are not reduced by increasing sample size. For instance, if a researcher samples for a political survey and the researcher's method is biased against Republicans (e.g., by including too many urban voters, who tend to be Democrats), increasing the sample size using the same biased sampling method yields a larger sample of voters who tend not to be Republicans. The larger sample is no less biased than the smaller one; it is equally biased. Thus, increasing sample size does not necessarily decrease bias.

Another method of sampling that many researchers regard as being essentially equivalent to simple random sampling is **systematic sampling**. In this type of sampling, every nth individual is selected. The number n can be any number, such as 2, in which case a researcher would select every second individual.[2] However, there is a potential problem with this method. Suppose someone has arranged the population in such a way that every second individual is somehow different from the others. Perhaps the population has been arranged in this order: man next to woman, next to man, next to woman, and so on. If a researcher draws every other individual, he or she will obtain a sample of all males or all females. Because a researcher cannot be sure that no one has ordered a list of the population in a way that might affect the sample, an alphabetical list (as opposed to any other kind, such as a classroom seating chart) is preferred, and the first individual selected should be chosen at random. Note that a researcher should go through the entire alphabetical list (up to the letter Z) because different national origin groups tend to concentrate at different points in the alphabet. Following this procedure yields a good sample, but note that it is a *systematic sample*, and it should *not* be referred to as a random sample.

■ TOPIC REVIEW

1. Is there a sequence or pattern to the numbers in a table of random numbers?
2. This topic explains how to use a table of random numbers to draw what type of sample?
3. What is the term for errors created by random sampling?
4. How can researchers minimize sampling errors?
5. Can researchers minimize the effects of a bias in sampling by increasing the sample size?
6. Suppose a researcher wants to sample from a population of 99 clients, and the random starting point in Table 26.1 is the first digit in the last row (Row #26). What are the numbers of the first two clients selected?
7. Suppose a researcher wants to sample from a population of 500 clients and the random starting point in Table 26.1 is the first digit in the fifth row (Row #5). What are the numbers of the first two clients selected?
8. If a researcher draws every other individual from a list of the population, he or she is using what type of sampling?
9. What is the potential problem with systematic sampling?
10. How can a researcher get around that problem with systematic sampling?

■ DISCUSSION QUESTIONS

1. Suppose a friend was planning to use simple random sampling in a research project from which he or she wants to generalize to all students on a campus. Would you recommend drawing names from a hat *or* using a table of random numbers? Why?
2. Suppose a friend predicts that candidate Smith will win a local election, and the prediction is based on the opinions expressed by his or her friends and neighbors. What would you say to help your friend understand that this method of sampling is unsound?

■ RESEARCH PLANNING

Will you use sampling to obtain participants for your research? If yes, do you plan to use random sampling, systematic sampling, *or* some other method of sampling? Explain.
Do you think that the method of sampling you plan to use might create a bias? Explain.

■ NOTES

1. Considerations for determining sample size will be covered in Topics 31, 32, and 33.
2. Divide the population size by the desired sample size to determine the value of n.

STRATIFIED RANDOM SAMPLING

As indicated in the previous two topics, simple random sampling gives each member of a population an equal chance of being included in a sample. Done correctly, the resulting sample is, by definition, *unbiased*, yet it may still contain *sampling errors*, which are errors created by chance (i.e., created by the random sampling process). The technical term for discussing the magnitude of sampling errors is **precision**. Results are more precise when researchers reduce sampling errors. The two major ways to reduce sampling errors are to increase sample size, which is discussed in Topics 32 and 33, and to use stratification in conjunction with random sampling, which is called **stratified random sampling**. A stratified random sample is a way of modifying the methods we have already seen.

Strata are layers. When you stratify a random sample, you create layers in the random or systematic selection of the sample. Stratified samples first create homogeneous groups from the population, and then make a proportional but random selection from each of the groups. This can help with several difficulties found in the previous methods, especially improving the representation of specific groups from the population.

To obtain a stratified random sample, first divide a population into strata. For example, researchers can easily divide a population into men and women because gender is typically identifiable. Once the two homogeneous groups are formed, the researcher draws randomly from the men, and then from the women. This is a very simple version of a stratified random sample.

Researchers usually draw samples by considering the total number of individuals they wish to have in the sample as a percentage of the population, and drawing the same percentage from each group rather than drawing the same number of people from each group.[1] Thus, if there are 600 women and 400 men in a population and a researcher wants a sample size of 100, he or she will not draw 50 men and 50 women. That does not accurately reflect the population. Instead, the researcher considers that 100 is 10% of the total population size of 1000 (600 women + 400 men = 1000 in the total population). Because 10% is needed, 10% of the women (i.e., $600 \times 10 = 60$) and 10% of the men (i.e., $400 \times 10 = 40$) are drawn. The resulting sample of 60 women and 40 men is representative of the population in terms of gender distribution (i.e., it accurately represents the same proportion of men and women as the population). Note that while this stratified random sample will be accurate in terms of its gender composition, the sample from each gender might not be representative of its respective group. For instance, the sample of 60 women drawn at random might be unrepresentative of the 600 women in the population due to errors created by random sampling (i.e., unrepresentative by the luck of the random draw). Nevertheless, for studies in which there might be differences associated with gender, it is better to ensure that men and women are represented in the correct proportions by using stratified random sampling than to take a chance on misrepresentation of gender that might be obtained by using simple random sampling.

Some students may believe that equal representation of each strata is better achieved by selecting the same numbers from each group to reach the sample total. To illustrate why this is wrong, suppose a researcher is trying to predict the outcome of a local proposition on funding from taxes for K–12 public education, and stratifies the sample into three surrounding districts. Fifty voters from District 1, District 2, and District 3 are randomly selected. District 1 stands to benefit the most from the new funding, and shows stronger support for the proposition. District 2 is evenly split, and District 3 is largely opposed. If they are all treated equally, the results from District 1 and District 3 may counterbalance one another, showing a weak victory or loss for the proposition. As it turns out, District 1 makes up 75% of the local voting population in the region, District 2 makes up 15%, and District 3 comprises only 10% of those who will vote on the proposition. By selecting 75% of the 150 people in the sample (112 people) from District 1, 15% or 23 people from District 2, and 10% or 15 people from District 3, the proportions match more closely to the distribution of voters, and are likely to give a more accurate prediction of a win for the education proposition.

If opinions on the issue of interest do not differ along the lines of gender in the first example, or district in the second, stratification by these characteristics will not increase the precision of the result. In other words, if men and women are the same in their opinions, it does not matter if a sample consists of all men, all women, or something in between because in any of these combinations, the approval rating will be about the same. In other words, the stratification variable of gender is irrelevant if those in the various strata are the same in terms of what is being studied. Thus, stratification will improve precision only if the stratification segments the population for a characteristic along which people are expected to predictably differ in the item being described, explained, or predicted.

Researchers are not confined to using just two variables for stratification. They can further increase precision (remember, this means reducing sampling errors) by using multiple strata to select a given sample. For instance, a researcher might stratify on the basis of both gender and age by drawing separate random samples from each of the four subgroups shown in Figure 27.1.

Having a larger number of strata is only better with variables that are both relevant and *independent* of each other. To see what is meant by independence, suppose a researcher stratifies on both age and number of years employed. Because older individuals have had more years in which to be employed, the two variables tend to be highly correlated. Thus, stratifying on age has probably already accounted to a great extent for years of employment (i.e., they are not independent of each other).

The primary purpose of stratification is to ensure that different subgroups are proportionally represented. In this instance, the goal in stratification is *not* to make comparisons

FIGURE 27.1 Stratification by gender and age.

Women Ages 18–39	Men Ages 18–39
Women Ages 40+	Men Ages 40+

across subgroups but to obtain a single sample that is representative in terms of the stratification variables.

Stratification shows yet one more way in which research methods are not simply a "plug and play" proposition that relies solely on mathematical or analytical formulas but depends heavily on logical, defendable decisions that reflect an understanding of the concepts and issues to result in high-quality work.

■ TOPIC REVIEW

1. What does stratification mean in random sampling?
2. What is the technical term for discussing the magnitude of sampling errors?
3. Is it possible for a random sample to contain sampling errors? What effect does stratification have on it?
4. What is the first step in stratified random sampling?
5. Does a researcher usually draw the "same number" *or* the "same percentage" from each stratum?
6. If the population of freshmen and the population of sophomores on a college campus are the same in their opinion on a particular issue on which a researcher will be conducting a survey, should the researcher stratify the sample based on class year?
7. Is it possible to stratify on more than one variable?
8. Is the primary purpose of stratifying to be able to compare subgroups (such as comparing freshmen and sophomores in Question 6)?

■ DISCUSSION QUESTIONS

1. Think of an issue on which you might want to conduct a survey using the students at your college or university as the population. Name the issue and two variables you think would be relevant for stratification purposes when drawing a stratified random sample. Defend your position.
2. Students were given a test on a research article they read for class. (The article reported on the use of stratified random sampling.) One test question asked, "What type of sampling was used in the research?" Students who answered using only the term "random sampling" lost a point for the question. The instructor's comment was that the answer was ambiguous. Do you think the instructor was right in taking off the point? Why? Why not?

■ RESEARCH PLANNING

If you planned to use simple random sampling (see Topic 26), do you now think your study would be improved if you used stratified random sampling instead? If yes, on what basis do you plan to stratify?

■ NOTE

1. If equal numbers are drawn, the responses from each stratum can be statistically weighted to make the statistical result reflect the population proportions.

TOPIC 28
CLUSTER SAMPLING

Simple random sampling, systematic sampling, and stratified random sampling are described in the previous two topics. These methods are referred to as probability sampling methods. In this topic, cluster sampling is considered.

Cluster sampling is another form of probability sampling. In this sampling method, researchers draw groups (or clusters) of participants instead of selecting individuals. It may be used when getting a list of all individuals that constitute a population is very difficult or impossible, but getting a complete list of a higher unit of analysis is not. For instance, it may be hard to get a list of all Methodists, all public high school students in California, or all people who have visited a national park, but possible to get a list of all Methodist churches, all public high schools in California, or all national parks.

Suppose a researcher wants to survey a sample of members of United Methodist churches throughout the United States. If the researcher obtains a membership list with addresses, he or she might draw a simple or stratified random sample of individuals and mail questionnaires to them. However, mailed questionnaires are notorious for their low response rates. The researcher might get a better response rate if he or she draws a sample of clusters—in this case, a sample of congregations—and contacts the ministers of the congregations to request that they personally distribute the questionnaires to their church members, collect the completed questionnaires, and mail them back to the researcher. If the ministers are convinced that the survey is appropriate and important, they might use their influence to help obtain responses from the members of their congregations (i.e., the clusters). Of course, for cluster sampling to be unbiased, a researcher must draw the clusters *at random*. This could be done by assigning a number to each congregation and using a table of random numbers to select a sample of the congregations (see Topic 26 for a description of how to use a table of random numbers).

Cluster sampling has a major drawback: each cluster tends to be more homogeneous in a variety of ways than the population as a whole. Suppose, for instance, that church members in the South tend to be more conservative than members in the North. Then, members of any one cluster in the South are unlikely to reflect accurately the attitudes of all members nationally. If a researcher draws only five clusters (i.e., congregations) at random, the researcher could easily obtain a sample in which most of the churches are in the South *or* most are in the North, potentially creating much sampling error, even if the five congregations provide a large number of participants. To avoid this problem, the researcher should draw a large number of clusters.[1] To help increase precision, the researcher could also stratify on geography and draw a random sample of clusters from each stratum, which would assure, for instance, that the North and South are represented in the correct proportions.

■ TOPIC REVIEW

1. Is cluster sampling a probability or nonprobability form of sampling?
2. To conduct a survey on a campus, a researcher drew a random sample of 25 class sections and contacted the instructors, who then administered the questionnaires in class. This researcher used what type of sampling?
3. What is a major drawback to cluster sampling?
4. What must researchers do in cluster sampling to obtain an unbiased sample of clusters?

■ DISCUSSION QUESTION

1. To study a sample of all nurses employed by hospitals in a state, a researcher drew two hospitals (clusters) at random, both of which happened, by chance, to be large public hospitals, each with hundreds of nurses, yielding a large sample. Are you impressed with the sample? Why? Why not?

■ RESEARCH PLANNING

In light of the topics covered so far on sampling, what type of sample do you plan to draw for your research? If you will be using a less-than-satisfactory sample, explain why it will be necessary to draw such a sample. How will you defend these choices or support them in your work to readers?

■ NOTE

1. Sample size for quantitative research is discussed in Topic 32. Note that statisticians consider each cluster to be a single participant. Thus, if five clusters are drawn, the sample size is 5. A comparison of sample sizes in both qualitative and quantitative research is discussed in Topics 32 and 33.

NONPROBABILITY SAMPLING AND QUALITATIVE RESEARCH

The previous topics described methods of **probability sampling,** in which samples are selected randomly and each person or unit has an equal, nonzero chance of being selected. Sometimes, probability samples are not possible or appropriate. In quantitative research, the goal is to create a sample that is representative of a larger population so that the statistical analysis of the numerical data will show relevant patterns and trends that support or refute hypotheses. In qualitative research, the method of analysis is not reliant on numerical data but is often based on direct experience through observation or extended interviews. Qualitative data and analysis often use the words of the participants and may be more intent on understanding the perspective of those directly involved in the issue, as well as how perspectives vary. Qualitative research may not try to generalize results to large groups, but it often does try to represent the experiences, outcomes, behaviors, opinions, language, or other elements about the group being studied.

Nonprobability samples do not guarantee that each person or element in the population has an equal chance of being selected. Several nonprobability sampling methods are presented here.

The first nonprobability method is called **purposive sampling** (also sometimes called **judgmental** sampling). When researchers use this method, they use their knowledge of the population to select individuals who they believe will be good sources of information. For instance, a researcher might observe over a long period that several members of the academic senate at a university consistently vote on the winning side on controversial issues. The researcher might decide that rather than interviewing a random sample drawn from the whole membership of the senate, he or she will interview only those who consistently vote on the winning side in order to predict the outcome of a new issue before the senate. Because these samples are not selected to be unbiased and representative of the population through random selection, their generalizability is more limited. Researchers frequently use purposive sampling in qualitative research. For more information on sampling in qualitative research, see Topic 33.

Several strategies for purposive sampling can help guide the researcher in selecting participants, and reduce the chance that bias taints the selection. The first, called **maximum variation sampling**, involves selecting a sample in which the widest range of variation on the dimensions of interest is represented. Another strategy for purposive sampling entails **extreme or deviant case sampling**. Looking at how cases are deviant can help define the category boundaries and shed light on the conventional case within a group. Conversely, **homogeneous sampling** is a form of purposive sampling that takes the opposite approach to maximum variation. It seeks to sample people who are similar to one another from a population that is larger and more diverse. Researchers may or may not describe their strategies when seeking a purposive sample, and these strategies do not have to be mutually exclusive.

Example 1 illustrates purposive sampling in which researchers investigated the experiences of those who became caregivers to parents as part of end-of-life care:

Example 1

Initially, sampling was purposive targeting bereaved family members who experienced transitioning their dying parents, primarily those enrolled in hospice. Two family members were recruited from a local college of health science, and two participants were recruited from a large church community. The remaining participants were recruited from two local hospice agencies.[1]

For the Example 1 study, the authors also explain that they conducted in-depth interviews, which allowed the researchers to develop the start of a theory. After this point, **theoretical sampling** was used. Like purposive sampling, theoretical sampling is based on the judgment of the researchers; however, instead of trying to represent various types of people, theoretical sampling selects additional participants based on information needed to corroborate, extend, or revise the emerging theory. For instance, in the Example 1 study, the researchers recruited social workers and nurses from residential facilities for the sample, and then recruited additional caregivers in families who did not have parents in hospice. The questions asked of these groups elicited information to fill gaps in the categories where a theory was being formulated.

Purposive sampling and theoretical sampling can be used independently, or, as in this example, they can be used sequentially. Typically, theoretical sampling is an *iterative* process, which means that the researchers alternate between theory development and collection of more data. Questions may be adapted in order to address the most needed data to inform the development of theory. When researchers find that respondents are giving answers that fit in the same theory, and no new data is emerging, this is typically called **saturation**. The technical term has a similar connotation to its more common meaning: when no more can be added or absorbed to something. It means the researchers have explored the categories many times, and have ceased to find any new properties that would fit into those categories.

An example of theoretical sampling comes from a qualitative article on how long-term marital couples are able to maintain stability, even as factors in social and personal life change. This study was interested in examining couples who had lived together for at least 10 years and had children in which the oldest child was at least 6 years of age.

Example 2

This analysis is based on interviews with 21 volunteer couples (i.e., 42 participants), completed as a part of the ongoing study. Participants were recruited via word of mouth and theoretically selected based on their relevance to the concepts of interest in this study (Corbin & Strauss, 2008). At the time of the interview, all were married, with relationships extending from 10 to 25 years. Most had two children. Four had one child, one had three, and one had four. Only one person reported a prior marriage.[2]

The article in Example 2 states that they selected participants "theoretically" and "based on their relevance to the concepts of interest in this study." To what concepts are they referring? The title of the article names three: flexibility, relational focus, and stability. Flexibility is defined in this study as the process of "how partners adjust to and are influenced by each other, situations, environments, and life changes."[3] Its importance to stability emerged from interviews. Interviews began with open concepts, asking couples to discuss what defines a good relationship or to describe how couples made choices about time spent apart and together. The researchers began to code and identify categories that emerged, consisting of "mutual decision making, mutual accommodation regarding household tasks, and mutual giving of personal time."[4] Additional participants were selected and questions may have been adjusted based on what additional information was needed to create saturation within the categories in the theory and ensure that other important categories were not overlooked.

Snowball sampling is another nonprobabilty method of sampling that can be useful when attempting to locate participants who are difficult to find. Suppose a researcher wants to study heroin addicts who have never had institutional contacts (e.g., never sought treatment or been arrested). How will the researcher find them? With the snowball technique, a researcher initially needs to find *only one*. If the researcher can convince this one individual that the research is important and that the data will remain confidential, this one participant might put the researcher in contact with several other potential participants. Each of these may help the researcher to contact several more. This technique is based on trust. If the initial participants trust the researcher, they may also identify other potential participants and convince them to trust the researcher. Of course, snowball samples should be presumed to be biased because individuals are not drawn at random. However, without the use of snowball sampling, there would be many special populations that researchers would be unable to study, such as successful criminals (i.e., criminals who have never been caught), homeless individuals with no institutional contacts, and others who are difficult to identify and locate. Both quantitative and qualitative researchers use snowball sampling for cases such as these.

In both qualitative and quantitative studies, researchers typically include a description of the participants in a study, as well as how they were selected. Qualitative researchers should plan to collect **demographic information** that will allow them to accurately account for the participants of the study at the point when they are ready to write about it. Occasionally, qualitative research articles only offer a thin description of how the sample was selected or the demographic composition of the sample. For instance, a report might simply say, "Fifteen male students who were enrolled in an introductory sociology class were interviewed." When thin descriptions are encountered, it may be safe to assume that a **sample of convenience** was used. This simply means that the sample was not selected by any other logic than participants being available and willing. This should be regarded as a flaw in sampling.

■ TOPIC REVIEW

1. Briefly define purposive sampling.
2. Who uses purposive sampling more: qualitative researchers *or* quantitative researchers?
3. What is maximum variation sampling?
4. What is the opposite of maximum variation sampling?

5. What is theoretical sampling?
6. What is the difference between purposive sampling and theoretical sampling?
7. True or false: purposive sampling and theoretical sampling can be used together.
8. In a qualitative study, why should you collect demographic data?
9. What is it called when a sample is selected solely on the logic of who is nearby and willing to participate? Is this an acceptable sampling method?
10. Which type of sampling is especially useful when attempting to locate participants who are difficult to find?
11. Suppose a researcher has identified an individual who has engaged in an illegal activity to be a participant in a research project, and then the researcher identifies others who have engaged in the same activity through the first individual's contacts. The researcher is using what type of sampling?

■ DISCUSSION QUESTIONS

1. Let's say you want to conduct a qualitative research study to determine the study habits of high school honors students. Consider how you might use the sampling principles presented here. What types of things might you consider to formulate your sampling strategy?
2. Name a population (other than those mentioned in the topic) for which snowball sampling might be better than other types of sampling. Explain the reason(s) for your answer.

■ RESEARCH PLANNING

If you are planning to conduct qualitative research, consider how you would approach your research question using purposive sampling or theoretical sampling strategies. What are some of the ways you could sample the group that interests you?

■ NOTES

1. From Martz, K., & Morse, J.M. (2016). The changing nature of guilt in family caregivers: Living through care transitions of parents at the end of life. *Qualitative Health Research.* doi:10.1177/1049732316649352
2. Nicoleau, A., Joo Kang, Y., Choau, S.T., & Knudson-Martin, C. (2014). Doing what it takes to make it work: Flexibility, relational focus, and stability among long-term couples with children. *Journal of Family Issues, 37*(12), 1639–1657. doi:10.1177/0192513X14543852
3. Ibid.
4. Ibid.

TOPIC 30

SAMPLING AND DEMOGRAPHICS

Demographics are the background characteristics that represent an indicator by which populations are described. These include characteristics such as gender, age, and income. When the data from a research study is analyzed, the demographic information is often the way that researchers analyze and discuss the outcomes of the study. Most studies collect basic information about age, gender, race, and some indicator of social class in the form of education, income, or both. Beyond that, researchers may decide to collect additional demographic characteristics based on their relevance to the study. Years married, number and ages of children, number of pets, health conditions, or occupation are all examples of demographics that may turn out to be important, depending on the topic of the study.

Consider a research project conducted with participants at a local substance abuse counseling center. By collecting demographic information on the participants, the researcher can provide the reading audience with a more accurate description of the individuals who constituted the sample for the study and how their responses differed across these groups. Readers can then make informed judgments regarding the extent to which the results may apply to their own settings. For instance, if the clients to whom a reader wants to generalize are similar in their demographics to the demographics of the participants in the study, the results are more likely to be generalizable.

Sometimes, the demographics for a population of interest are known, and these data can be useful for analyzing and interpreting the results of a study. For instance, suppose that a researcher is studying students at a specific college. The college has data about the student population indicating that 20% of the students in the population are Asian American. If a researcher draws a sample of the population and obtains a sample in which only 10% of the respondents are Asian American, he or she can make adjustments when completing statistical analysis to **weight** the results of the Asian American respondents in the sample. It works in a way that is similar to curving a grade. The responses of Asian Americans would be adjusted to a worth that is equal to 20% instead of 10% of the sample in the analysis, allowing the weight of Asian American responses to match their proportion in the known population.

Even if a researcher does not make a statistical adjustment based on the difference between the demographics of a population and a sample, it is still worthwhile to know how closely a sample reflects a population on important demographics. When reporting results, researchers often compare the sample demographics with those of the population, and account for areas where the sample differs from the population demographics.

Many studies rely on participants to actively volunteer into a research study. Whenever possible, it is important to collect demographics that permit the researcher to compare those who volunteered with those who were offered but did not volunteer to participate. Consider research on an after-school reading program in which the program is offered to all students, but only 30% volunteer to participate. From school records, it may be possible to provide information on demographic differences between the volunteers and nonvolunteers, such as previous grades in reading, gender differences, differences in age, and so on. Such information could be of value to readers who are interested in the application of the program in their local settings.

In experiments, a special type of sampling bias results from what researchers call **mortality**. As indicated in Topic 4, experiments are studies in which researchers administer treatments in order to examine their effects on participants. Consider an experiment in which a new therapy is administered to an experimental group while the control group receives no therapy. If some of the participants drop out of the experiment at midcourse, *mortality* is said to have occurred. Because mortality does not occur at random, the result is presumed to bias the sample. For instance, those in the experimental group who experience less relief from the therapy may get discouraged and drop out of the experiment before it is completed. This would bias the results of the experiment in favor of those for whom the therapy is effective.

Because of mortality, it is important for experimenters to mention in their research reports whether there was mortality and, if so, the number and percentage who dropped out from each group. In addition, information on the demographics of those who dropped out and those who completed the experiments should be reported. For instance, did those who dropped out have more severe symptoms to begin with? Did the dropouts tend to be older? Answers to these types of questions can help readers to assess the severity of the effects of mortality on the outcome of experiments.

■ TOPIC REVIEW

1. What are demographics?
2. Are all demographic variables equally relevant in all studies? Why or why not?
3. If a researcher compares the demographics of a sample with its population and finds that a subgroup is underrepresented, what is one way to address it?
4. Is it important to compare the demographics of those who participated in a study with those who were asked but did not participate? Why?
5. If some of the participants drop out of an experiment at midcourse, what is said to have occurred?

■ DISCUSSION QUESTION

1. Consider a survey on campus services for freshmen. Name three demographic variables that might be especially relevant for this study.

■ RESEARCH PLANNING

What demographic information might you collect from your participants that would be especially relevant to your topic or research question?

Do you anticipate the need to weight any demographic information mentioned in this topic? If so, in what area might you experience this? Consider how the sampling strategy might allow you to avoid the need for weighting.

TOPIC 31

SAMPLE COMPOSITION AND BIAS

Sample size is typically one of the first questions people have when it comes to sampling. As important as sample size is, it is secondary to the larger question of bias.

To understand why bias is more important, consider this example: A student is conducting a survey on whether the main cafeteria on campus should open during evening hours. Being a commuter with only day classes, the student goes to the cafeteria at lunchtime and asks every 10th student who enters to participate in the survey. Of the 100 participants in the survey, 65% say they would not use the cafeteria in the evening, 15% have no opinion, and 20% say they would go to the cafeteria during evening hours.

After considering the results, the student decides that he should have used a larger sample, so he obtains another 100 participants in the same way (asking every 10th student entering the cafeteria at lunchtime). This time, the results are 55% who say they would not use the cafeteria in the evening, 30% with no opinion, and 15% who want evening hours. Being very cautious, the student samples again, and this time obtains a 60% no/20% no opinion/20% yes split. Combining results from the three surveys, the student obtains the total results shown in Table 31.1 in the bottom row.

For all practical purposes, the three results indicate the same sentiment: only a minority want evening hours. With a total sample size of 300, the student might feel rather comfortable that he or she has pinned down an answer close to the truth. However, do you see the possible problem with his method of sampling? The student sampled only those who entered the cafeteria at lunchtime. The sample could easily be biased against those who are on campus in the evenings, and those are the students most likely to use the cafeteria in evening hours. The student can continue to increase the lunchtime sample size, but the increase has no benefit to correcting the bias. Instead, the student's results would gain accuracy by correcting for the bias by varying the time of day when data is collected. In fact, even if the sample is smaller, the study is likely to be more representative. As a rule, small, unbiased samples tend to yield more accurate

TABLE 31.1 **Combined Sample Results from Three Samples**

	Would not use evening hours	Would use evening hours	No opinion
Sample 1	65%	20%	15%
Sample 2	55%	15%	30%
Sample 3	60%	20	20%
Total	**60%**	**18.3%**	**21.7%**

results than biased samples, even if the sizes of the biased samples are large and the sizes of the unbiased samples are small.

Three of the most common sources of bias were covered in Topic 25 on biased and unbiased sampling. They include underrepresentation of some members within the population, as would be the case in the example above. Other common ways that samples are biased through sample selection processes are through a failure to ensure that population members have one and only one chance of being included, and through the difference between those who volunteer and those who do not. It can be tricky to identify biases based on differences between those who respond and those who do not, but researchers may compare the sample with the known parameters of the population to establish the degree to which the sample is representative of the population.

Once biases are addressed, sample size is the next consideration. Larger samples are of benefit in research because they increase **precision**. When researchers say that they have highly precise results, they are saying that the results will vary by only a small amount from sample to sample, which is what will happen if each sample is large. Notice that in the cafeteria example, the results of the three samples were reasonably close, so a researcher could correctly say that there is a good degree of precision. However, because of the bias in the method of sampling, it would be more accurate to say that the results are *precisely wrong* to the extent that the bias has consistently thrown the results off in the same direction each time a sample was drawn. This helps to emphasize the role of the researcher's careful thought, planning, and use of sampling strategies to ensure a quality sample, rather than relying on a number to define an adequate sample.

Thus, researchers should strive first to obtain an unbiased sample and then to seek a reasonably large number of participants. The next topic addresses sample size in quantitative studies, followed by Topic 33, which addresses sample size in qualitative studies.

■ TOPIC REVIEW

1. Is sample size the primary consideration when judging the adequacy of a sample?
2. Does increasing sample size reduce bias?
3. Does increasing sample size increase precision?
4. What are the three main types of bias to account for?
5. If a researcher uses a very large sample, is it still possible for the results to be wrong?
6. How could the researcher correct the bias in the above study about evening cafeteria hours?
7. True or false: "If the sample size is large, it will improve results, even if there is bias."

■ DISCUSSION QUESTIONS

1. A magazine editor conducted a poll by printing a questionnaire in an issue of the magazine for readers to fill out and mail back. Several thousand readers returned completed questionnaires. Suppose a friend reads the results of this poll and is convinced that it reflects the views of all adults in the United States. What would you say to convince him that he might be wrong?

2. Consider the statement "The larger the sample, the better." Explain why this statement might be misleading to a novice researcher.

■ RESEARCH PLANNING

Take notes on the ways that your data collection choices could lead to biases. What options might you have for varying your data collection or correcting for the potential bias?

SAMPLE SIZE IN QUANTITATIVE STUDIES

"How many participants will I need?" The answer is not as straightforward as it may seem. Sample size is one of the many decisions that researchers must make and be able to support with logic. Major factors that influence the quantitative researcher's choice of sample size include the purpose of the study, the population size from which the sample is being drawn, the amount of variability within the population, the risk of selecting a sample that is a poor representation of the population, and the amount of precision wanted from the results.

Sample size expectations differ depending on the goal of the study. For instance, researchers frequently conduct **pilot studies**, which are studies designed to obtain preliminary information on how new treatments and measures work. For instance, when studying a new drug, a researcher might conduct a pilot study on the maximum tolerable dose. Also, a researcher might try out a new measure, such as a questionnaire, to determine if any questions are ambiguous, or if there are questions that participants refuse to answer. Pilot studies are usually conducted with small sample sizes, such as 10 to 100. On the basis of the results, treatments and measures can be modified for use in more definitive future studies with larger samples.

If the research plan is to analyze data using statistics, a probability sample—otherwise known as a random sample—is needed. Topics 26 through 28 covered the main ways that probability samples are drawn. As students and new researchers learn to use statistics, they will find that sample size relates to mathematical properties. Remember that statistics are a type of analysis that approximates information from a sample to a known population. Sample size is determined by identifying the *minimum* number of people or units needed to represent that population well and to produce useful results when subjected to statistical analysis.

To offer a good approximation of the population, a sample needs to be large enough to adequately represent the population and its variability in the relevant areas of inquiry. Most studies have constraints on time, effort, and money that can be spent to complete data collection. Collecting more than the minimum number needed does not hurt a study, but it may also do very little to help create more accurate results. This is because, as more people are added, the effect of each person is a bit less to the total.

To illustrate this principle, consider the following two cases in Table 32.1, in which the sample size was increased by 50 participants.

It is clear that Researcher A gets a much bigger payoff for increasing the sample size by 50 because it doubles the sample size, which gives a big boost in precision. Researcher B, on the other hand, gets a very small increase in precision because the addition of 50 to the original sample of 3,000 has little influence on the results. The responses of the 50 additional participants will be overwhelmed by the responses of the first 3,000.

TABLE 32.1 Illustrates Increasing Sample Size

	Original Sample Size	Add to sample	New Sample Size	Added sample portion of population
Researcher A	50	+50	100	50%
Researcher B	3,000	+50	3,050	1.6%

Population size can affect the appropriate sample size, especially if the population is under 20,000. When the population is larger than 20,000, the recommended sample size does not change much based on population size. Because of this principle of *diminishing returns*, even the most important and prestigious national surveys are often conducted with only about 1,500 respondents. This book's authors reviewed sample sizes across articles in five journals published by the American Psychological Association and found that sample sizes ranged from 25 to 766, with a median of 82.[1] It is a good idea to review the literature in your area of study to see the sample size ranges of studies similar to your own.

Table 32.2 provides some helpful estimates for sample sizes in survey research that has a goal of description. The recommended sample sizes (n) correspond to a population size (N) that has an error of 5%. That is, the true percentage in the whole population should fall within 5% of the percentage obtained from the sample.

Notice that until the population size is over 400, the sample size is over half of the total. This further illustrates a practical application of the principle of diminishing returns. The recommendations in Table 32.2 are based on a few simple assumptions and should not be accepted as a rule but rather a guideline. If samples sizes are smaller than those listed, it may still be possible to conduct statistical analyses, but the margin of error will be larger. There are many sample size calculators online that allow the user to determine some basic parameters, including population size and margin of error, as well as determine the right sample size.[2]

Important considerations for determining sample size include variability, the risk of selecting a sample that is a poor representation of the population, and the precision that the researcher wants. Researchers can obtain accurate results from a small sample if a

TABLE 32.2 Recommended Sample Sizes (n) for Populations (N) with Finite Sizes[3]

N	n	N	n	N	n	N	n
10	10	150	108	750	254	10,000	370
25	24	200	130	1000	278	20,000	377
50	44	300	169	1500	306	50,000	381
75	63	400	196	2000	322	75,000	382
100	80	500	217	5000	357	100,000	384

population has very little variability (i.e., the population is homogeneous) and a **normal distribution** (values revolve around a central, most common value; more in Topic 61). For instance, the population of healthy babies born at 40 weeks is homogeneous and converges toward a consistent average. Human babies only have limited variation at birth, thankfully. Studying a random sample of only 100 babies is likely to give a researcher about the same information as studying a random sample of 1,000.

By contrast, if a population is very heterogeneous, a researcher needs a large sample. Suppose, for instance, a researcher wants to study the use of healthcare in the last six months among adults in a large metropolitan area. There undoubtedly is great variability, ranging from no use to extensive use. If the researcher draws a small sample of 50 individuals from such a diverse population, the researcher might obtain a result with major errors, such as not having a single individual with extensive use of healthcare in the sample. If the researcher also wants to categorize those in the sample by the type of health insurance they have, an even larger sample will be needed to capture a sample that represents all the categories in the population.

When researchers want to document something that is rare, such as incidence of heart attacks among men aged 18 to 30, a larger sample is needed because it will occur to so few individuals. If a researcher drew a small sample, such as 25 participants, and followed them for a year, it is quite likely that no heart attacks would occur, but it would be a mistake to conclude that no heart attacks occur in this age group. Studies of this type might rely on datasets from very large samples that were collected by others in order to have an adequate sample size.

When researchers are looking for small differences, they also need larger sample sizes to minimize the risk of drawing a nonrepresentative sample. Suppose the population of women voters is just slightly more in favor of a ballot proposition than is the population of men voters. In small random samples of these voters, the risk of selecting a nonrepresentative sample is high. Sampling errors could easily overwhelm the small difference and might even produce a result in which it appears that the men are slightly more in favor of the proposition than are women. Using large samples in this case is necessary if a researcher wants to identify the correct direction and size of such a small difference.

■ TOPIC REVIEW

1. Does the purpose of the study matter for sample size?
2. True or false: "Once you know the population size, the sample size is an easy calculation."
3. What are pilot studies?
4. Do researchers usually use small *or* large samples in pilot studies?
5. If a researcher suspects that a trait is rare in a population, should he or she use a small *or* a large sample to identify the incidence of the trait?
6. Suppose a researcher suspects that there is only a very small difference in the math abilities of boys and girls at the sixth-grade level. Should the researcher use a small *or* a large sample to measure this difference?
7. Suppose the population consists of church members in the Southern Baptist Convention. If a researcher believes the members of this population are very homogeneous in their belief in an afterlife, should the researcher use a small *or* a large sample to identify the percentage who hold such a belief?

8. What do N and n stand for in Table 32.2?
9. If the population size is 5,000, what is the recommended sample size?
10. At what population size does the sample size stop changing considerably?

■ DISCUSSION QUESTION

1. Some research articles based on small samples in academic journals are characterized by their authors as pilot studies. What justifies the publication of pilot studies? Why might they be rejected?

■ RESEARCH PLANNING

If you are planning a quantitative study, what is your anticipated sample size based on the information in this topic and the topics in this part thus far? Explain the basis for your decision. What factors affect your sample size considerations?

■ NOTES

1. The journals are *Journal of Counseling Psychology*, *Journal of Educational Psychology*, *Cultural Diversity and Ethnic Minority Psychology*, *American Journal of Orthopsychiatry*, and *Professional Psychology: Research and Practice*.
2. Examples of sample size calculators intended for research purposes are www.raosoft.com/samplesize.html and www.surveysystem.com/sscalc.htm. Online survey software may also offer a similar guideline or calculator—just be sure that the guidelines are intended for your type of research or discipline.
3. Adapted from a combination of Krejcie, R.V., & Morgan, D.W. (1970). Determining sample size for research activities. *Educational and Psychological Measurement, 30,* 607–610, and the use of the Raosoft sample size calculator with 50% response distribution for 5% margin of error.

SAMPLE SIZE AND DIVERSITY IN QUALITATIVE RESEARCH

Qualitative researchers are not collecting data that will be analyzed using statistical methods, so the mathematical and probabilistic rules used to determine quantitative sample sizes and selection do not have the same relevance. Topic 29 discussed differences in sampling strategies. In qualitative research, sampling is still tied to analytical methods, but is more reliant on the judgment of the researcher. As a result of this difference, qualitative research has often been subject to criticism for being less rigorous. However, qualitative researchers often respond that the two types of research have different logics and base the evaluation of rigor on different characteristics.

Qualitative data is collected in a number of ways: through interviews, observation, focus groups, or other modes of rich data collection in which the data from each subject is more extensive than quantitative data. Qualitative methods allow researchers to collect local knowledge and give voice to participants. Qualitative researchers are often interested in gathering data that is *in a context*. Context here means information about things such as the particular organization, geographic location, or period of time that may contribute to understanding the responses of the people included in the study.

Qualitative researchers are not trying to *generalize* to a known population, but still may be interested in exploring a topic that adds knowledge about a process or a concept. Often, a first question is whether the research focuses on capturing information within one case or will include more than one case, comparing the data for similarities or differences. Addressing this decision focuses the researcher on the theory, concept, process, or other underlying aspects of the research, allowing the researcher to refine the research question.

For instance, a professor might want to understand why so few women choose to major in engineering. For such a study, sampling women only from one campus would be appropriate. However, it might also be valuable to seek participants from multiple campuses. The researcher might want to find out about the differences in the size and composition of the campuses from which the women were selected and compare women's responses based on these differences as one way of gaining understanding of their choices. The use of participants from *diverse sources* is a methodological strength of a qualitative study when the researcher has a broader interest than just a single source (such as a single college campus). Example 1 illustrates how one group of researchers sought participants from diverse sources for a qualitative study.

Example 1

To begin the sampling procedure, 15 well-regarded mental health clinicians with a minimum of 5 years of professional experience were chosen as interviewees. These clinicians were chosen because of their: (a) involvement in therapeutic services to clients with developmental disabilities and severe and persistent mental illnesses;

(b) long-standing involvement with clients' interdisciplinary teams working with parents; and (c) noted consistent excellence of work in the field serving the DD population, both in treating clients and training employees and direct support service staff. Each key informant was asked to nominate two professionals: licensed social workers, group home coordinators or supervisors, or licensed registered nurses with case loads of at least 20 clients within the large metropolitan area of the initial sample group.[1]

The researchers in Example 1 also formulated criteria for the nominations of additional professionals, which included level of experience and the excellence of their work. Many qualitative researchers develop samples by placing themselves in a context and coming to know those involved, or using experts and key informants to reach a larger group. Another way is to recruit from a selected setting and create ways to allow those in the setting to opt in to the study. Example 2 is a qualitative study that explores what role family plays when African Americans choose to pursue doctoral degrees. Semi-structured interviews were conducted with 41 African American students who were currently enrolled as doctoral students in any discipline at one of two research-intensive programs—one at a private university and one at a public university. The researchers explained their sampling approach as follows:

Example 2

I sent emails to doctoral program coordinators at both institutions requesting they forward an announcement to students soliciting participants. I also attended a graduate student association meeting at each campus. A total of 30 participants responded. Snowball sampling was used to recruit the remaining participants (Stage & Manning, 2003).[2]

Snowball sampling, discussed in Topic 29, is a form of sampling in which people who are already participating can refer other appropriate participants. Often, multiple forms of sample recruitment are utilized as was the case in both examples. This is fairly common because different methods may work best at different phases of data collection.

Qualitative researchers usually use fewer participants than quantitative researchers. The literature on qualitative research methods points out that few guidelines exist for determining sample sizes for nonprobabilistic samples.[3] The literature on sample size for qualitative research varies in recommendations for a minimum sample size, usually between 20 and 50 participants. The authors reviewed sample sizes for qualitative research articles in five journals published by the American Psychological Association and found that qualitative research studies ranged from 10 to 26 participants with an average of 13.[4] To be published, sociological studies generally require a slightly larger sample size—20 or more.

Because of the inductive nature of much qualitative research, the exact sample size may not be determined at the outset of the study but will rely on the analysis that takes place as more data is collected. Researchers often rely on the concept of **saturation,** first covered in Topic 29. To recap, saturation relies on simultaneous analysis, in which major and minor themes of the research emerge. When adding several participants fails to yield new information that leads to the identification of additional themes or categories within a theme, the researcher might conclude that the data collection process has become saturated. Saturation suggests that new types of information are unlikely to be obtained by increasing the sample size. Thus, the point of saturation may determine the final sample size.

Most sources will say that sample sizes rely on the type of research, the topic, and the judgment of the researcher. The sampling strategy also has an effect. Deviant case sampling may be good with as few as one case, and homogeneous sampling strategies may start to find saturation in 10 cases. Maximum variation sampling is a frequently used purposive sampling strategy, and typically requires the largest minimum samples because of its goal of determining that variability has been exhausted.[5] This is often determined by getting redundant answers.

■ TOPIC REVIEW

1. Do qualitative samples rely on rules of probability for determining the appropriate size?
2. Are qualitative researchers always interested in problems that extend beyond one location or institution?
3. The use of participants from *diverse sources* is a methodological strength of a qualitative study when the researcher has what?
4. How might a qualitative researcher obtain participants for a sample?
5. On the basis of this topic, what was the average range of sample sizes for qualitative studies?
6. At what point might a qualitative researcher conclude that the data collection process has become saturated?

■ DISCUSSION QUESTION

1. Qualitative methods have been subject to many criticisms aimed at the sampling methods used. What questions or concerns do you have with qualitative sampling methods? What strengths are related to qualitative approaches to research?

■ RESEARCH PLANNING

If you are planning to conduct qualitative research, which approach do you think you will take to planning your sampling strategy? Even if you plan to collect data based on a model of reaching saturation, do you have an estimated range for the sample size you think your research project will require? Consider whether you will collect from more than one site or from people in more than one role.

■ NOTES

1. Van Ingen, D.J., Moore, L.L., & Fuemmeler, J.A. (2008). Parental overinvolvement: A qualitative study. *Journal of Development & Physical Disabilities, 20,* 449–465.

2. McCallum, C.M. (2016). 'Mom made me do it': The role of family in African Americans' decisions to enroll in doctoral education. *Journal of Diversity in Higher Education, 9,* 50–63.

3. Gues, G., Bunce, A., & Johnson, L. (2006). How many interviews are enough? An experiment with data saturation and variability. *Field Methods, 18,* 59–82. doi:10.1177/1525822X05279903

4. The journals are *Journal of Counseling Psychology, Journal of Educational Psychology, Cultural Diversity and Ethnic Minority Psychology, American Journal of Orthopsychiatry,* and *Professional Psychology: Research and Practice.*

5. Sandelowski, M. (1995). Sample size in qualitative research. *Research in Nursing & Health, 18,* 179–183.

SAMPLING IN THE MODERN WORLD

Statistics have become commonplace. They are reported in the news and are presented in much of the information we consume. Examples of research collection from the samples those statistics rely on also abound in surveys conducted through social media, email, and phone. Surveys ask your opinion of consumer products, to review a restaurant you recently ate at or book you read, or what candidate you are planning to vote for. Obviously, today's communication technology has developed rapidly and continues to evolve, but you may not realize that the use of sampling is also a modern phenomenon. Go back a century, and it was practically nonexistent as a research method.

Sampling has developed as a research method across disciplines over the 20th century. Even though some types of sampling predate written history (testing a part to determine characteristics of the whole), sampling for research is a modern phenomenon on which all scientific observation, statistical or not, has come to depend.[1] Very little sampling was used in research prior to the last decade of the 19th century, and sampling methods developed at the turn of the century only became popular in the 1930s.[2] The U.S. Census first used sampling strategies in a test survey on unemployment in 1937.[3]

For most of the 20th century, sampling relied on landline phones and mailing addresses that were shared by households. The selected sample received a call or a paper survey form in the mail along with a return envelope. Sometimes, door-to-door methods were used to collect data in person. These methods had difficulties that researchers had to surmount. First, they all involved expenses to mail surveys, place phone calls, or knock on doors to collect information. Second, methods of data collection were not guaranteed to reach an individual but were more likely to reach a household, which contained a variable number of adults and children.

The accuracy of quantitative research relies in large part on the ability to keep errors low, and one of the primary concerns is sampling errors. The revolution in information and communication technology has changed the sampling problems of the past. Now it is much cheaper and easier to reach people from any distance using a multitude of options. But remember the basis of a simple random sample? Each individual must have an equal, nonzero chance of selection. Usually, this means that each person has one and only one chance to be selected.

Reaching truly random samples of the general population through the Internet and phones faces difficulties, some of which are new and some are new variations on the same challenges sampling has always faced. Some people have phones and computers while others do not. With the proliferation of cell phones, some people have both a landline and a cell phone, and research indicates nearly half of all American adults now have only a cell phone. This means some people have no chance of selection, others have one chance, and others have multiple chances.

Many polling agencies and research centers have been studying how cell phones impact survey sample selection. Most telephone surveys use the household as the unit for sampling, which arose out of the fact that a landline phone is shared by the household. Cell phones, however, are rarely a collective item. They belong to individuals instead of the household and may belong to people of all ages. Even though there are banks of hundreds of contiguous numbers that are wireless only, simply selecting from these numbers does not resolve all issues with using phone numbers for selection. Those owned by anyone under 18 years of age can create problems for surveys that are meant only for adults. While a screening question can eliminate those individuals, it creates issues with the sample selection. Also consider a researcher attempting to use area code prefixes as an indicator of geographic location in selecting a sample. Cell phones now have "number portability" that allows people to keep the same cell phone number when they move to a new area code.

Web-based research also faces issues with sampling, but its low cost and ease of use makes it appealing. Its value depends on the credibility of the data, just as with traditional mail methods. Reaching people on the Internet or through email with Internet surveys is easier and much less expensive than acquiring a mailing list, and printing and mailing out surveys (although survey data is still collected this way sometimes).

Internet surveys are easy to handle for both respondents and researchers. Internet surveys can be completed and returned faster and with fewer steps required on the part of the respondent, and the data is already digitized for ease of analysis by researchers. The interactivity and nonlinearity possible online allow questions to include multimedia audio and video, and **branching** (in which the next question varies depending on prior answers) becomes a seamless process. In addition, the data is already input in a spreadsheet as a part of the survey process, reducing the time, cost, and potential for human error when data must be transitioned from answers on paper to a computer in order to be analyzed.

Internet surveys are not just much less costly to create and send out. Increasing sample size has a marginal cost that is virtually zero. This may seem like an argument for increasing sample size, but remember Topic 31 that discussed why sample size is less important than sample bias. Surveys or censuses based on large convenience samples are unlikely to produce credible data. But how can a sample other than a convenience sample be selected? One of the biggest challenges to Internet surveys is sampling. Currently, there is not a systematic method for accomplishing a traditional probability sample of the general population using the Internet. It is possible to mix mediums by mailing invitations or to go completely digital, emailing invitations. The approach may depend on the information that is available and the methods for selection. Lists of just email addresses can work for sampling organizations, but more information than an email address may be needed if a stratified sampling technique is to be used.

The Internet can significantly bias who can be reached because not all individuals have access to the Internet. This may be more significant for some demographic groups such as those with lower incomes, lower education, those living in rural areas, or those age 65 and older. Researchers should consider other factors that might lead to the subjects in their research to be less likely to use email or the Internet or less proficient with its use in a way that could affect participation, or uneven use among one's group of interest in ways that might bias samples. If a group or subgroup that a researcher is trying to sample is likely to be underrepresented using this method, it poses a serious biasing issue for a study. The researchers must consider whether an Internet approach is best, or how it can be supplemented.

Internet surveys are not all created equal, so their value must be evaluated based on the purpose for which they are intended and the claims or generalizations researchers apply in analysis.

■ TOPIC REVIEW

1. How long have sampling methods for research been around?
2. Much data collection in the past had to figure out how to create equal nonzero chances for people to be selected into a sample from a household. Why is that?
3. Why is it a challenge to draw a simple random sample using phone numbers now?
4. Is it still necessary to select a random sample when sampling is done using the Internet?
5. What are some examples of questions that Internet surveys may support better than traditional surveys?
6. What is the major consideration raised by this topic that may result in bias in an Internet survey?

■ DISCUSSION QUESTION

1. What are some examples of groups that could yield quality samples for an Internet survey? What makes them suited to this approach? What are some of the possible problems with surveying on the Internet and how could these issues be addressed?

■ RESEARCH PLANNING

If you are considering a survey that uses digital methods and requires random sampling techniques, what are some ways that you might ensure your sample meets the standards of random sampling? Are there ways that you can stratify your sample to improve results? Will you offer any alternative forms of data collection to resolve potential biases in the sample?

■ NOTES

1. Wright, T., & Farmer, J. (2000). *A Bibliography of Selected Statistical Methods and Development Related to Census 2000*. Bureau of the Census Statistical Research Division, Statistical Research Report Series No. RR 2000/02.
2. Ibid.
3. U.S. Census Bureau History Staff. (2016). Developing sampling techniques. *Data Collection*. Retrieved June 20, 2016 from www.census.gov/history/www/innovations/data_collection/developing_sampling_techniques.html.

PART 5
Measurement

This part covers the essentials of measurement with an emphasis on how to assess the validity of tests and measures. Validity and reliability are explored in detail in Topics 35 through 41. Topic 42 explores various ways that researchers interpret measurement scores. Finally, Topics 43 and 44 discuss the distinguishing features of measures of optimum and typical performance. Topic 45 discusses how measurement concepts are used in qualitative research.

INTRODUCTION TO VALIDITY

When talking about measurement, especially in quantitative research, it is important to understand **validity.** Validity is a concept that is used in relation to **measures,** which is a generic term for measurement devices (e.g., tests, questionnaires, interview schedules, or personality scales).[1]

Researchers call a measure **valid** to the extent that it measures what it is designed to measure and accurately performs the function(s) it is purported to perform. For instance, consider an achievement test in American history that emphasizes knowledge of dates, places, and events in the westward spread of settlement in the United States. It will be only *modestly valid* when administered to students whose instruction in history emphasized a critical appraisal of social and economic forces and movements over facts and figures. Likewise, an employment test is likely to be only *partially valid* if it only tests applicants' ability to use Microsoft Word, and the job to which they are applying includes the use of several other programs.

It is important to note that validity is *relative* to the purpose of testing. If the purpose is to measure the achievement of students exposed to instruction in critical thinking, a test that measures only factual knowledge will be largely lacking in validity. For the purpose of measuring the achievement of students exposed to instruction in which the acquisition of factual knowledge is emphasized, the same test will be much more valid. Thus, before researchers can assess the validity of a particular measure, the purpose for measuring must be clearly identified.

Also, note that validity is a *matter of degree.* Therefore, it is appropriate to discuss *how valid* a test is—not *whether* it is valid. Given the imperfect state of measurement practice, it is safe to say that no test is perfectly valid.

Consider some reasons why perfect validity is elusive. First, almost all tests tap only a *sample* of the behavior underlying the constructs being measured. Consider the construct of aptitude for college (i.e., having the abilities to succeed in college). College aptitude tests emphasize verbal and mathematical skills but do not assess other behaviors that relate to college success, such as the ability to use a computer to do homework, knowledge of how to use an academic library, command of effective study. Even within the domains that are tapped by a college aptitude test, only a small sample of verbal and mathematical problems can be presented within a test of reasonable length. In the same way as researchers sample participants from a population (see Part 4 of this book), some samples of material and skills covered by tests are better than others, and all samples are subject to error.

Another reason that perfect validity is elusive is that some traits researchers may want to study are elusive and inherently difficult to measure. Consider the trait of cheerfulness. Almost everyone has known individuals whose cheerfulness is contagious. However, how can researchers measure this trait in a systematic way in order to study it? Researchers could, for instance, ask a series of questions on how participants interact with other individuals in various types of contexts, how they view adversity, and so forth. On the other hand, researchers might observe participants and rate them on the cheerfulness they exhibit in their interactions with others (e.g., Do they smile? Is the tone of their voice upbeat? and so on). While these procedures probably identify certain aspects of cheerfulness, even taken together, they fail to capture the *full essence* of the trait. This illustrates the old principle that the whole may be greater than the sum of its parts. To compound the problem, researchers often examine only some of the parts when they attempt to measure a given trait (e.g., researchers look at only certain behaviors that indicate cheerfulness, not all possible cheerful behaviors, and do this in only certain specific settings, not all possible life circumstances).

The problem of elusiveness, at first glance, seems to plague those with a quantitative orientation more than those with a qualitative orientation because quantitative researchers seek to reduce elusive constructs, such as cheerfulness, to numerical scores, no matter how difficult to measure directly they may be. Qualitative researchers, on the other hand, tend to measure in ways (such as unstructured interviews) that yield words to describe the extent to which traits are present. Yet unless qualitative researchers refer to specific behaviors and events in their reports, they will fail to describe results in enough detail for readers to accurately understand the meanings that have been attached to a construct such as cheerfulness. While qualitative researchers' descriptions (including quoting participants' words) are less artificial than the numerical scores obtained by quantitative researchers, qualitative researchers can find it as difficult to describe the essence of a trait, such as the feelings a genuinely cheerful individual creates when interacting with others, as it is to create quantitative data that captures it. The next three topics explore the major methods researchers use to assess the extent to which measures are valid.

■ TOPIC REVIEW

1. What is the generic term for any type of measurement device?
2. A measure is said to be valid to the extent that it does what?
3. Suppose a researcher purchases a commercial reading test that is highly valid for students who receive reading instruction that emphasizes phonics. Is it possible that the test is of limited validity for students who are taught with a method that does not emphasize phonics?
4. According to this topic, is it safe to say that no test is perfectly valid?
5. Tapping only a sample of the behaviors underlying the construct a researcher wants to measure has what effect on validity?
6. If a trait is elusive, is it easy *or* difficult to measure with a high degree of validity?

■ DISCUSSION QUESTIONS

1. Have you ever taken an achievement test in school that seemed flawed in its validity? If so, describe the test and state why you believe it was seriously flawed. In your discussion, mention the purpose for testing.
2. Name a trait you think is *elusive* and thus may be difficult to measure with great validity. Discuss different ways the trait could be measured.

■ RESEARCH PLANNING

Will you use or create any measures in your research (e.g., tests, questionnaires, interview schedules, or personality scales)? Have you considered how to translate the quality you wish to capture into measurements? If you will be using measures, do a little research by looking up some measures that have already been validated. How did they capture concepts? Can you use any existing measures, or can you use anything you have learned to improve the validity of your own measure?

■ NOTE

1. Note that some researchers use the term instrument as a synonym for the word measure. The term *instrumentation* is sometimes used as the heading for the "measure" section of a research report in older research literature.

TOPIC 36

JUDGMENTAL VALIDITY

As explained in the last topic, validity reflects the extent to which a measure (such as a test or questionnaire) captures the information it is meant to measure or accurately performs the function(s) it claims to perform. Validity is assessed in a few ways based on dimensions of the measure that help to establish its validity. **Judgmental validity** consists of assessments that are based on professional knowledge. There are two forms of judgmental validity: **content validity** and **face validity.**

Content validity, as the name suggests, is an assessment of a measure based on the appropriateness of its contents. In other words, do the questions or other measurements used actually produce responses that address the construct in question? Content validity is often determined by having participants complete the measure and then having experts analyze the items in the measure and the answers they elicit to determine whether they reflect the concept that the measure was attempting to describe.

For achievement tests, this type of validity is essential. Suppose a group of researchers want to build an achievement test on the material in the first four parts of this book. What steps could the researchers take to maximize the content validity of the test?

First, they would need to consider the types of test items to be used and the amount of time given to take the test. For instance, it is possible to include many more multiple-choice items than essay items in a given amount of testing time. Assume the researchers decided to write 35 multiple-choice items to be administered in a 50-minute period. The researchers could write one item on each of the 34 topics. This would ensure that the test covered a broad sample of the material. Then, the researchers could allocate any remaining items to topics deemed most important. The researchers would also need to decide which skills to measure. They could test primarily for facts and definitions (e.g., "Which of the following is the definition of validity?") or for higher-level understanding through application (e.g., "Which one of the following statements indicates something about the content validity of a test?").

Although the above example has been simplified, it illustrates three principles for writing achievement tests with high content validity. First, a broad sample of content is usually better than a narrow one. Second, important material should be emphasized. Third, questions should be written to measure the appropriate skills, such as knowledge of facts and definitions, application of definitions to new situations, drawing inferences, making critical appraisals, and so on. Of course, the skills should be those covered in instruction. Keeping these principles in mind, researchers can make *judgments* of the content validity of achievement tests.

Although content validity is most closely associated with achievement testing, it is sometimes applied when evaluating other types of measures. For instance, if researchers want to measure the broad construct called *self-concept* with a series of questions, they could consider sampling from each of the narrower constructs that constitute it, such as physical self-concept, academic self-concept, social self-concept, and so on. A broad sample of all the elements that constitute *self-concept* should be covered. If the researchers believe one type of self-concept is more important than others for their research purpose (e.g., academic self-concept for a study in a school setting), they might emphasize one type over the others by asking more questions about it. Finally, the researchers will need to write the questions in such a way that they elicit common, shared meanings from the examinees. To do this, the researchers should consider the participants' educational levels and the meanings they are likely to attach to particular words in the questions. Will the participants find some words too difficult to understand? Are some terms ambiguous in their meaning? Careful consideration of these points regarding the contents of measures helps to improve their validity.

Face validity judges whether a measure appears to be valid *on the face of it*. In other words, upon superficial inspection, does it seem to measure what it claims to measure? Consider, as an example, a survey that attempts to measure sexism. If the test includes statements with which to agree or disagree, and one of those statements is "I am sexist," that may seem valid on its face. It does appear to measure the construct ("sexism") that it is designed to measure. However, many sexist people may not be willing to directly identify themselves with a term that carries a negative social value. Individuals in research situations are likely to adjust their answers to conform to socially acceptable answers, so the most direct items may be less successful around prejudicial behaviors. Statements that measure attitudes less directly, such as "Women should take more responsibility for childcare" or "In a heterosexual relationship, the man should earn more money than the woman," may produce more valid responses. Even though the face validity might be higher with the direct statement "I am sexist," the second items may also be considered to have face validity because they seem to measure what they seek to measure.

In cases like these that attempt to investigate behaviors or attitudes participants may not want to admit to, researchers may deliberately use measures with *low face validity*. For instance, in a survey on sexism, pollsters may ask about a variety of unrelated topics even though they were concerned only with attitudes related to sexism. The face validity of the survey questions may be deliberately diluted with questions about other topics in the hope of reducing the potential sensitivity of the questions on sexism. In general, low face validity is desirable when researchers want to disguise the true purpose of the research from the respondents. This type of deception can, of course, raise ethical issues (see Topic 11).

Face validity is considered a weak form of validity, but researchers usually do prefer to use tests that *look like* they are related to their purpose, in addition to having content validity. It is possible for a test to have high face validity for a certain purpose while having low content validity. For example, a test of anxiety based on reports of sensations such as butterflies in the stomach or sour stomach may have high face validity, but these symptoms are subjective and have not shown good content validity when used in anxiety measures. Content validity has been better established for many other measures, such as "feeling of suffocation" and "fear of losing control."[1]

■ TOPIC REVIEW

1. What is judgmental validity based on? What are the two types of judgmental validity?
2. True or false? "To improve content validity, it is usually desirable to cover only a narrow sample of content from the broad content area to be covered by an achievement test."

3. Is content validity relevant only to achievement tests?
4. Which type of validity is based on superficial inspection?
5. Which type of judgmental validity is more valuable to research design?
6. Is it possible for a test to have high face validity but low content validity?
7. When might a researcher deliberately use a measure with low face validity?

■ DISCUSSION QUESTIONS

1. Suppose an instructor fails to tell students the types of items (e.g., multiple-choice or essay) that will be on a midterm examination. Could this affect the validity of the results? Explain.
2. Have you ever taken an achievement test in which the content emphasized was different from the content you concentrated on while studying for the test? If so, describe the discrepancy, and speculate on what caused it.

■ RESEARCH PLANNING

Consider any questions or measures you are planning to use in your research. If you had to explain the items' validity to a critic, how would you justify your questions or measures in terms of judgmental validity? Do you anticipate that your measure(s) will have high or low face validity? Explain the reason.

■ NOTE

1. Beck, A.T., & Steer, R.A. (1990). *Manual for the Beck Anxiety Inventory.* San Antonio, TX: Psychological Corporation.

TOPIC 37

EMPIRICAL VALIDITY

Empirical[1] **validity** is also referred to as predictive validity or criterion-related validity. It is when researchers make planned comparisons to see if a measure yields scores that relate to the chosen **criterion** (a standard or principle used to judge). For instance, if one compares performance on a college entrance exam with students' subsequent college grade point averages, this is an assessment of empirical validity. Another example of this approach to validity is offered in Example 1.

Example 1

Nine applicants for the position of administrative assistant were administered a pre-employment test, yielding scores from 15 to 35. Due to a labor shortage, all nine were hired even though some had low test scores. After six months on the job, the employees were evaluated on job performance by their supervisors on a scale from 1 (poor performance) to 10 (excellent performance). Here are their scores and ratings:

Employee	Test Score	Supervisor Rating	Placement
Jose	35	9	Top third on test.
Jane	32	10	
Bob	29	8	
Fernando	27	8	Middle third on test.
Sue	25	7	
Debbie	22	8	
Milly	21	6	Bottom third on test.
Ling	18	4	
John	15	5	

Comparing the test scores with the supervisor ratings provides information about the validity of the pre-employment test. In this example, the supervisor rating is the *criterion* by which the test is being judged. Because the purpose of a pre-employment test is to *predict* success on the job, the most appropriate test of validity is **predictive validity**: To what extent does the employment test predict the outcome (in this case, the supervisor rating)?

To begin to assess the validity of the employee test in Example 1, a researcher can examine the table. First, notice that those in the bottom third on the test are also in the bottom third in terms of ratings, suggesting that the test is highly valid for identifying those who will get low ratings on the job. Next, notice that the results for the top and middle thirds are more mixed. For instance, Bob, who is in the top third on the test with a score of 29, has a rating of 8, which is the same as the ratings of Fernando and Debbie, who are in the middle third. Thus, while the test has some validity at these high levels, it is not perfectly valid.

A researcher can obtain more information on the test's predictive validity by looking at the rank order of individuals on the test in comparison to their rank order on the ratings. In Example 1, the individuals are already ordered from high to low in terms of test scores. Notice that their order on ratings is to some extent similar but not the same. For instance, Jose has the highest test score, but only the second-highest rating. Sue scored higher than Debbie on the test, but Debbie exceeds Sue on the ratings. Despite exceptions such as these, the overall ordering of individuals by the test is similar to their ordering in terms of supervisors' ratings.

Another way to look at a test's predictive validity is to compute its **validity coefficient**. A validity coefficient is a *correlation coefficient*[2] used to express validity. Correlation coefficients are described in detail in Topic 67. At this point, only some basic properties of validity coefficients will be considered. Coefficients range from 0.00 (no validity) to 1.00 (perfect validity).[3] In practical terms, a coefficient of 1.00 indicates that the ranks on the test are identical to the ranks on the criterion (the supervisor rating). A coefficient of 0.00 indicates that there is no relationship between performance on the test and the ranks on the criterion. In other words, knowing the test scores is of no benefit when predicting the supervisor rating. The data in Example 1 have a validity coefficient of .89, indicating a very high degree of validity—higher than is usually found in validity studies of this type.

Higher validity coefficients are better, but how high should predictive validity coefficients be to indicate the measure is valid? For an employment test validated against supervisor ratings, a knowledgeable researcher would be surprised to obtain a coefficient that is greater than about .60 and would not be at all surprised to obtain one as low as .20, indicating poor validity.

Why are employment tests only modestly to poorly valid? For two reasons: First, success on the job is a complex construct involving many traits, such as interpersonal skills (e.g., getting along with coworkers), psychomotor skills (e.g., typing), work habits (e.g., being punctual), and so on. It is not reasonable to expect a single test (especially a paper-and-pencil test) to predict all these traits successfully. Second, coefficients are not higher because criteria such as supervisors' ratings are themselves less than perfectly reliable and valid. Thus, even if a test were perfectly valid, the coefficient would be less than 1.00 if the supervisors failed to put the employees in the order that objectively reflects their job effectiveness. (Note that human judgments are subject to biases and other sources of error.)

Sometimes, researchers determine the empirical validity of a test that is *not* designed to predict future behavior. For instance, a new self-administered version of the Addiction Severity Index (ASI) was validated by correlating scores on it with scores obtained using the expensive and time-consuming original version, which involves a lengthy, structured clinical interview. The original version, which had been widely accepted as being highly valid, was the *criterion* (or gold standard) by which the new version was judged. In this study, the Drug Domain subscale on the self-administered version of the ASI had a *validity coefficient* of .62, which is moderately high, indicating that the less expensive version of the ASI provided information reasonably similar to the more expensive original version.[4]

Another approach is to correlate scores on a test that is being validated with scores on a *different test* of the same trait. For instance, scores on the *Beck Depression Inventory* were

TABLE 37.1   Types of Criterion-Related Validity*

	What is the criterion?	When is the criterion measured?
1. Predictive validity	A measure of the outcome that the test is designed to predict.	After examinees have had a chance to exhibit the predicted behavior.
2. Concurrent validity	An independent measure of the same trait that the test is designed to measure.	At about the same time that the test is administered.

*Both types of criterion-related validity employ the empirical approach. That is, they are based on data that have been collected (planned empirical data collection)—not subjective judgments or theory.

correlated with scores on the *Revised Hamilton Psychiatric Rating Scale for Depression*, which resulted in a validity coefficient of .71. This relatively strong correlation indicates that to the extent that one of the measures is valid, the other one has a similar degree of validity.[5]

A validity coefficient that is obtained by administering the test and collecting the criterion data at about the same time is called a **concurrent validity coefficient** (as opposed to a **predictive validity coefficient**). Notice that in both predictive and concurrent validity, researchers validate by comparing scores with a criterion. Table 37.1 shows the relevant features of both.

■ TOPIC REVIEW

1. What is the term for the standard by which a test is judged?
2. How is *empirical* defined in this topic?
3. What question does predictive validity answer?
4. If a test is perfectly valid, what value will its validity coefficient have?
5. In light of this topic, should a researcher be surprised to get a validity coefficient of 0.95 for a paper-and-pencil employment test when validated against supervisors' job-performance ratings?
6. If a test has no validity whatsoever, what value will its validity coefficient have?
7. If a researcher collects the criterion data at about the same time the test is being administered, he or she is examining what type of empirical validity?

■ DISCUSSION QUESTIONS

1. Suppose a researcher validated a new multiple-choice reading test by correlating the test scores with teachers' ratings of students' reading abilities (i.e., the scores on the test were correlated with the ratings made by teachers). What is your opinion on using teachers' ratings for this purpose? Could teachers' ratings themselves be less than perfectly valid? Explain.
2. Suppose a researcher wanted to validate a new measure of self-esteem. Name a criterion that might be used in a criterion-related validity study. Be prepared to justify its use.

3. The validity of an achievement test might be established by using either content validity (see Topic 36) *or* concurrent validity (e.g., correlating the scores with teachers' judgments of students' achievements). In your opinion, which approach to validity is more useful for achievement tests? Should both be used?

■ RESEARCH PLANNING

How will you evaluate the empirical validity of any measures you will be using in your research? Explain. (Note that if you use a published measure, information on empirical validity may already be available in the manual for the measure or in a research report that used the measure.)

■ NOTES

1. The definition of *empirical* that applies to this discussion is "relying on or based on observation rather than theory."
2. See Topic 67 on the Pearson Correlation Coefficient to learn more about this statistic.
3. It is also possible to obtain negative coefficients, but they are very rare in validity studies. Negative correlation coefficients are discussed in Topic 67.
4. Butler, S.F., Budman, S.H., Goldman, R.J., Newman, F.L., Beckley, K.E., Trottier, D., & Cacciola, J.S. (2001). Initial validation of a computer-administered Addiction Severity Index: The ASI-MV. *Psychology of Addictive Behaviors, 15,* 4–12.
5. Beck, A.T., Steer, R.A., & Brown, G.K. (1996). *Manual for the Beck Depression Inventory—Second Edition.* San Antonio, TX: The Psychological Corporation.

JUDGMENTAL-EMPIRICAL VALIDITY

The type of validity that relies on subjective judgments *and* empirical data (i.e., data based on observations) is **construct validity**. A **construct** stands for a collection of related behaviors that are associated in a meaningful way. For instance, "depression" is a construct that stands for a personality trait manifested by behaviors such as lethargy, flat affect when speaking, loss of appetite, loss of sexual drive, preoccupation with suicidal thoughts, difficulty concentrating on tasks, and so on. Notice that each of these is an *indicator* of depression—the construct itself does not have a physical being outside of its indicators. That is, observers infer its existence based on the *collection* of related indicators. The emphasis on *collection* is important because any one indicator may be associated with several constructs. For instance, although loss of appetite is an indicator of depression, it may also be an indicator of anxiety, fear, physical illness, and so on. Thus, loss of appetite is indicative of depression only when it is found in association with a number of other indicators of depression.

To determine the construct validity of a measure, researchers begin by hypothesizing about components that make up the construct they wish to measure. How should it affect or relate to other variables? For instance, researchers might hypothesize that students who are depressed will earn lower grades and be more likely to drop out of college than students who are not depressed. Note that this is a *hypothesis* (see Topic 24) because it *predicts* a relationship between depression and grades earned in college. Also, note that the researchers arrived at the hypothesis by making a subjective judgment regarding the likely effects of the indicators of depression on grades. If the researchers test the hypothesis using empirical methods, they are conducting a construct validity study.

Consider how this works for a new 50-question depression *scale*.[1] To determine this scale's construct validity, the researchers could test the hypothesis stated above using a sample of college students as participants. First, suppose the researchers find *no* relationship between the scores obtained on the depression scale and success in college. What does this mean? Either (1) the scale lacks validity for measuring depression (i.e., it measures something else that is not related to grades earned in college) or (2) the hypothesis is wrong. If the researchers hold firmly to their belief in the hypothesis, they will have to conclude that the empirical evidence argues against the validity of the scale.

Next, suppose the researchers find a relationship between scores obtained on the new depression scale and performance in college. What does this mean? Either (1) the depression scale is, to some degree, valid for measuring depression or (2) the depression scale measures a variable other than depression that is also related to grades earned in college. This other variable could be many things. For instance, maybe the scale is heavily loaded with signs of depression that are also signs of anxiety so that it is more a measure of anxiety than depression. Because debilitating anxiety may lead to poor grades in college, the scores on the scale may relate to grades in college because it measures anxiety, not depression.

At this point, it should be clear that determining construct validity is a complex matter that involves both judgment and empirical data. Also, it should be clear that this method offers only *indirect* evidence regarding the validity of a measure. Notice that direct evidence on the validity of a depression scale could be obtained by determining *criterion-related validity* (see Topic 37). For instance, this could be done by correlating scores obtained on the depression scale with clinical psychologists' judgments on how depressed each participant is. This is direct evidence because the researcher would be comparing scores from a depression scale with some other established measure of depression, not with an entirely different variable such as grades earned in college.

Consider another example: the construct called *dependence on others*. A researcher might hypothesize that younger children are, on average, more dependent on adults than are older children. If the researcher tests the hypothesis and finds that the scores on a dependence scale fail to relate to age among children, this result would argue against the validity of the dependence scale. On the other hand, if the researcher finds the predicted relationship between the dependence scores and age, this empirical evidence would suggest that the scale might have validity.

Because the evidence generated by construct validity studies is indirect, researchers should be very cautious about declaring a measure to be valid on the basis of a single study. Instead, researchers hope to see a series of construct validity studies for a given measure—testing various hypotheses derived by considering how the construct should be related to other variables—before reaching firm conclusions.

From one perspective, the indirect nature of the evidence obtained in construct validity studies may be regarded as a weakness. However, when there are a series of construct validity studies on a given measure, researchers gain insight into how meaningful the scores are in various contexts. This gives richness to researchers' understanding of how well a measure works, which is a strength of this approach to validity.

Note that construct validity requires *judgments* about the nature of relationships as well as *empirical evidence* regarding whether a measure provides scores consistent with the judgments. Hence, construct validity is classified as *judgmental-empirical* in this book.

Historically, construct validity has been most closely associated with personality scales. However, its proper application can yield useful information about all types of measures. It is often desirable to examine a given measure in several different types of validity studies. The types of validity considered in Topics 35, 36, 37, and this topic are summarized in Table 38.1.

TABLE 38.1   Comparison of Major Approaches to Validity

Approaches to validity	Types	How determined
Judgmental	Content	Make expert judgments on the appropriateness of the content.
	Face	Make judgments based on superficial appearance.
Empirical	Predictive	Correlate test scores with criterion scores obtained after examinees have had a chance to achieve the outcome that is supposedly predicted by the test.
	Concurrent	Correlate test scores with criterion scores obtained at about the same time the test is administered.
Judgmental-Empirical	Construct	Hypothesize a relationship between the test scores and scores on another variable. Then, test the hypothesis.

■ TOPIC REVIEW

1. How is the term *construct* defined in this topic?
2. Is fear a construct?
3. To determine construct validity, researchers begin by hypothesizing what?
4. Does confirming a hypothesis in a construct validity study offer "direct" *or* "indirect" evidence on the validity of a test?
5. In Table 38.1, which two types of validity are classified as solely empirical?
6. In Table 38.1, which two types of validity are classified as solely judgmental?
7. Why is construct validity identified as judgmental-empirical in this book?

■ DISCUSSION QUESTIONS

1. In your opinion, what are some of the indicators of (or behaviors associated with) the construct called *industriousness*?
2. To determine the construct validity of an industriousness scale, a researcher hypothesized that scores earned on it should be correlated with the number of promotions employees received on the job. Do you think this is a good hypothesis for a construct validity study? Explain.

■ RESEARCH PLANNING

Does your study work with any constructs? What components make up your construct or are related to or affected by it? What are some of the measures you can use as indicators of your construct? How would you argue for this item's construct validity in your research report?

■ NOTE

1. Measures of personality traits are often called *scales* so they can be distinguished from *tests* of cognitive skills, which have right and wrong answers.

RELIABILITY AND ITS RELATIONSHIP TO VALIDITY

A test is said to be **reliable** if it yields *consistent* results. It is easy to see what this means by considering an extreme example. Suppose a professor writes a midterm exam on research methods that contains only four multiple-choice items. The items are on four different important concepts that were emphasized during instruction. Thus, the exam is *valid* in the sense that it covers appropriate content. However, students who have thoroughly mastered the course content should be concerned about taking such a test because it would be very easy to misinterpret a question or to miss a key term in it and get it wrong, yielding a score of 3 out of 4, or only 75% correct, despite knowing the material. On the other hand, students who have moved through the semester in a fog—not understanding even basic concepts—should be pleased at the prospect of taking this exam. With only four multiple-choice items, the odds of getting a few right by guessing, and thus passing the test, are reasonably high.

Now suppose some students complain about their scores on the midterm, so the professor writes four new multiple-choice items, and again, the items are all on appropriate content. After administering the test at the next class meeting (without announcing there would be a second test, so students are not motivated to study again), should the professor expect to obtain the same scores as he or she did the first time? In all likelihood, no. Some students who were lucky in guessing the first time will have their luck wash out. Other students who misinterpreted a key term in a question will not do so on the new set of items. Examining the scores from the two tests provides the professor with information on the *consistency of results* or *reliability*. In this case, he or she would probably find that the scores are rather inconsistent from one test to the other.

What can the professor do to increase the reliability of the midterm? Obviously, the professor can increase the length of the test. This reduces the effects of the occasional ambiguous item and the effects of guessing. After realizing this principle, the professor instructs a graduate assistant to prepare a 100-item test overnight. The assistant, being pressed for time, takes the easy route and pulls a standardized test off the shelf. Although it has 100 items, they are on educational psychology, which includes some research concepts but also much material not covered in the research methods class. Administering this test should give highly reliable results because it contains a large number of test items. If the professor administers it twice, for instance, students who have a good command of educational psychology should do well on both tests. Also, those who have little knowledge of educational psychology will have little chance of getting a good grade by guessing on such a large number of items and, thus, should do poorly on both administrations. However, the professor has a new problem: The test lacks **validity** because it covers the wrong content (see Topics 35 through 38 to review the concept of validity). This example illustrates an important principle: *A test with high reliability may have low validity.*

Here is another example of this principle: An employer wants to reward the best employees with end-of-year bonuses. The employer decides that to be perfectly fair, she should use a completely objective method for determining who should get the bonuses. To do this, the employer examines the employees' time cards and selects those who were never late for work during the previous year to receive bonuses. Notice that this method of measurement is highly reliable because of its high level of objectivity. Thus, another individual could independently perform the same measurement procedure and, if careful, identify exactly the same employees for bonuses, yielding consistent (reliable) results. But is the procedure valid? Probably only minimally so because the employer's measurement technique is limited to only one simple characteristic. Those who are outstanding in a number of other ways (such as identifying more effective ways to advertise products) but who were late to work even once are excluded from getting bonuses. Thus, the procedure is reliable, but it is of questionable validity.

This leads to the next principle: When evaluating measures, *validity is more important than reliability*. This should be clear from considering the example of the employer basing bonuses on employees' time cards. A complex measure involving subjective judgments of employees' performances that taps a variety of important types of behavior and achievement on the job would be much more valid (even if it turned out to be only modestly reliable) than a highly reliable measure that considers only punctuality measured by examining time cards.

Finally, there is a third principle: *To be useful, a measure must be both reasonably valid and reasonably reliable.*

To understand the complex relationship between reliability and validity, consider Figures 39.1 through 39.4.

In Figure 39.1, the darts are aimed in a valid direction (toward the target), and all the throws are consistently directed, indicating that they are reliable.

In Figure 39.2, the darts are also aimed in the direction of the target, but the throws are widely scattered, indicating low consistency or reliability. The poor reliability makes it

FIGURE 39.1 Reliable and valid.

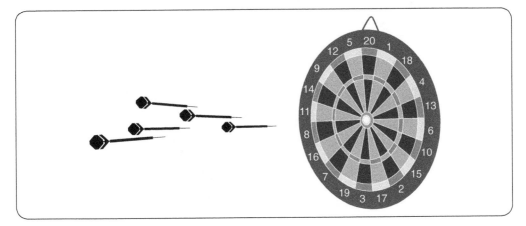

unlikely that most of the darts will hit the target. Thus, poor reliability undermines the valid direction in which the darts are pointing.

In Figure 39.3, the darts are not pointing at the target, which makes it invalid, but there is great consistency in the throws, which indicates that it is reliable. (In other words, it is reliably invalid.)

In Figure 39.4, the darts are not pointing at the target, which makes it invalid, and the lack of consistency in the direction of the dart throws indicates its poor reliability.

Of course, Figure 39.1 represents the ideal in measurement. For most measures in the social and behavioral sciences, however, researchers expect the aim to be off by at least a small amount, which would indicate less-than-perfect validity. They also expect some scatter in the darts, which would indicate less-than-perfect reliability.[1] Clearly, the first priority should be to point the darts in the correct *general direction*, which promotes validity. Then, researchers should work on increasing reliability.

FIGURE 39.2 Unreliable, which undermines the valid aim of the darts. Less useful than Figure 39.1.

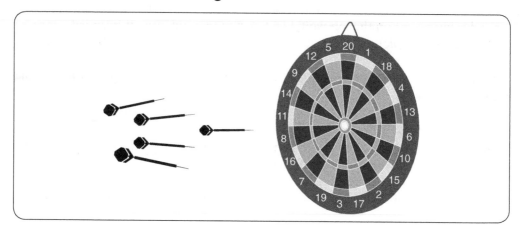

FIGURE 39.3 Reliable but invalid. Not useful.

FIGURE 39.4 **Unreliable and invalid. Not useful.**

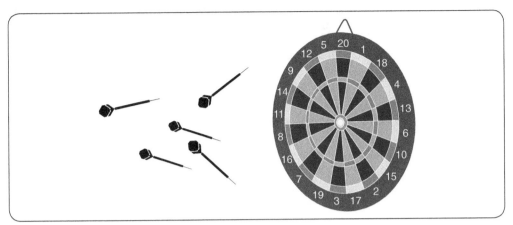

■ TOPIC REVIEW

1. A test is said to be reliable if it yields what?
2. Should a researcher expect a very short, multiple-choice test to be highly reliable?
3. Is it possible for a test with high reliability to have low validity?
4. Overall, is "validity" *or* "reliability" more important when evaluating a measure?
5. If a test is highly reliable but highly invalid, is it useful?
6. In light of this topic, should a researcher expect any tests to be both perfectly reliable and perfectly valid?
7. Professional test makers tend to be more successful in achieving high validity than in achieving high reliability. Is this statement true *or* false?

■ DISCUSSION QUESTIONS

1. Consider the example of the employer who was trying to identify the best employees by using a measure of punctuality because it was reliable, even though it was not especially valid. Name one or two other traits that might be examined in evaluating employees. Comment on whether each of your suggestions can be measured reliably. Also, comment on whether you think each is more valid than punctuality for determining which employees should receive bonuses.
2. Suppose you were offered a choice between two midterm examinations for your research methods class. The first one contains eight short essay questions, and the second contains 38 multiple-choice questions. Both are on appropriate content. Which would you prefer to take? Why? In your opinion, which one is likely to be more reliable?

■ RESEARCH PLANNING

Will you be evaluating the reliability of any measures you will be using in your research? Explain. (Note that reliability will be considered in more detail in the next topic.)

■ NOTE

1. Examination of the technical manuals for published tests indicates that professional test makers usually are more successful in achieving high reliability than in achieving high validity. This is because it is relatively easy to increase reliability by increasing the number of objective-type test items, while the tasks that need to be undertaken to increase validity vary greatly from construct to construct and may not be obvious.

MEASURES OF RELIABILITY

How can a researcher determine reliability? The classic method is to measure twice and then compare the two sets of measurements to see if they are consistent with each other.

First, consider how **interobserver reliability** might be determined. Suppose a researcher wants to test the hypothesis that tall individuals are waited on more quickly in retail stores than short individuals. To do this, the researcher could observe unobtrusively[1] to (1) classify each customer as tall, medium, or short, and then (2) count the number of seconds from the time each customer enters the store to the time a salesperson greets the customer.

Because judgments of height made from a distance might not be reliable, the researcher could have two observers independently observe. The researcher could then determine the *percentage* of participants that were rated to fit in the same height category (tall, medium, or short) *by both observers*. How high should the percentage be? Although there is no standard answer to this question, it is clear that if the percentage gets too low (let's say less than 60% agreement), the researcher has a problem with either one or both of the observers. Such a lack of consistency in their judgments would cast serious doubt on the meaningfulness of the results of the study.

Measurements of the number of seconds it took for the customer to receive service might also be unreliable if, for instance, the observers are distracted by other events, are inattentive to the task, and so on. To check on this possibility, the researcher could compare the measurements reported by the two observers. When there are two quantitative scores per participant (such as the number of seconds for each customer to be waited on, as indicated by each of the two observers), the researcher can check on the degree of relationship between the scores by computing a **correlation coefficient**.[2] A similar measure was used in Topic 37 to evaluate empirical validity. When researchers use *correlation coefficients* to describe reliability, they call them **reliability coefficients**. This coefficient also varies in value from 0.00 to 1.00, where a 0.00 indicates no reliability and a score of 1.00 indicates perfect reliability.[3] In other words, when the score is 1.00, the timing of the customers based on the observations of one observer is the same as those based on the observations made by the other observer. When researchers use reliability coefficients to describe the agreement between those rating the measurement of height or observing the time, they are called **interobserver** or **interrater reliability coefficients**.[4]

Reliability measures study the consistency of different aspects of measurement. For instance, when studying interrater reliability, researchers usually obtain the two measurements *at the same time* (i.e., the two observers observe the same participants at the same time). They are seeking to compare the raters to see if they are rating the same incidence in the same or very similar ways.

By contrast, in **test-retest reliability**, researchers measure at *two different points in time*. This reliability measure seeks to know more about the reliability of the test, not the observers. Suppose a researcher wants to know the reliability of a new test designed to assess the ability to learn college-level math. The researcher might administer the test one week and then re-administer it two weeks later. Because the ability to learn college-level math should not change very much from week to week, the researcher would expect the scores from the two administrations to be consistent. Once again, for two sets of scores, the researcher would compute a correlation coefficient, which would indicate the *test-retest reliability* of the test.

Some published tests come in two parallel (or equivalent) forms that are designed to be interchangeable; they have different items that cover the same content. When they are available, **parallel-forms reliability** should be determined. This is usually done by administering one form of the test to examinees and then, about a week or two later, administering the other form to the same examinees, thus yielding two scores per examinee. A good design could also divide the group, testing each half with one version of the test in the first round and then flipping the test used for the second round. This helps to control for the **practice effect** (influence on performance as a result of practicing a task). When the sets of scores are correlated, the result indicates the *parallel-forms reliability* of the test.

How high should a reliability coefficient be? Most published tests have reliability coefficients of 0.80 or higher, so researchers should strive to select or build measures that have coefficients at least this high, especially if researchers plan to interpret the scores for *individuals*. For *group averages* based on groups of participants of about 25 or more, measures with reliability coefficients as low as 0.50 can be serviceable. To understand why researchers can tolerate rather low reliability coefficients in research where they are examining averages, first keep in mind that reliability coefficients indicate the reliability of *individuals' scores*. Statistical theory indicates that averages are more reliable than the scores that underlie them because, when computing an average, the negative errors tend to cancel out the positive errors. For instance, suppose a researcher wants to compare the average age of parents who read extensively with their sixth-grade children with the average age of parents who do not. Asking children their parents' ages is likely to be unreliable. However, a researcher might expect about half of the children to overestimate the ages and half to underestimate them. To the extent that this is true, the averages may be reasonably accurate because the underestimates will cancel out the overestimates.

■ TOPIC REVIEW

1. Researchers need to use at least how many observers to determine interobserver reliability?

2. When there are two quantitative scores per participant, researchers can compute what statistic to describe reliability?

3. Do researchers usually measure at two different points in time to estimate interobserver reliability?

4. Do researchers usually measure at two different points in time to estimate test–retest reliability?

5. According to this topic, most published tests have reliability coefficients that are about how high?
6. According to this topic, serviceable reliability coefficients may be how low if researchers are examining group averages?

■ DISCUSSION QUESTIONS

1. In your opinion, which of the following variables mentioned in this topic would probably be easier to measure reliably: (1) height of customers based on observations made from a distance *or* (2) number of seconds from the time each customer enters a store until a salesperson greets him or her, also based on observations from a distance? Explain your choice.
2. For which of the following would test-retest reliability (with the measures administered two weeks apart) probably be more appropriate: (1) a questionnaire on voters' opinions on the honesty of two presidential candidates *or* (2) a questionnaire on prejudice against minority groups? Explain your choice.

■ RESEARCH PLANNING

What items in your study may need to be tested for reliability? What methods will you use to examine reliability in your study? What evidence would you offer to a skeptic reading your work that shows the measure is reliable?

■ NOTES

1. Researchers attempt to measure unobtrusively to avoid changing participants' behavior. For instance, if salespeople know that researchers are observing them, the salespeople might modify their normal behavior toward customers.
2. See Topic 67 for a detailed discussion of correlation.
3. Correlation coefficients may also be negative, as discussed in Topic 67. In the unlikely event that a researcher obtains a negative when studying reliability, it should be interpreted as representing no reliability.
4. These terms are interchangeable. The preferred term may vary by discipline.

INTERNAL CONSISTENCY AND RELIABILITY

Two methods for estimating the reliability of a test (such as an achievement test) or a scale (such as an attitude scale) were covered in the previous topic: test-retest reliability, in which a test[1] is administered twice, and parallel-forms reliability, in which two alternative forms of a test are administered. In both of these types of reliability, examinees are being assessed for their consistency over time and must take a test twice, with a week or two intervening between the administrations. Thus, if a test is less than perfectly reliable (i.e., the scores are not perfectly consistent), which is usually the case, variables associated with time can be partly responsible. For instance, at the time of the first administration, an examinee might be emotionally upset and not do well on the test, while the same examinee might not be upset at the time of the second administration and perform much better. Such time-associated variables obviously reduce the consistency of the scores from one administration of the test to the other, reducing reliability (and the reliability coefficient).

A different approach to reliability is to test the consistency of scores *within the test itself*—not across two test administrations. This class of reliability estimates is known as estimates of **internal consistency**. It is examining the degree to which the items within the test are measuring the same concepts. Scores from a single administration of a test can be used to examine the internal consistency of test scores—that is, did the test taker perform consistently across all items in the test. One way to determine this is to compute the **split-half reliability** of a test. Another that has become more common is **Cronbach's** alpha.

To determine the *split-half reliability*, a researcher administers a test but scores the items in the test as though they consisted of two separate tests. Typically, researchers do this by performing what is known as an odd-even split. Specifically, a researcher scores all the odd-numbered items and obtains a score for each examinee. Then, the researcher scores all the even-numbered items and obtains a second score for each examinee. This process results in two scores per examinee. Then, the researcher correlates the two sets of scores, yielding what is known as a *split-half reliability coefficient*. As with other types of reliability coefficients, these can range from 0.00, which indicates a complete absence of reliability (i.e., the scores on the odd-numbered items have no relationship to the scores on the even-numbered items), to 1.00, indicating complete consistency in the ordering of the two sets of scores.[2]

An alternative to the split-half method for estimating internal consistency is **Cronbach's alpha**, whose symbol is **α**. While the computation of alpha is complex, the concept is relatively easy to understand. Like the split-half method, it is based on a single administration of a test. After the test has been administered, mathematical procedures are used to obtain the equivalent of the average of all possible split-half reliability coefficients. For instance, an odd-even split could be used, yielding a split-half reliability coefficient. Then, the split could be the first half of the test versus the second half of the test, and a second split-half reliability coefficient could be obtained. Yet another split (maybe items 1–5 and items 11–15 for one half of a 20-item test versus the remaining items) could be used to obtain a third split-half reliability coefficient. After continuing in this way until all possible splits have been used, a researcher could average all the split-half reliabilities and obtain a value equivalent to Cronbach's alpha. Fortunately, the formula devised by Cronbach makes it possible to obtain this value without physically rescoring various splits over and over.

Because computer programs can be used to easily compute alpha, it has become much more commonly used than the split-half method, which depends on only a single split. Thus, the split-half method is reported primarily in older literature.[3]

Having high internal consistency is desirable when a researcher has developed a test designed to measure a single unitary variable, which is usually the case. For instance, if a researcher builds a test on the ability to sum one-digit numbers, students who score high on some of the items should score high on the other items and vice versa. Thus, the researcher should expect high internal consistency (i.e., a high value of α such as .80 or more). In contrast, if the researcher builds a general achievement test with some math items, some social studies items, some vocabulary items, and so on, the researcher would expect less internal consistency (a lower value of α).

In review, test-retest reliability and parallel-forms reliability measure the consistency of scores over time, while internal consistency methods (split-half and alpha) measure consistency among the items within a test at a single point in time.

■ TOPIC REVIEW

1. Which two methods for estimating reliability require two testing sessions?
2. Does the split-half method require one *or* two administrations of a test?
3. What is meant by an odd–even split?
4. If a split-half reliability coefficient equals 0.00, what does this indicate?
5. What is the highest possible value for a split-half reliability coefficient?
6. To obtain alpha, mathematical procedures are used to obtain the equivalent of what?
7. Does alpha estimate the consistency of scores over time?

■ DISCUSSION QUESTION

1. Suppose a researcher prepares a poorly written test in which some items are ambiguous. Speculate on the effect of the ambiguous items on split-half reliability.

■ RESEARCH PLANNING

Will you be considering the measures you will be using in your research? If so, which method (split-half or alpha) will you use? Explain.

■ NOTES

1. In this topic, the term *test* is being used to refer to both tests and scales.

2. As indicated in Topic 39, the larger the number of items in a test, the more reliable it tends to be. However, the split-half method estimates the reliability of a test only half as long as the full test. To correct for this underestimate, an adjustment using the Kuder-Richardson Prophecy Formula should be made.

3. Other older methods for estimating internal consistency are obtained by using Kuder-Richardson's Formulas 20 and 21. Like the split-half method, these have given way to Cronbach's alpha.

NORM- AND CRITERION-REFERENCED TESTS

Tests designed to facilitate a comparison of an individual's performance with that of a norm group are called **norm-referenced tests** (**NRTs**).[1] For instance, if an examinee takes a test and earns a *percentile rank* of 64, the examinee knows that he or she scored higher[2] than 64% of the individuals in the norm group. Often, the norm group is a national sample of examinees, but it also may be an entire local population (such as all seniors in a school district) or a sample of a local population (such as a random sample of all seniors in a state).

In contrast, tests designed to measure the extent to which individual examinees have met performance standards (i.e., specific criteria) are called **criterion-referenced tests** (**CRTs**).[3] For instance, suppose a researcher wants to test student nurses on their ability to administer an injection. The researcher might draw up a list of 10 behaviors that must be performed correctly for a student to pass the test, such as measuring the correct amount of medication, using a sterile needle, and so on. In this case, performing all the behaviors correctly is the criterion (i.e., performance standard).[4] Notice that the interpretation of an examinee's test score is independent of how other students perform. For instance, an examinee with nine items right might be the best in a group, but he or she, along with everyone else, will have failed the test because the standard is to perform all 10 behaviors correctly. Thus, being higher or lower than others who take the same criterion-referenced test is irrelevant to the interpretation.

Researchers who build norm-referenced tests (NRTs) approach the task differently from those who build criterion-referenced tests. NRTs are intentionally built to be of medium difficulty. Specifically, items that are answered correctly by about 50% of the examinees in tryouts during test development are favored in the selection of items for the final versions of the tests. It is essential that an NRT be of medium difficulty because this facilitates the comparison of an individual with a group. This can be seen most easily at the extremes. For instance, if a researcher foolishly built an NRT that was so easy that all participants in the norm group got every item right, the researcher could not interpret scores in terms of who has a higher or lower score than other examinees because everyone would have the same score. The same problem would occur if a researcher built an NRT that was so difficult that all the examinees got all the items wrong.

In contrast, when building CRTs, item difficulty typically is of little concern. Instead, expert judgment is used to determine the desired level of performance and how to test for it. These judgments are influenced very little by how difficult a task is. This approach is often appropriate. For instance, it would be inappropriate for the professors at a nursing school to drop a test of whether nurses can measure the correct amount of medication before injecting it simply because it is too difficult for their students. Because of its importance, the item should be retained regardless of its difficulty.

The need to have items of medium difficulty in NRTs is the basis of a major criticism of this type of test. Specifically, the criticism is that building NRTs is primarily driven by statistical considerations (i.e., item difficulty) and not by content considerations. Of course, those who build NRTs do carefully consider the content that a test should cover, but important content may be deleted if the items that measure it are very easy or very difficult in tryouts of the items.

Which type of test should be favored in research? The answer depends on the research purpose. Here are two general guidelines:

Guideline 1

If the purpose is to describe specifically what examinees know and can do, criterion-referenced tests should be used.

> *Example*: To what extent can voters understand a ballot proposition?
> *Example*: Have students mastered the essentials of simple addition?

Guideline 2

If the purpose is to examine how a local group differs from a larger norm group, norm-referenced tests should be used.[5]

> *Example*: How well are students in New York doing in reading in comparison with the national average?

■ TOPIC REVIEW

1. A norm-referenced test is designed to facilitate a comparison of an individual's performance with what?
2. Are norm groups always national samples?
3. What is the definition of a criterion-referenced test?
4. In which type of test do test designers favor items that will be answered correctly by about 50% of the participants?
5. In which type of test are items typically selected on the basis of content they cover without regard to item difficulty?
6. Which type of test should be used in research where the purpose is to describe specifically what examinees can and cannot do?

■ DISCUSSION QUESTIONS

1. Assume you are a parent, and your child's second-grade teacher offers to provide you with *either* scores on a "norm-referenced test" *or* a "criterion-referenced test" of your child's basic math ability. Which would you choose? Why?
2. For research on the percentage of students whose swimming skills are good enough for them to save themselves if they jump into the deep end of a pool, which type of test would you choose? Explain.

■ RESEARCH PLANNING

If you will use tests in your research, are they norm-referenced tests or criterion-referenced tests? How does this influence the report you can make on the results? How would this change if you were to change test types? If you compare this to your hypotheses or research question, do these statements match with the mechanism you have chosen to use as a measure?

■ NOTES

1. Some individuals use the terms *norm-referenced tests* and *standardized tests* interchangeably. However, it is better to reserve the term *standardized* for describing tests that come with standard directions for administration and interpretation. Both *norm-referenced tests* and *criterion-referenced tests* may be standardized.

2. Strictly speaking, a percentile rank indicates the percentage of those in a norm group that an examinee scored *as high as or higher than.*

3. The term *criterion-related validity* is used in Topic 37. Note that the word *criterion* is being used here and in Topic 37 to mean a *standard.* In Topic 37, using a standard for validating tests is discussed. Here, the discussion concerns using a standard to interpret the scores of individuals. These are, of course, separate matters, even though the same adjective is used in both cases.

4. Performance standards are established by expert judgments and may be less than 100% correct, depending on the trait being measured. For instance, on a typing test, a test administrator might require only 95% accuracy. Of course, performance standards are not always expressed as a percentage. Instead, descriptive labels such as *expert, novice,* and so on can be used.

5. To make predictions, researchers need tests that differentiate among participants. For instance, if all examinees earn the same score on a college admissions test, the scores cannot be used to predict who will and who will not succeed in college. Because norm-referenced tests are specifically built to make differentiations by being of medium difficulty, they are also useful in prediction studies.

MEASURES OF OPTIMUM PERFORMANCE

When researchers measure achievement, aptitude, or intelligence, they want examinees to strive to do their best—to perform at their optimum. An **achievement test** measures *knowledge and skills individuals have acquired.* When researchers investigate the effectiveness of direct, planned instruction, they should use achievement tests designed to measure the objectives of that instruction. To the extent that the tests do that, they are *valid* (i.e., they measure what they should).

Multiple-choice tests of achievement are frequently used by researchers because they are easy to administer and score. Indeed, multiple-choice tests are often appropriate when a researcher wants a quick snapshot of participants' achievements. Researchers can also measure achievement by having participants write answers to open-ended questions (e.g., essay questions) by evaluating participants' overt performances (e.g., a musical performance), or by assessing products (e.g., a portfolio of watercolor paintings). Scoring of the latter types is more time-consuming than scoring multiple-choice tests and may be *unreliable* unless researchers make sure that the scorers know specifically what characteristics of the essays, performances, or products they are to consider and how much weight to give to each characteristic in arriving at the scores. For instance, to evaluate the ability of a student nurse to give an injection, a researcher could develop a list of desirable characteristics, such as "measures the appropriate amount of medication," "checks the name on the patient's wristband," and so on. These can be the basis for a *checklist* (a list of desirable characteristics of a product or performance, each of which is awarded a point) or a *rating scale* (e.g., "excellent," "above average," "average," "below average," "poor"—terms that are applied in evaluating each characteristic).

An **aptitude test** is designed to *predict some specific type of achievement.* An example is the College Board's *Scholastic Aptitude Test* (SAT), which is used to predict success in college. The validity of an aptitude test is determined by correlating the scores participants earn (such as SAT scores obtained during high school) with a measure of achievement obtained at a later date (such as college freshman GPA). Other widely used aptitude tests are reading readiness tests (designed to predict reading achievement in the first grade by measuring whether examinees can identify shapes, and know basic concepts such as color names, etc.) and algebra prognosis tests (designed to predict achievement in algebra by measuring basic math skills that are used in algebra).

The most widely used aptitude tests are developed by commercial test publishers. Typically, they have low to modest validity (with validity coefficients of about 0.20 to 0.60). The modest predictive validity of aptitude tests is understandable because they measure only some of the skills needed for achievement in a particular area. For instance, many other skills such as persistence in the face of difficulty, study habits, and physical characteristics like being chronically ill can affect achievement but are not measured by aptitude tests.

Published aptitude tests, however, usually have high reliability (with reliability coefficients of .80 or higher).

An **intelligence test** is designed to *predict intellectual ability in general*, not any one specific type of achievement. The most popular intelligence tests (1) are culturally loaded and (2) measure knowledge and skills that can be acquired with instruction (with questions such as "How far is it from New York to Los Angeles?"). The arguable assumption underlying intelligence tests is that all individuals are exposed to such information, and more intelligent individuals are more likely to retain the information. Almost all contemporary experts on measurement, however, reject the notion that such tests measure innate (inborn) intelligence. At best, intelligence tests measure skills that have been acquired in some specific cultural milieu. Commercially available intelligence tests of this type have low to modest validity for predicting achievement in school—a degree of validity that can be achieved with less controversial aptitude tests.

Extensive efforts have been made to develop culture-free intelligence tests. Typical efforts in this area concentrate on nonverbal tasks because of the high cultural load of language usage. These tests are usually less predictive of subsequent achievement than the more traditional intelligence tests, possibly because achievement is accomplished in a cultural context in which language is critical.

Research on intelligence can be controversial when, for instance, researchers assume that intelligence tests measure innate ability or that they measure all aspects of intelligence. Historically, differences between groups in intelligence test results have been used to argue there are innate differences in ability based on gender, race, or ethnicity that justify discriminatory programs such as eugenics. Increasing awareness of these widespread misinterpretations of intelligence test scores and the structural limitations of intelligence tests (e.g., arguable assumptions underlying them) has meant intelligence tests are used in research much less frequently now than they were several decades ago.

TOPIC REVIEW

1. Which type of test is designed to predict achievement *in general*?
2. An algebra prognosis test is an example of what type of test?
3. A test designed to measure how much students learn in a particular course in school is what type of test?
4. A test designed to predict success in learning a new set of skills is what type of test?
5. A list of desirable characteristics of a product or performance is known as what?
6. How can researchers increase the reliability of scoring essays, products, and performances?
7. According to this topic, are intelligence tests good measures of innate ability?

DISCUSSION QUESTIONS

1. Did you ever take an achievement test on which you did not perform up to your optimum? If yes, briefly describe why. Was the test maker or test administrator responsible for your less-than-optimum performance? Were you responsible? Other factors? Explain.

2. Name a specific type of achievement that can be most accurately measured using a checklist or rating scale. State why a scale or checklist would be better than a multiple-choice test.

■ RESEARCH PLANNING

Will you be using an achievement test, aptitude test, or intelligence test in your research? Have you selected it yet? What is it designed to predict? Is it designed to be culture-free? If yes, do you believe it is fully culture-free?

Scales that have choices from "strongly agree" to "strongly disagree" are known as **Likert-type scales**.[1] Each item in a Likert-type scale should present a clear statement on a single topic. For instance, to measure attitudes toward school, a researcher might ask respondents to indicate their degree of agreement or disagreement with statements such as "In the mornings, I look forward to going to school" and "I get along well with my teacher." To reduce response bias (such as marking "Strongly agree" to all items without considering the individual items or just being generally inclined to respond positively), it is a good idea to provide some positive and some negative statements and score them according to whether the associated answers are correspondingly positive or negative. For instance, if five points are awarded for strongly agreeing to a positive statement toward school, a researcher would award five points for strongly disagreeing with a negative statement toward school. Researchers call this process **reverse scoring**.

Of course, the statements in a Likert-type scale should be derived from an analysis of the possible components of the attitude. For attitude toward school, a researcher might have several statements concerning attitudes in each of these areas: (1) learning in academic areas, (2) relationships with classmates, (3) relationships with teachers and staff, (4) participation in extracurricular activities, and so on. Such an analysis helps to assure that the contents of the attitude scale are comprehensive, which will contribute to its content validity (see Topic 36).

In short, when researchers measure personality traits, they want respondents to indicate what they are typically like, not how good they can make themselves look. This is quite different from measurement of cognitive skills with achievement, aptitude, and intelligence tests on which researchers want respondents to show their best.

■ TOPIC REVIEW

1. Do researchers usually want participants to show their best when measuring personality traits?
2. In this topic, what is the main reason for administering personality measures anonymously?
3. What do researchers reduce by observing behavior unobtrusively?
4. Loosely structured stimuli are used in which type of personality measure?
5. According to this topic, which type of personality measure is seldom used in personality research?
6. What is the range of choice in a Likert-type scale?
7. Is content validity a relevant concern when creating a Likert-type scale for measuring attitudes?

■ DISCUSSION QUESTIONS

1. Have you ever given a socially desirable response that was not true of you when being interviewed or answering a questionnaire? Would you? If yes, briefly describe why. Is there anything the interviewer or questionnaire writer could have done to increase the odds that you would have been more forthright?

2. Write three statements that could be used with a Likert-type scale to measure attitudes toward your research methods class. Each should be on a different aspect of the class, such as the textbook, the instructor, and so on. Two should be positive statements and one should be negative. Explain how they would be scored.

RESEARCH PLANNING

Will you be using a measure of typical performance in your research? If so, to what extent might it be subject to the influence of social desirability? What are some possible ways to design your research to avoid answers that are biased by social desirability?

Will you be measuring attitudes? If yes, will you use a Likert-type scale? Explain how you will use this scale. What thoughts do you have on the different categories of the scale in relation to your measure that make this scale an appropriate and useful measure?

NOTE

1. Named for social psychologist Rensis Likert, who popularized this psychometric scale in the 1930s as a part of his PhD thesis. The proper pronunciation of Dr. Likert's name is "Lick-urt"—not "Lie-kurt"—although this is the more common pronunciation people use when referring to the scale.

MEASUREMENT IN QUALITATIVE RESEARCH

This topic describes some of the specific techniques that qualitative researchers use to establish the dependability and trustworthiness of their data.[1] One technique is **data triangulation**, which is the use of multiple sources or multiple methods for obtaining data on the research topic. When data collected in different ways points to the same conclusion, it strengthens the researcher's argument and mitigates the weaknesses of any one method.

To triangulate data for a qualitative study that examines gender differences in professional behavior in an employment setting, a researcher might interview employees and other groups, such as supervisors and the human resources personnel responsible for hiring. To the extent that the various sources provide similar information, the data can be said to be corroborated through data triangulation.

The methods used to collect data can also be triangulated. For instance, a researcher studying child-rearing practices might conduct individual interviews with parents and then observe parents in a public or home setting. This would be an example of **methods triangulation** because two qualitative methods were employed to collect the data from one group of participants.

To contrast the two types of triangulation, *data triangulation* typically includes two or more types of participants in the data collection but uses the same type of method (interviews), while *methods triangulation* uses multiple methods (interviews and observation) to collect data from participants. The participants may include only one type (such as parents) or different groups (parents, grandparents, childcare providers). When a researcher combines qualitative and quantitative methods, it is referred to as *mixed methods* (see Topic 51).

Another approach to assure the integrity of qualitative research is to form a *research team*, with each member of the team participating in the collection and analysis of data. This can be thought of as **researcher triangulation**, which reduces the possibility that the results of qualitative research represent only the idiosyncratic views of one individual researcher.

Sometimes, it is helpful to form a **team of researchers with diverse backgrounds** (see Topic 49 on consensual qualitative research). For instance, for a study on the success of minority students in medical school, a team of researchers that consists of both medical school instructors and medical school students might strengthen the study by providing more than one perspective when one is collecting and analyzing the data.

Consider the issue of studying age discrimination in the workplace. Age and gender diversity in the research team helps to provide a "comprehensive view" of the data obtained in interviews on age and gender discrimination in public employment, as seen in Example 1.

Example 1

Diversity in a research team: Age and gender issues were analyzed by all three researchers. A comprehensive view of the different meanings of age and gender issues was obtained by using a research team consisting of a 40-year-old man, a 55-year-old woman, and a 62-year-old man.

Interviews and focus groups are typically audio-recorded and then transcribed. Sometimes, transcription is challenging because of technical difficulties or participants not speaking distinctly. In addition, transcribers sometimes make clerical errors. Therefore, **checking the accuracy of a transcription** helps to ensure the quality of the data. This can be done by having an independent person compare the audiorecordings with the transcription. Often, it is sufficient to have this person check only a sampling of the transcription. If the sampled sections are satisfactory, it may be assumed that the entire transcription is accurate.

In the analysis of qualitative data, the members of a research team should initially work out some basics for coding the themes in the data and then work independently (without consulting each other) to code a sample of the data. When they compare the results of their analyses, the results are considered dependable to the extent that they agree. This technique employs what is called **interobserver agreement**.[2] When there are disagreements, they can often be resolved by having the researchers discuss their differences until they reach a consensus. This process is described in more detail in Topic 49.

The use of an outside expert can also help ensure the quality of the research. A researcher's peer (such as another experienced qualitative researcher) can examine the process used to collect data, as well as the resulting data and conclusions, and then provide feedback to the researcher. This process is called **peer review**. Under certain circumstances, the peer who provides the review is called an **auditor**, which is also discussed in Topic 49.

The dependability of the results can be further enhanced by a process called **member checking**. This term is based on the idea that the study participants are "members" of the research team. This process allows participants to check specific aspects of the researchers' results and analysis. Researchers can use this feedback to determine whether their results ring true to the participants. Member checking typically takes place early in the analysis phase to review early interpretations of data, or may only be used as a way to verify the accuracy of transcripts. Member checking is often only conducted once. This allows researchers to adjust the description of the results, although caution must be used if the topic is controversial or the findings unflattering to participants.

Member checking can include participants in meaningful ways, but it is important to prepare for this inclusion so that it damages neither the integrity of the research nor the rapport with participants. For instance, if transcripts are being reviewed, it may be helpful to prepare the participant for what they will receive and to provide precise instructions on what they should do. If transcripts are verbatim and lengthy, researchers can create a copy that is easier to review by removing content that will not be considered in the analysis, correcting grammar, and cleaning up other speech patterns so that the transcript is shorter and easier to review as a written document.[3] Ultimately, it is also important to realize that participants may need options and guidance on reading transcripts, and may feel sensitive to how they sound and to issues of dignity around what they said rather than only focusing on checking for the accuracy of their comments. Member checking can be fraught with problems if introduced without a clear plan, or late in the analysis process when conflicts between the researcher and participant outlooks could create dilemmas to completing the project. Certainly, research on sensitive topics should be especially mindful of how such a process is carried out to produce a constructive experience.

■ TOPIC REVIEW

1. Suppose a researcher interviewed participants and then observed the behavior of the same participants. Is this an example of "data triangulation" *or* of "methods triangulation"?
2. In data triangulation, how many types of participants are used?
3. What is the name of the type of triangulation that reduces the possibility that the results of qualitative research represent only the idiosyncratic views of an individual researcher?
4. Is it ever desirable for a team of researchers to consist of individuals with diverse backgrounds?
5. In peer review, what is a peer?
6. Who are the members in "member checking"?

■ DISCUSSION QUESTION

1. Which techniques described in this topic seem most useful to improving a qualitative study's dependability and trustworthiness, and which seem the least useful? Explain your reasoning.

■ RESEARCH PLANNING

If you are planning to conduct qualitative research, which of the techniques described in this topic, if any, do you plan to use to ensure that your data has integrity? Explain your choice(s).

■ NOTES

1. The terms *dependability* and *trustworthiness* in qualitative research loosely correspond to the terms *reliability* and *validity* in quantitative research.
2. In qualitative research, this is sometimes called *intercoder agreement*. In quantitative research, this concept is called *interobserver reliability* or *interrater reliability*.
3. Suggestions adapted from Carlson, J.A. (2010). Avoiding traps in member checking. *The Qualitative Report, 15*(5), 1102–1113. Retrieved from www.nova.edu/ssss/QR/QR15-5/carlson.pdf

PART 6
Qualitative Research Design

Qualitative research collects data that will be analyzed as words. This section discusses the basic approaches to qualitative research, starting with the methods by which it is collected. Topic 46 discusses the widespread use of interviews in qualitative research designs, and Topic 47 provides an overview of focus groups and observation as qualitative methods of data collection. Topics 48 and 49 explain two approaches for qualitative research designs, each of which involves specific processes for evaluating data. Because qualitative research is *inductive*, many decisions about the research process must be made in advance. Data collection and analysis often purposely intermingle to improve the results. Topics 50 and 51 discuss research methods that build upon the earlier topics: case studies and mixed methods research.

INTERVIEWS IN QUALITATIVE RESEARCH

Interviews are by far the most widely used type of measure for collecting data for qualitative research. Interviews vary from **structured** to **unstructured**, with the most common type being a **semi-structured interview.** In the semi-structured approach, an **interview guide** or **interview protocol** is formulated in advance (the "structured" part) but interviews may follow the flow of the conversation in each individual interview rather than follow the guide exactingly.

Semi-structured interviews are popular in part because thinking through question wording carefully in advance allows researchers to consider if the question is complete, or if it is biased or leading. Semi-structured interviews combine this strength with the ability to deviate from the guide in order to collect the most useful information. For instance, if a participant does not seem to understand a question, it can be reworded by the interviewer. If a response is too terse, the interviewer can ask additional questions, such as "Can you tell me more about it?" The interviewer can also probe with additional follow-up questions in order to explore unexpected, unusual, or especially relevant material revealed by a participant.

Although semi-structured interviews are the most common, a **structured interview** may be preferable in some types of studies. For example, **longitudinal research** in which people will be interviewed repeatedly in intervals that may be weeks, months, years, or decades apart, the interviews may benefit from more rigid structure to ensure consistency and the ability to compare results over time. By contrast, **unstructured interviews** may be used in exploratory research when flexibility is needed to allow interviewees to bring up information that matters most to them. A **life story interview** is a type of unstructured interview.

In interviews with structure, an **interview protocol** includes written directions for conducting the interview, such as the script to begin the interview, question prompts, or any other notes that may help the interviews maintain consistency where needed, as well as a standard set of predetermined questions to be asked of all participants. Ideally, the questions should be pilot-tested with at least a few individuals who will not be participants in the study. On the basis of the pilot test, the questions may be revised, if necessary. Also, when possible, the predetermined questions should be reviewed by experts in the area being investigated and revised as needed.

Initial interview questions should be designed to *establish rapport*. Example 1 shows three of the nine questions researchers asked in order to establish rapport with first-year university students at the beginning of an interview. Notice that the questions are quite general and do not deal with the direct topic of the research (self-handicapping, defensive pessimism, and goal orientation). These might also be thought of as warm-up questions.

Example 1

Sample interview questions to establish rapport with first-year university students:

- So now that you are at the university, what do you think?
- Is the university what you expected?
- Are you enjoying the university?[1]

Example 2 shows how a research team investigating medical treatment outcomes described their use of predetermined questions. Notice that they commenced with "broad, open-ended questions," followed by increasingly specific questions as the data collection progressed.

Example 2

Use of predetermined questions in a semistructured interview: A set of predetermined questions guided but did not limit the conversation. Interviews were about half an hour in length and commenced with broad, open-ended questions inviting participants to describe in their own words what assisted or impeded recovery during the six months immediately following discharge from treatment. As data collection progressed and emerging categories became apparent, participants were asked increasingly specific questions. In addition, summary statements and reflections were frequently made to validate responses and verify accurate understanding.[2]

Qualitative interviewing is a complex activity that requires skill that is acquired through practice. Interviews of all types are often face to face, and researchers frequently record interviews after obtaining permission. There are several advantages to these interviewing conditions. One is that face to face offers the richest responses in an interview situation. Face-to-face interviews allow researchers to note factors such as intonation, gestures, and facial expressions that convey the meaning of what was said. Recording allows the interview time to be focused on building rapport and active listening instead of trying to take notes and missing opportunities to improve the data. Recorded interviews also allow data to be shared among research teams more easily.

Typically, researchers are not simply following a predetermined script but are listening for cues to follow up with questions that may elicit important information on issues that need clarification. Interviews are typically transcribed in part or full, and the interview transcripts are treated as data. As we will see, this data is then analyzed, often by coding for themes and concepts.

A novice who is planning qualitative research should conduct some practice interviews with individuals who will not be participants in the study. If possible, these practice interviews should be observed by an experienced qualitative researcher, who then provides feedback. Even those with experience often benefit from testing a new interview guide to work out any areas that are unclear or do not flow well in advance of the actual data collection. Researchers typically provide time expectations for interviews. Interviews can vary greatly in length but most range between an hour and 90 minutes. It is possible to conduct shorter or longer interviews. For interviews that take more than two hours, researchers may consider scheduling more than one session with a person in order to avoid fatigue, especially if the topic matter could be stressful for the interviewee.

It is important that an interviewer maintain neutrality in question wording and in affect during the interview session. Many interviewers examine their research problem in relation to their own background and attitudes before conducting the interviews, a process referred to as **self-disclosure**, in order to make explicit any concerns with bias. For instance, if a team of qualitative researchers is planning to study child-rearing practices of recent emigrants from Asia, the researchers should consciously think about how they themselves were raised, any experience they have raising children, and any attitudes they have toward Asian Americans that might predispose them to skew the interview. The purpose of self-disclosure is to clear the air as well as to clear the mind before conducting the interviews. In some published reports of qualitative research, brief summaries of the researchers' self-disclosures are included.

Interviews should include a portion in which relevant **demographic information** is collected. This may be as a part of the interview, in a short form that the interviewee completes at the beginning or end of the interview process, or at another time.

■ TOPIC REVIEW

1. Which type of interview is most widely used for data collection in qualitative research?
2. What does an interview protocol consist of?
3. With whom should a pilot test of the interview questions be conducted?
4. The initial questions should be designed to do what?
5. In a semi-structured interview, is it ever acceptable for an interviewer to ask questions not included in the list of predetermined questions?
6. Why might a researcher use an unstructured interview?
7. What is the name of the process through which an interviewer can consider any personal biases?

■ DISCUSSION QUESTION

1. In semi-structured interviewing, what are some ways that an interviewer can design research collection to avoid biasing results?

■ RESEARCH PLANNING

If you are planning to conduct qualitative research using interviews, how do you plan to gain experience or test your interview guide before conducting your research?

■ NOTES

1. Martin, A.J., Marsh, H.W., Williamson, A., & Debus, R.L. (2003). Self-handicapping, defensive pessimism, and goal orientation: A qualitative study of university students. *Journal of Educational Psychology*, *95*, 617–628.
2. Cockell, S.J., Zaitsoff, S.L., & Geller, J. (2004). Maintaining change following eating disorder treatment. *Professional Psychology: Research and Practice*, *35*, 527–534.

OTHER METHODS FOR COLLECTING QUALITATIVE DATA

Basic characteristics of interviews were described in the previous topic. This topic explores some additional methods that are used in qualitative research design. Some qualitative designs use **focus groups** instead of one-on-one interviews. A focus group is a type of group interview in which participants are asked to respond to a set of questions that express similar and differing views and discuss them among the group. Focus groups usually consist of 6 to 12 participants. The group is led by a **facilitator**,[1] as opposed to an interviewer. Focus groups typically last for about an hour. Also, it is typical to use two or more focus groups in a given research project.

The facilitator presents the topic to be discussed and tries to create a nonthreatening environment in which all group members feel free to express their opinions, attitudes, and experiences—often with the goal of encouraging members to express views that differ from those of other participants. Similar to semi-structured interviews, focus groups typically follow a predetermined set of questions (also known as a *questioning route*), but may do so in a format that varies in the degree of structure. The facilitator works to ensure that all participants have an opportunity to provide opinions and all relevant aspects of the topic are discussed. The facilitator will also probe for additional information when necessary.

Focus groups are typically recorded so that the facilitator has the opportunity to focus on the complex job of facilitating the discussion. Similar to interviewing, facilitation involves active listening, probing, and keeping the conversation within the topics, but it also requires moderating interactions and the level of participation from all members of the focus group. Facilitation benefits from practice in resolving various scenarios and learning to redirect conversation, maintain rapport, and ask valuable questions. Often, focus groups include an assistant for the facilitator, who can operate the recording equipment and ensure that individual focus group participants can be matched with recordings later. An assistant may also take notes related to body language or other relevant aspects of the dynamics among the group to help with interpretation and analysis when the focus groups recording is transcribed.

A clear benefit of using focus groups is that the method reveals *the evolution of perceptions in a social context*. It is interesting to note that the focus group method began as a business marketing research tool when marketing researchers realized that the perceptions of an individual in isolation may be different from perceptions that develop in a social context. For instance, a new product that initially seems satisfactory to an individual may be seen as less desirable after he or she has discussed it with other individuals who may have different perspectives on it.

Example 1 shows a brief description of how data were collected with the focus group method in a study on stress.

Example 1

Description of data collection using focus groups: Each of the four groups of medical students who experienced the recovery teaching intervention participated in a 1-hour focus group at the beginning and at the end of their placement. A topic guide was used by the author to guide the discussion, and students were encouraged to talk to one another: asking questions, exchanging anecdotes, and commenting on each other's experiences and points of view.[2]

Interviews and focus groups rely on the narratives of participants rather than on actual behaviors. This can raise issues with the representation of reality. Sometimes, understanding how participants perceive matters and talk about them is relevant to the goal of the research. However, sometimes the narratives that participants produce raise complex issues about what constitutes reality.

For instance, when participants describe how they were treated in some situation, an interview primarily exposes how participants perceive it rather than how it might be objectively measured. Qualitative researchers may be more interested in how people construct reality through narrative rather than how it may be objectively described through quantitative data. Examining perceptions is known as a **phenomenological approach** to acquiring knowledge about the world. Almost all qualitative researchers are in some sense phenomenologists.[3]

Another common method of collecting qualitative data is through direct observation and participation with a group. Researchers who use these observational methods often refer to this as **field research.** When the focus is cultural and the approach is immersive, the research may be referred to as **ethnography**. Direct observation is either **nonparticipant observation** or **participant observation**. In *nonparticipant observation*, the researcher observes individuals without becoming involved in their activities. Observing people requires permissions when done in private settings, but the setting may allow the observer to be unobtrusive. An example of this type of observation is sitting at the back of a classroom to observe student/teacher interactions. A particular concern with this type of observation is that the participants' behavior may change from its normal course when they know they are being observed.

In *participant observation*, the researcher becomes a member of the group being researched and, thus, makes any observations while participating in the events of the group and interacting with other members. For instance, someone who wants to study the experiences of temp workers might become a temp worker. Likewise, someone who wants to understand the perspective and actions of an environmental activist group might join the activities of the group. Researchers may run into limits regarding participant observation due to skills or clear identity differences that make participation in a group more challenging. A woman may find it difficult to study an all-men's choir; a man may not be able to effectively participate in a group of women seamstresses. Clearly, a person with no medical background is unlikely to be able to carry out participant observation on nursing from the role of a nurse. However, some researchers have found clever ways to study hard-to-reach groups. Others take radical steps to pursue study, such as Loïc Wacquant, a French sociologist who became a boxer in Chicago in order to study the world of boxing, or Peter Moskos, who became a police officer in Maryland to write his dissertation on policing the poverty stricken neighborhoods of Baltimore.[4] Note that participant observation without revealing to those who are being observed that research is being conducted raises serious ethical problems. Field research requires strong observational skills and careful, detailed note taking. Its main strength is in capturing not just what people report but what they do in real-life settings.

■ TOPIC REVIEW

1. Examining perceptions is known as what type of approach to acquiring knowledge?
2. A focus group usually consists of about how many participants?
3. What are the two names for the individual who leads a focus group?
4. According to this topic, what is a clear advantage of using focus groups?
5. What is the name of the type of observation in which the researcher observes as an outsider?
6. When the emphasis in field research is on cultural issues, what may the research be referred to as?

■ DISCUSSION QUESTION

1. Do you think you would rather analyze and interpret data from individual interviews or from focus group discussions? What are the strengths and weaknesses of each? What makes them easier or harder to analyze?

■ RESEARCH PLANNING

If you are planning to conduct qualitative research, would interviews (see Topic 46), focus groups, or field research best provide you with the information you need to answer your research question? Will you use more than one of these methods in your study? Examine the relationship between your chosen design and your research question.

■ NOTES

1. Facilitators can also be called *moderators*.
2. Feeney, L., Jordan, I., & McCarron, P. (2013). Teaching recovery to medical students. *Psychiatric Rehabilitation Journal, 36*, 35–41. doi:10.1037/h0094745
3. Both qualitative and quantitative researchers are interested in perceptions and realize that objective factual reality is elusive. The distinction between methods is in the degree to which the two types of researchers rely on perceptions for understanding a research topic and is often clear based on differences in the focus of research questions across these methods.
4. Both of these sociologists wrote books on their studies. See Wacquant, L. (2006). *Body & Soul: Notebooks of an Apprentice Boxer*. Oxford, UK: Oxford University Press, or Moskos, P. (2008). *Cop in the Hood*. Princeton, NJ: Princeton University Press.

GROUNDED THEORY AND RESEARCH DESIGN

Grounded theory is a set of principles and practices that is widely used in qualitative research. Originating with sociologists Barney Glaser and Anselm Strauss in the mid-1960s, grounded theory is actually not a theory but a method for making qualitative research more systematic. Qualitative research was declining in the 1960s, in part because quantitative methods that rested on hypotheses and allowed for generalization became popular in the social sciences during that period. A gap began to open between experimental research, which became more focused on the concrete, and the more abstract world of theory. While experiments and quantitative work were concerned with testing existing theories, new theories waned. In this climate, qualitative work suffered from a reputation of not being scientific enough because it was perceived as being biased, impressionistic, and anecdotal.

Glaser and Strauss helped to revive qualitative methods by formulating approaches that *grounded* theory within a more systematic, qualitative approach. *Grounded theory* refers to an *inductive method* of data collection and analysis that can lead to theories of behavior.

In the inductive approach, which is characteristic of all qualitative research, there is no hypothesis that begins the research. Instead, researchers start with the data and develop theories that are *grounded* in the data. By contrast, quantitative researchers typically start with an existing theory or deduce a new one from existing information and then collect data to test the theory. They do not typically try to develop their own theories based on the data they collect. Quantitative research uses a *deductive method* instead of an *inductive* one.

To put it more simply, quantitative researchers test existing theories, or deduce theories from what is already known and then collect data and analyze it to test the theories with research. In contrast, qualitative researchers collect data and begin to analyze their observations and the responses of participants for patterns that can be explained by theories. The way that data is collected reflects these differences. Quantitative data is often collected by offering participants closed-answer questions that limit possible responses. The researcher may never see or meet the people who participate in the research by answering questions. In many cases, participants are only involved in the research for the length of time it takes to complete a survey or experimental activity. By contrast, qualitative researchers typically do meet the people who participate in the research. In fact, they enter the participants' world, where they may observe or participate in activities with them over weeks, months, or years. Interviews with participants are lengthy and consist of open-ended questions.

As a qualitative method, grounded theory rests on the involvement of the researcher simultaneously in data collection and data analysis. The data is transcribed in lengthy field notes and interview transcriptions. Researchers carefully review all the information that has been collected looking for **themes** from the responses of different people. Throughout the research process, grounded theory researchers use **constant comparison** to test their ideas about the patterns they see. **Constant comparison** is a technical term that refers to constantly comparing each new element of the data with all previous elements that have been coded in order to establish and refine categories. While this is being done, the analysis focuses on similarities and differences in the data that might be accounted for by a core idea.

Coding themes is a way of analyzing the data for theory building. Researchers read the words of their participants and identify the concepts that are represented in each passage. The first phase of coding is **open coding**. Interview transcripts are examined for broad themes that pertain to one's topic of research (such as the ideas or experiences of the participants) in order to allow them to be categorized. As researchers read each passage, they identify themes and code the passage with its theme so that they are able to begin to group together all passages by code to see what has been said on a specific theme. Example 1 shows how the researchers of a grounded theory article on education and health describe it:

Example 1

Open coding is a process for finding the right label for a phenomenon. It helps to ask questions such as 'What is it?' and 'What does it represent?' about each sequence, comparing the text step by step to label similar phenomena as being equal (Strauss and Corbin 1996). Moreover, a concept is developed around the phenomenon; this is called categorizing.[1]

In this study, the authors were interested in discovering how education influences health. They began by coding education, reported health behaviors, "material resources" such as income and working conditions, "social resources" such as social support, and "psychological resources" such as a sense of control or goal achievement. From this, they developed categories. Categories begin to conceptualize the data. Subcategories are also developed, when possible. In keeping with the inductive approach, categories and subcategories should be suggested by the data during data analysis, not developed prior to analyzing the data. Categories and subcategories developed at this stage should be regarded as preliminary and subject to change during the remainder of the analysis, as data continues to be collected. Preliminary notes on any overarching themes noticed in the data should also be made at this point.

In the health and education article, categories include living and working conditions, socialization, awareness, responsibility, and information. In this case, socialization, especially by parents, was found to influence both health behaviors and level of education attained. Likewise, awareness had to do with the ability to recognize health issues without resorting to "mythical" or "irrational" explanations for the issue.

Next, the grounded theory approach proceeds to **axial coding**. At this stage, the data is reexamined and reorganized to identify relationships between categories and themes in coding. In the article on education and health, the researchers in Example 2 describe axial coding in this way:

Example 2

While the aim of open coding 'is to open up the inquiry' (Strauss 1987, p. 29), during the axial coding, data are grouped in a new way to develop and create the connection between categories and subcategories (Strauss and Corbin 1996).[2]

MEASURES OF TYPICAL PERFORMANCE

As indicated in the previous topic, when researchers measure achievement, aptitude, and intelligence, they encourage examinees to perform their best. In contrast, when researchers measure deep-seated personality traits such as attitudes, interests, and dispositions, they want to determine participants' *typical* levels of performance. For instance, when selecting employees to work as salespeople, an employer might want to know how assertive each applicant typically is, not just how assertive they claim to be in their responses to an assertiveness scale (a series of questions that are scored to get an overall assertiveness score). When measuring such traits, a major concern is that applicants might indicate what is *socially desirable* rather than their true level of assertiveness in order to increase their chances of employment.

Individuals are often hesitant to reveal they have *socially undesirable* traits even when they have nothing directly to gain by being deceitful. Thus, the responses of participants in research projects may frequently be influenced by perceived social desirability. Reducing the influence of social desirability increases the validity of personality measures.

There are three basic approaches to reducing social desirability as a factor in participants' responses. First, by administering personality measures anonymously, researchers may reduce this tendency. Another approach is to observe behavior unobtrusively (without the participants' awareness—to the extent that this is ethically possible) and rate selected characteristics such as aggressiveness. A third approach is to use *projective techniques*. These provide loosely structured or ambiguous stimuli such as ink blots. As participants respond to these stimuli, such as by telling what they see, they are presumed to be projecting their feelings and beliefs and revealing them in their responses. For instance, a test administrator might infer that participants whose responses to ink blots contain numerous references to aggressiveness are themselves aggressive. When participants are unaware of the specific traits an investigator is looking for, the tendency to give socially desirable responses is reduced.

The literature is quite mixed on the validity and reliability of popular projective techniques, which ask respondents to interpret pictures, complete sentences, or provide word associations, with some studies showing that they can be remarkably deficient. Thus, they are best used for limited purposes and only by those who have had formal training in their administration and scoring. For instance, they are seldom used in personality research because (1) they are time-consuming to administer and score; (2) they do not naturally lend themselves to numerical results because the interpretations are usually in words; and (3) their validity is highly suspect. Instead, researchers usually use objective-type personality measures in which participants respond to statements or questions with restricted choices such as true-false, scales from "strongly agree" to "strongly disagree," and checklists in which respondents check off the characteristics they believe are true of themselves.

Researchers review transcripts of the interviews and any other data sources, such as memos written during data collection, with the purpose of finding relationships between the categories and themes identified during open coding. Some important types of relationships that might be noted are (1) temporal—usually precedes Y in time; (2) causal—X caused participants to do Y;[3] (3) associational—X and Y usually or always occur at about the same time but are not believed to be causally connected; (4) valence—participants have stronger emotional reactions to X than to Y; and (5) spatial—X and Y occur in the same place *or* X and Y occur in different places.

In the final stages of the grounded theory approach, qualitative researchers develop a **core category**, which is the main overarching category under which the other categories and subcategories belong. They also attempt to describe the *process* of how the categories work together (or in opposition to each other) in order to arrive at the conditions or behaviors contained in the core category.

In the education and health article, the core category is "health competence." Many factors were influenced by education, but the authors mainly propose that education influences health through health competence.

■ TOPIC REVIEW

1. Does the grounded theory approach use the "inductive approach" *or* the "deductive approach"?
2. Grounded theory was developed to help qualitative research in what way?
3. The grounded theory approach starts with what type of coding?
4. When coding is reviewed and connected to concepts, what is this called?
5. What is the second type of coding in the grounded theory approach?
6. In which type of coding is there an emphasis on identifying relationships?
7. What is the technical term that refers to checking each new element of the data against all previous elements that have been coded in order to establish and refine categories?
8. What are grounded theory researchers looking for in the final stages of research?

■ DISCUSSION QUESTION

1. Do you think that the "inductive approach" (such as grounded theory) or the "deductive approach" (such as quantitative research) is more likely to yield important information for your research interest? Are there topics where they are equally likely to do so? How would each approach differ in focus?

■ RESEARCH PLANNING

If you plan to conduct qualitative research, how would you design your research to use the grounded theory approach? Investigate resources to help you learn more about how to code qualitative data, including the approach to coding as well as the practical tools you can use to code the data and analyze it. This may include how to code in programs you already own, or you may want to find out what qualitative data analysis (QDA) software is available to you or is most commonly used in your discipline.

■ NOTES

1. Flandorfer, P., & Fliegenschnee, K. (2010). Education and health: Theoretical considerations based on a qualitative grounded theory study. *Vienna Yearbook of Population Research*, *8*, 237–259. doi: 10.1553//populationyearbook2010s237
2. Ibid.
3. Participants' claims that "X caused me to do Y" should be viewed with caution because participants sometimes are not sufficiently insightful about the causes of their behavior.

CONSENSUAL QUALITATIVE RESEARCH DESIGN

In Topic 48, grounded theory research was discussed as a general overarching approach that qualitative researchers use to analyze data. It is a method that is popular in sociology but can also be found in other social sciences and education research. Another qualitative approach that is commonly found in counseling and psychology is **consensual qualitative research (CQR)**.[1] It is good for these disciplinary areas because the method is best suited to studying the inner experiences of individuals. Both qualitative approaches are *inductive* (see the previous topic for a discussion of the differences between inductive and deductive approaches) and involve coding qualitative data, which consists primarily of interview transcripts but may include field notes.

CQR borrows ideas from grounded theory, which preceded it, as well as from other qualitative approaches. CQR and grounded theory differ not only in the disciplines more likely to use them, but also in the role of involving multiple researchers. While it is possible to use a research team in grounded theory, CQR relies on the use of a team of researchers as a basic requirement. The research team should include diverse perspectives. The researchers work together to arrive at a consensus on the meaning of the data collected. This process of building consensus is integral to the CQR method, and is adopted to strengthen the analysis by teasing out nuances in meaning and mitigate the biases of any individual researcher.

In practice, samples in CQR are often as small as 10–15 people and are from a homogeneous population. Best practices suggest that samples should be a minimum of 12.[2] They are often selected based on recent experience with the phenomenon under study and are considered very knowledgeable about the area being studied. All project stages from formulating a semi-structured interview schedule to coding and analysis involve feedback from the research team.

Once data is collected, the first step in the CQR method is to **code into domains**. This refers to segmenting the data (such as interview transcripts) into groups according to the topics they cover. Most studies begin with a list of the domains that were represented in the interview questions. After the members of the research team have split up the data and completed domain coding, they meet to discuss and refine the domains until they reach unanimous agreement on them.

The next step is to **develop core ideas within domains**. This is done by writing short summaries (i.e., abstracts) that reduce the original ideas of participants to fewer words. Initially, the researchers work independently in developing core ideas, which should remain as close to the participants' perspective and words as possible and should work to avoid assumptions or interpretations. Team members read the summaries to familiarize themselves with the cases and the primary research team meets to review and reach agreement about the domains and core ideas.

The third step in CQR is called **cross-analysis**. In this step, the core ideas are grouped into categories based on similarities, and higher level generalizations begin to emerge (i.e., the results are becoming less specific and more abstract). The cross-analysis begins to summarize across cases.

Example 1 shows how one team of researchers described the above three steps.

Example 1

Description of the use of CQR by a research team (bold added for emphasis): The CQR method (Hill et al., 2005, 1997) is characterized by the following three steps: **(1) developing domains and coding data into domains, (2) constructing core ideas (abstracts) from the data within each domain, and (3) conducting a cross-analysis by categorizing the consistencies across cases**. Hence, the analysis in this study was first done case by case, and later the data were examined across cases. At each step, the data were independently coded by each analysis team member, and then the team members met to engage in consensual discussion. Specifically, at the first step, each analysis team member independently assigned each segment of data to various domains (e.g., stress, coping, relationships) and then met as a group to discuss the coding. After all of the data were coded into domains, at the second step, each team member again individually summarized the content of the raw data within each domain for each case, and then they met again as a team to engage in consensual discussion. The consensus versions of the summaries served as the core ideas (abstract) of the data. Subsequently, at the third step, the team members discussed possible categories that could be used to cluster similar core ideas across cases, independently coded the data, and then met again to discuss the coding.[3]

In CQR, there may be an external **stability check**, which can be done by examining data in addition to the interview transcripts (perhaps eyewitness accounts or physical evidence), if it is available.

Internal stability is examined in CQR by determining the extent to which each category was general, typical, or variant. Usually, domains that apply to all the participants are called **general**; those that apply to half or more of the participants are called **typical**; and those that apply to less than half but more than two of the participants are called **variant**. When writing up the results, researchers who use CQR usually use these labels throughout their Results sections. Emphasis on enumerating the number of participants to which each domain applies is a distinctive feature of CQR. Example 2 shows a portion of the Results section of a CQR study in which there is enumeration.

Example 2

Enumeration in the results of a CQR study (bold added for emphasis): Results for European American therapists yielded one **typical** and two **variant categories** (neither of the variant categories emerged for the African American sample). As a **typical category**, these participants stated that, like their African American counterparts, they would address race when they deemed it relevant to the therapy process or relationship. . . . In the first **variant category**, these participants reported that if a client raised the topic of race, the therapist would respond.[4]

The CQR method requires the use of an **auditor.** The auditor is an outside expert who usually reviews the work of the research team after each major step in a study, not just at its conclusion. In a report on a CQR study, the following should be described briefly: the credentials of the auditor, the steps at which the auditor supplied feedback, and whether changes were made on the basis of the auditor's feedback. If changes were made, the types of changes made should be mentioned.

■ TOPIC REVIEW

1. Unlike the grounded theory approach in Topic 48, CQR is *deductive*. Is this statement true *or* false?
2. In what discipline are CQR studies most likely to be found?
3. What is the first step in analyzing data using the CQR approach?
4. Which step includes writing short summaries of participants' ideas?
5. What is done in the cross-analysis?
6. In CQR, what term is used for domains that apply to all the participants?
7. Does the auditor review the work of the research team only at the conclusion of the study?

■ DISCUSSION QUESTION

1. What strengths does building consensus in a research team offer to qualitative research? What qualities help to make the CQR processes avoid bias? What are its weaknesses as a qualitative method?

■ RESEARCH PLANNING

If you are planning to conduct qualitative research, and you anticipate using CQR, who will you involve in your research team? Why does this qualitative approach fit your research topic better than grounded theory?

■ NOTES

1. For more information on CQR, see Hill, C.E. (ed.). (2012). *Consensual Qualitative Research: A Practical Resource for Investigating Social Science Phenomena*. Washington, DC: American Psychological Association.
2. Hill, C.E., Knox, S., Thompson, B.J., Nutt Williams, E., & Hess, S.A. (2005). Consensual qualitative research: An update. *Journal of Counseling Psychology*, 52(2), 196–205.
3. Wang, Y.-W., & Heppner, P.P. (2011). A qualitative study of childhood sexual abuse survivors in Taiwan: Toward a transactional and ecological model of coping. *Journal of Counseling Psychology*, 58, 393–409.
4. Knox, S., Burkard, A.W., Johnson, A.J., Suzuki, L.A., & Ponterotto, J.G. (2003). African American and European American therapists' experiences of addressing race in cross-racial psychotherapy dyads. *Journal of Counseling Psychology*, 50, 466–481.

DESIGNING CASE STUDY RESEARCH

Case study research (CSR) shares many similarities to the other approaches discussed so far in Part 6. It uses many of the same principles of research design and analysis as the other qualitative approaches and uses the same methods to collect data, often multiple forms of rich qualitative data collection, such as observation and interviews. The major advantage of case studies is the "close reading" of social life they can provide.

The main distinguishing characteristic of CSR is its focus on a single or small number of "cases" of a phenomena or event. A **case** may be defined in a number of ways. It could be an individual, or it could be a group of varying sizes, such as a family, village, or organization. The definition of what can constitute a case is not limited in the research methods literature, and can also consist not of a particular group but of a specific time period or an event. Even though what can constitute a case is not constrained by its definition in the literature, the researcher is best served by selecting a unit for a case or cases around which they can establish clear boundaries defining where it starts and ends.

CSR differs from cross-sectional research because it does not investigate the relationships between limited variables. It has been called "the research equivalent to the spotlight or the microscope" for qualitative social science research.[1] This is because CSR takes an **idiographic** approach to research, which means that researchers attempt to describe an individual phenomenon holistically, accounting for as many factors as possible, with an emphasis on detailed, contextual analysis. In CSR, the focus of research is on not only the "case,"—the individual, group, or event—but also the **context**, that is the environment that surrounds the individual, group, or event being studied. It is also possible for CSR to serve as an exploratory study that can inform future **nomothetic** studies on the same issue. A nomothetic study focuses on only a few variables and investigates their relationship carefully, often attempting to explain how much one or a small set of variables explain another variable or an outcome, with the hope of producing data that can be generalized to a population.

CSR has been employed across many disciplines, including sociology, psychology, health research, business, and education, but its popularity has been subject to ups and downs based on methodological critiques that the research results are merely anecdotal. Those accustomed to quantitative approaches can easily criticize CSR for relying on a very small sample size as well as the critiques that qualitative research methods typically face. However, CSR is organized to investigate cases systematically. Studies may take place over long stretches of time, from a month to several years. It is this systematic, detailed, and thorough look that requires researchers to limit cases to just one or at most a few. When individuals or small groups constitute the case, then the number of cases is likely to be in the single digits and will rarely be more than 15.

CSR can be a powerful method for researchers who want to explain a complex whole and make connections between factors in a real-time, real-life scenario. Researchers who collect rich data through observation and interviews must keep careful, organized documentation. The amount of data can be substantial. The goal is for researchers to have as little impact on the environment where they observe as possible so that the data they collect reflects the real behavior of the participants. Taken together, these experiences tend to give case study researchers a broad appreciation for their participants' experiences.

To gain a better understanding of how this works, consider CSR completed by Cronin, as briefly summarized here. Cronin's case study investigated "how students engage in learning in healthcare settings." The study recruited five students, aged 16–18, through a health studies program. The students had little to no prior experience in a healthcare environment. Little prior research had tried to discover how new students learn or the effect that work placements have on recruiting students into a healthcare field.[2] In this study, "cases" consisted of individual students, who were placed in different healthcare environments to work. Data was collected over a two-year period by interviews and observations, as well as documentation provided by student journals, program curricula, and placement information. Constant comparative analysis (similar to grounded theory, see Topic 48) was used throughout to find emerging categories. The study was able to consider how learning is affected by both the constantly changing context of the healthcare environment and the participants' responses to it. CSR is well suited to studying learning in workplaces where the environment is complex and chaotic and learning is heavily dependent on how willingly individuals engage with the environment.

CSR tends to have a lot of data, and the researcher must gain a close familiarity with the data collected through multiple methods, with the goal of identifying categories, themes, and patterns. Like grounded theory, data collection and analysis in CSR are simultaneous and iterative, which gives researchers a chance to adjust data collection tools, build theory gradually, and refine ideas during the study. Although this method is flexible, it maintains rigor by being systematic in data collection and creating a transparent "chain of evidence" with the data that is available for review. As with other *inductive* methods, researchers ideally approach data collection with as little predetermined theory as possible.

When there is only one case, the researcher may evaluate one type of data, such as observation, formulating initial categories, themes, and theories before moving on to the next type of data, such as interviews. When different forms of collected data corroborate one another, the trustworthiness of the findings is strengthened.

If there are multiple cases, data analysis often begins by considering within-case data from a single individual first. Patterns, themes, and categories developed in the within-case review will be tested to see similarities and differences across cases. Another approach to multiple case analysis is similar to consensual qualitative research (see Topic 49). Multiple researchers may each review one type of data—or one case, if there are multiple cases—and then compare results to see where there are similarities and differences. This helps to strengthen the findings. Researchers are more able to defend CSR against criticism when they have a clear purpose and a rigorous approach.

■ TOPIC REVIEW

1. What is the distinguishing principle of case studies?
2. How many cases are typically in a case study research project?

3. True or false: you can have only one case in case study research.
4. What can constitute a case?
5. What is the term when one tries to describe everything in a research scenario?
6. What is one type of data collection that CSR has in common with other qualitative methods?
7. What is one main way that CSR differs from other qualitative methods?

■ DISCUSSION QUESTION

1. Do you think a method with only one or two cases can produce results on which generalizations or a theory can be based? Why or why not? What could a researcher do to improve the quality and integrity of a case study research project?

■ RESEARCH PLANNING

If you considered a case study approach to a research interest or question you have, what would constitute a case? (Remember that a case does not have to be an individual; it might be a group, event, or period of time.) What would be the boundaries around the case? What types of data collection methods and time frame would you need to do a case study project? Would your project be idiographic or an exploration to set up a nomothetic research project?

■ NOTES

1. C. Cronin cites this comparison from Hakim, C. (1987). *Research Design: Strategies and Choices in the Design of Social Research*. London: Routledge in her 2014 article, Using case study research as a rigorous form of inquiry. *Nurse Researcher, 21*(5), 19–27.
2. Cronin, C. (2014). Using case study research as a rigorous form of inquiry.

MIXED METHODS DESIGNS

Sometimes referred to as "the third methodological movement," mixed methods research combines qualitative and quantitative research techniques in one project. This approach is characteristic of how popular writing in books, magazines, and journalism present real-world problems using statistics to provide context for stories and personal stories to illustrate data. Many qualitative researchers use their introduction or literature review to frame their work with statistics, and quantitative researchers may use the introduction, literature review, or concluding discussion to connect their data to a larger context, meaning, or significance. Presenting both types of information can make an argument stronger.

Mixed methods research takes this logic one step further. Instead of simply including a review of both types of research in the reporting of a problem, mixed methods includes at least one qualitative and one quantitative component of original research in the study design. Many disciplines, including sociology, nursing, and evaluation research, converged on the concept of mixing methodologies to address complex research problems in the late 1980s, but it would take a decade before a mixed methods approach gained wider recognition.

Mixed methods designs vary. They can combine any types of quantitative and qualitative research, including experimental or quasi-experimental designs or case studies. Each component of the study is referred to as a **strand**; for instance, if qualitative interviews and a quantitative survey were used, each of these would be a *strand* of the research.

At this point, it may seem that every project would benefit from using both qualitative and quantitative methods, but this is not always the case. Mixed methods designs are still greeted with some skepticism. First, conducting a project that has multiple, diverse types of data collection requires mastery of both qualitative and quantitative analysis skills. The research design is more complex than a single-method design and likely includes extra time, money, and staff. This requires a solid rationale from the researcher or research team to justify that the research really benefits from two different types of data and cannot be adequately addressed with only one. Many research questions can be answered using just qualitative or just quantitative data.

Studies that are best suited to mixed methods are those that need the results to be explained, or exploratory studies that need to be generalized. Consider a study evaluating a healthy eating program that is introduced at a high school. The researcher wants to collect qualitative data from those participating in the program to see where the program works well and where students have difficulty complying or understanding how to follow the program. At the end, the researcher also needs to evaluate the program's overall effectiveness in order to see if there was a net positive effect on health. This may involve a pretest/posttest model that uses quantitative methods. Other examples are when a second method can greatly enhance the first method, or a theoretical stance needs to be employed. For instance, a study attempts to theorize the differences in recovery among cancer survivors in order to help understand the best post-treatment services to offer this patient population. A survey may reveal resources or attitudes that best support this process, but to theorize why, researchers may need more in-depth information about how these resources or attitudes helped, or to explore counterfactual cases where the same resources were not helpful and see if the differences between the lives or the services can help to identify factors that contribute to better care.

Mixed methods studies may be **fixed,** which is when a mixed methods design is used from the start, or **emergent,** which is when the need for both types of data is discovered after work is in progress. Qualitative and quantitative data are typically collected separately, but, in some cases, it may mean that data is collected only once but analyzed in both ways. The main design questions with mixed methods revolve around timing, priority, and level of interaction between the methods used—in other words, are the methods connected or independent during any or all of the phases of the research design.[1] Notice how variations on mixed methods designs presented next vary by these dimensions to achieve different types of results.

First, designs may be based on a **simultaneous** or **sequential** approach. In **simultaneous** approaches, both qualitative and quantitative data are collected at the same time. In **sequential designs**, one data type is collected first, followed by the collection of the second type of data.

Simultaneous designs may be **convergent,** in which the data are collected *independently* but then mixed and interpreted in one analysis, or they may be **embedded**, in which collection of one type of data is dominant, and the other is much smaller or exploratory and is nested in the larger, dominant set of data. Embedded models can also be **sequential.** One example is a quantitative survey that also carries out a small subset of qualitative interviews as a pilot to help determine the best questions and closed-choice responses to include in a specific part of the quantitative survey. Often, embedded models use the less dominant data to answer a secondary or preliminary question without which the research would seem incomplete. Embedded models may also keep one type of data collection small due to constraints in resources needed to collect both types of data equally.

Sequential designs are typically described as **explanatory** or **exploratory.** This helps to distinguish the overall purpose of the research and suggests a sequence of data collection.[2] *Explanatory* designs are most appropriate to research that analyzes relationships or trends using a quantitative approach, but also wants to be able to address underlying mechanisms or reasons. The above example of research on services for cancer survivors fits this design. In *exploratory* designs, the researcher begins with a qualitative approach to a research question but wants to also be able to generalize the findings. The initial findings are used to create a quantitative instrument that is used in a second phase to collect data and discover if the qualitative results are reflected in a larger population as well.

Longstanding tensions and contentious divides can exist between qualitative and quantitative camps of research in some disciplines, but these methods are not inherently incompatible. However, as noted earlier in this topic, carrying out a mixed methods study requires more skills from researchers and involves a more time-consuming and costly plan with more areas to potentially troubleshoot. For these reasons, researchers embarking on a mixed methods design should have clear reasons for collecting both types of data and a careful, detailed plan.

■ TOPIC REVIEW

1. What characteristic defines mixed methods research?
2. What are each of the types of research called in a mixed methods design?
3. True or false: mixed methods research requires that all data be collected at the same time.
4. When a mixed methods design is selected at the beginning, what is the design called?
5. What is the difference between a simultaneous and sequential research design?
6. This topic suggests that three dimensions are key to planning a mixed methods design. One is timing. What are the other two?
7. If a mixed methods design first collects qualitative data and then collects quantitative data, what is the name of the design type?

■ DISCUSSION QUESTION

1. Are you convinced that not all research would benefit from the use of mixed methods? Consider what makes a research question best suited to the use of a mixed methods design, keeping in mind the different possible types of designs presented.

■ RESEARCH PLANNING

If you considered expanding your current study to use a mixed methods design, what would you want to explore in the new strand of your research? Which design would make the most sense to answer your question?

■ NOTES

1. Creswell, J.W., & Plano Clark, V.L. (2011). *Designing and Conducting Mixed Methods Research*. Thousand Oaks, CA: SAGE Publications.
2. Ibid.

PART 7
Designing Experimental Research

Researchers design experiments so that participants are given treatments in order to observe effects on their behavior. Part 7 describes various designs for experiments. Specifically, in Topics 52, 55, and 56, designs for true experiments, pre-experiments, and quasi-experiments are explained and illustrated. Topic 53 discusses threats to internal validity in experiments, in which the question "Did the treatments, in fact, cause the observed differences?" is posed. Topic 54 addresses external validity of experiments, which addresses the question "Can a researcher generalize beyond the experimental setting?"[1] Finally, Topic 57 explains various confound effects in experimental research. Learning about experimental research design benefits from knowing the concepts presented thus far in the book, and builds on concepts that were first introduced in Part 5 on Measurement.

TRUE EXPERIMENTAL DESIGNS

As discussed in Topic 4, the purpose of an experiment is to explore cause-and-effect relationships. In this topic, we will examine some specific designs for experimental studies. First, consider a classic design for exploring cause-and-effect relationships:

Design 1

Assign participants at random to groups.	Group A: (Experimental group)	Pretest	Experimental treatment	Posttest
	Group B: (Control group)	Pretest	Control condition	Posttest

Design 1 is the **pretest-posttest randomized control group design**. By assigning participants at random to groups, researchers are assured that there are no biases in the assignment.[2] That is, the two groups of participants are equal except for random differences.

In Design 1, if the experimental group makes greater gains from pretest to posttest than the control group *and* if the two groups have been treated the same in all respects except for the experimental treatment, the difference is attributable to only one of two causes: (1) the treatment or (2) random errors. Part 8 of this book discusses how researchers can use inferential statistics to assess the role of random errors in creating any observed differences. Thus, researchers can tolerate random errors because the results can be interpreted in light of their possible effects. There are no generalizable statistical techniques for assessing the influence of bias. Hence, researchers use random assignment to avoid bias in the assignment to the two conditions (experimental and control conditions).

Researchers can simplify the representation of Design 1 by using symbols suggested by Campbell and Stanley (1963): R (which stands for random assignment to groups), O (which stands for observation or measurement, whether pretest or posttest), and X (which stands for experimental treatment). There is no symbol for control condition, so it is represented by a blank. Note that a control condition may include some type of treatment (in education, it might be a traditional form of instruction; in medicine, it might be a placebo). Thus, the control condition is the standard by which the effectiveness of the experimental treatment is judged. Using symbols, Design 1 looks like this:

R	0	X	0
R	0		0

The advantage of using a pretest is that it permits researchers to determine how much each group has *gained*, not just whether they are different at the end of the experiment. However, sometimes having a pretest causes a problem because it can sensitize participants to the experimental treatment and, in effect, become part of the treatment. For instance, by taking a pretest at the beginning of an experimental course of instruction, participants can gain an overview of what will be covered, the depth to which the material will be covered, and so on. Thus, changes observed in the experimental group may be the result of a *combination of the pretest and the treatment*. This problem is called **pretest sensitization** (also called the **reactive effect of testing**). It can be overcome by conducting an experiment without a pretest, as shown in Design 2, which is the **posttest-only randomized control group design**.

Design 2

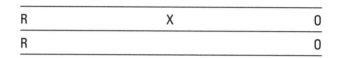

R		X	0
R			0

At first, the lack of a pretest may seem to be a flaw, but remember that the comparability of the two groups in Design 1 was achieved by assigning participants at random to the two groups. This initial comparability is also achieved in Design 2 above by this random assignment. In other words, it is not the pretest that makes the two groups comparable; it is the random assignment that does.

Researchers can have the best of both designs by using the **Solomon randomized four-group design**, which is a combination of Designs 1 and 2. Solomon's design is shown in Design 3. Because it has four rows of symbols, it has four groups. The first two rows are the same as Design 1, while the bottom two rows are the same as Design 2. In effect, the Solomon design is two experiments conducted at the same time.

Design 3

R	0	X	0
R	0		0
R		X	0
R			0

The advantage of the Solomon design above is that researchers can compare the first two groups to determine how much gain is achieved and can also compare the last two groups to determine whether the treatment is more effective than the control condition in the absence of a pretest (without pretest sensitization). The only potential drawback to Design 3 is that a researcher must begin with a reasonably large pool of participants so that when they are divided into four groups, each of the groups will have a sufficient number to yield reliable results. How many is enough? The answer is complex, but generally speaking, it probably would be unwise to use the four-group design instead of a two-group design if the total pool of participants is fewer than 48.

All three of the preceding designs are called **true experimental designs**. True experimental designs are easy to spot because they are all characterized by random assignment to treatments.

Sometimes, it is not possible to assign participants at random. For instance, for ethical and legal reasons, a researcher might not be able to withhold a particular treatment from individuals. In such a case, the researcher might treat an entire group with a treatment mandated by law and use another group that is not required to have the treatment as the control group. Because the participants were *not* assigned at random to treatments, such experiments are *not* true experiments.

■ TOPIC REVIEW

1. What is the purpose of an experiment?
2. In an experiment, how can researchers ensure that there are no biases when they assign participants to groups?
3. In a diagram for an experimental design, the symbol O stands for what?
4. In a diagram for an experimental design, the symbol X stands for what?
5. What is the name of the potential problem caused by the pretest in the pretest–posttest randomized control group design?
6. What is the name of the true experimental design that has no pretests?
7. What is a potential drawback to the Solomon randomized four-group design?
8. True experimental designs are easy to spot because they are all characterized by what?

■ DISCUSSION QUESTION

1. Briefly describe an experimental problem for which a researcher probably would not be able to assign participants at random to conditions.

■ RESEARCH PLANNING

Could your research interest be investigated with a true experimental design? If so, how could you use the designs proposed in this topic?

■ NOTES

1. This part highlights some of the main ideas in the classic work of Campbell, D.T., & Stanley, J.C. (1963). *Experimental and Quasi-Experimental Designs for Research.* Chicago, IL: Rand McNally.
2. See Topic 26 for a discussion of how to select participants at random. If half of them are selected at random to be the experimental group and the rest are designated as the control group, the researcher has used random assignment to groups.

THREATS TO INTERNAL VALIDITY

Suppose a researcher observes major changes in participants' behavior in an experiment. Is it reasonable to attribute these changes to the effects of the treatment(s)? Depending on the design of the experiment, there may be explanations for the changes other than the treatment. These alternative explanations are called **threats to internal validity**. It is easiest to understand them in the context of a poor experiment with no control group (specifically, one in which a researcher pretests, treats, and then posttests one group of participants). Using the symbols described in the previous topic, the design looks like this:

O   X   O

Suppose the treatment (X) was designed to improve participants' self-concept, and the researcher observed an average gain of nine points in self-concept from pretest (the first O) to posttest (the second O). Of course, the treatment could be responsible for the increase. Another possibility is the internal threat called **history** (i.e., other environmental influences on the participants between the pretest and posttest). For instance, perhaps some of the participants were part of a winning team during the same period of time that the treatment was being administered. The improved self-concepts could have resulted from the experience of winning and not from the treatment.

Another threat in this design is **maturation**. Perhaps the participants matured (e.g., became older, wiser, or smarter) during the period between the pretest and posttest, and the increase is due to maturation and not to the treatment.

Instrumentation, as it is sometimes called, is also a threat. This refers to possible changes in the measurement procedure from the time it was used as a pretest to the time it was used as a posttest. For instance, the particular observers who made the pretest observations may have been less astute at noticing signs of good self-concept than the observers who made the posttest observations.

Another threat is **testing**, which is defined as the effects of the pretest on the performance exhibited on the posttest. For instance, while taking the pretest self-concept scale, the participants may have learned to interpret the questions differently by the end of the test. Their posttest performance might be affected by this learning experience that occurred while they took the pretest.

Statistical regression is a threat that occurs only if participants are selected on the basis of their extreme scores. For instance, perhaps a large group of students was administered a self-concept scale, and those in the lowest 20% were selected for treatment in the experiment. A fundamental principle of measurement is that those who are extremely low on a screening test will, on average, tend to have a higher score when tested again, purely because some of them will be so classified because of random errors created by the less-than-perfect reliability of the measures researchers use—whether or not the treatment is effective.[1]

Another threat to internal validity can occur when researchers use two comparison groups that are *not* formed at random. Suppose, for instance, that a researcher uses the students in one school as the experimental group and those in another as the control group. Because students are not assigned to schools at random, the researcher is using **intact groups** (i.e., previously existing groups). This is diagrammed by putting a dashed line between the symbols for the groups, which indicates that the groups were intact, as shown here:

0	X	0
0		0

Notice that when researchers do not assign participants to the two groups at random, there is a very strong possibility that the two groups are not initially the same in all important respects, which is the threat called **selection**. Selection can *interact* with all the other threats to internal validity. For instance, consider **selection–history interaction**. Because the selection of participants for the two groups was not at random, they may be systematically subjected to different life experiences. It may be that the teachers in the school with the experimental group took a self-concept workshop, which was not part of the treatment, and applied what they learned to their students. Thus, the improvement in self-concepts may be the result of the teachers' efforts and not of the treatment. Another example is **selection–maturation interaction**. Perhaps the two groups, on average, were at somewhat different developmental stages at the time of the pretest, which would have led to different rates of maturation in the two groups, which could affect self-concept.

Selection can also interact with a threat called **mortality** (i.e., differential loss of participants from the groups to be compared). For instance, those in an experimental school may have a higher dropout rate than those in a control school. If those who drop out have lower self-concepts, the posttest mean for the experimental group will be higher than the pretest mean, resulting in a statistical change in the average that is not the result of the treatment. At the same time, the control group will not exhibit as much change because it has a lower dropout rate.

All threats to internal validity can be overcome by using a **true experimental design** (see Topic 52), in which participants are assigned at random to experimental and control conditions. Because random assignment has no bias (or favorites), both the experimental and the control group are equally likely to experience the same environmental events (have the same history), mature at the same rates, drop out at the same rates, and so on.

■ TOPIC REVIEW

1. What is the name of the threat that indicates that taking a pretest may affect performance on a posttest?

2. Suppose an experimental group is being taught letters of the alphabet as a treatment. At about the same time, the students are watching an educational program on

television, from which they learn the names of the letters. What is the name of the threat that this problem illustrates?

3. If observers are more tired and less astute when making posttest observations than when making pretest observations, what threat is operating?

4. What is the name of the threat posed by nonrandom assignment of participants to experimental and control groups?

5. If infants naturally improve in visual acuity and thus perform better at the end of an experiment than at the beginning, what threat is operating?

6. Under what circumstance will statistical regression operate?

7. How can researchers overcome all the threats to internal validity?

■ DISCUSSION QUESTION

1. Suppose a researcher gave a series of wellness workshops over a six-month period and then determined that five of the participants had quit smoking during the six-month period. The researcher's interpretation was that the workshops caused the decrease in smoking. Is this interpretation flawed? Explain.

■ RESEARCH PLANNING

If you are planning to conduct an experiment, consider which threats, if any, it will be subject to. Are there any steps you can take to help control or learn about these threats?

■ NOTE

1. Statistical regression is difficult to grasp without a solid background in measurement theory. However, some students may recall the principle of *regression toward the mean* from their study of other sciences. Those who are very low will, on average, tend to be higher on retesting (closer to the mean, on average), and those who are very high will tend to be lower on retesting.

THREATS TO EXTERNAL VALIDITY

External validity and **internal validity** (see Topic 53) are separate considerations and it is important to differentiate between them. In relation to experiments, internal validity is concerned with the question "Is the treatment, *in this particular case*, responsible for the observed change(s)?" Threats to internal validity are potential alternate explanations for the observed changes other than the treatment. Threats to internal validity are controlled by using true experimental designs (see Topic 52).

By contrast, the external validity of an experiment is concerned with "To whom and under what circumstances can the results be generalized?" Even if an experiment has excellent internal validity, it may not be appropriate to generalize the results to other populations because of the threats to external validity. Likewise, a study with high external validity might have poor internal validity. This can happen if threats to internal validity have confounded a researcher's understanding of the cause for the observed changes. Thus, each of these types of threats should be considered and evaluated independently.

Consider this example: A researcher drew a sample from a population and divided it into an experimental group and a control group. To conduct the experiment, the researcher administered the experimental treatment and control condition in a laboratory on a college campus. Suppose the results of the experiment showed that the experimental group improved significantly more than the control group. Can the researcher accurately **generalize** from the sample to the population (i.e., is it accurate to assume that the treatment administered to the experimental group will work as well in the population as it did in the sample)? Also, will the treatment be as effective in the population's natural setting as it was in the artificial laboratory setting? The answers depend on the extent to which the experiment is subject to what researchers call **threats to external validity**.

The first threat is **selection bias** and its interaction with the experimental (independent) variable. As indicated in Part 4 of this book, if a sample is biased, a researcher's ability to generalize to a population is greatly limited. In a strict scientific sense, no generalizations should be made when bias is present. If a biased sample of participants is used in an experiment (such as using the students who happen to be in one professor's class), a researcher will not know whether the effects of the treatment (observed in that class) can be expected if the treatment is administered to the entire population. Of course, the way to control this threat is to select the participants for an experiment at random from a population because a random sample is, by definition, unbiased.

Another threat is the **reactive effects of experimental arrangements**. This threat is present if the experimental setting is different from the natural setting in which the population usually operates because the effects that are observed in the experimental setting may not generalize to the natural setting. For instance, if a treatment is administered in a laboratory to fifth-graders, the responsiveness of the students may be different from the responsiveness of the population of fifth-graders when the treatment is used in public school classroom settings. In other words, it can be risky to generalize from an experimental setting to a natural setting. The way to control this threat is to conduct experiments under natural conditions when possible.

The possible **reactive effect of testing** (also called **pretest sensitization**) is another threat. This threat refers to the possibility that the pretest might influence how the participants respond to the experimental treatment. For instance, if a researcher gives a pretest on racial prejudice and then administers a treatment designed to lessen prejudice, participants' responses to the treatment may be affected by the experience of taking the pretest. That is, having to think about prejudice (while taking the pretest) might change participants' sensitivity to the treatment. This is a problem when researchers want to generalize about how well the treatment will work in the population *if* the population will not be given a pretest. As indicated in Topic 52, researchers can conduct true experiments without pretests, thereby eliminating this threat.

Multiple-treatment interference is a threat that occurs when a group of participants is given more than one treatment. For instance, at first, a researcher might give participants no praise for correct answers, then start giving them moderate amounts of praise, and finally give them large amounts of praise. Suppose the researcher finds that large amounts of praise work best. Will it work in the same way in the population? The generalization will be risky if those in the population will *not* first be given the no-praise condition, then the moderate-praise condition, and, finally, the large-praise condition. In other words, the fact that these participants first received small and then moderate amounts of praise might make their responses to large amounts of praise different from the responses of a population that will receive *only* large amounts of praise. To put it a different way, treatment(s) given earlier in an experiment might affect the effectiveness of treatments given later to the same participants.

■ TOPIC REVIEW

1. Which type of validity deals with the question of whether a researcher can generalize with confidence to a larger population in a natural setting?
2. Which type of validity deals with whether the treatment is directly responsible for any changes observed in the experimental setting?
3. What is the name of the threat that warns researchers to be careful in generalizing the results to a population when an experiment is conducted on a nonrandom sample?
4. Suppose a single random sample of workers in a factory is exposed to five different reward systems in succession, with each system being used for one month. What is the name of the threat that reminds researchers that the research results for the last reward system may not generalize to the population of workers?
5. Suppose an experimental classroom has research observers present at all times. What is the name of the threat that reminds researchers that the results may not generalize to other classrooms without observers?
6. If a pretest causes a change in participants' sensitivity to a treatment, what threat is operating?

■ DISCUSSION QUESTION

1. Work together to describe a hypothetical experiment on racial prejudice that has high internal validity but low external validity.

■ RESEARCH PLANNING

If you are planning to conduct an experiment, which threats to external validity, if any, will your experiment be most vulnerable to? Are there any steps you can take to document these effects or design your study to reduce them?

PRE-EXPERIMENTAL DESIGNS

The three designs discussed in this topic are called **pre-experimental designs** because they use the elements of an experiment but lack the necessary ingredients to be a quasi-experiment or true experimental design, such as pretest and posttest, and control group. They have limited value for investigating cause-and-effect relationships because of their poor internal validity. One of the designs was introduced in Topic 53: the **one-group pretest-posttest design**. Its diagram is shown here as Design 4.[1]

Design 4: *One-group pretest-posttest design*

O	X	O

As indicated in Topic 53, changes from pretest to posttest in Design 4 may be attributable to *history, maturation, instrumentation, testing,* and *statistical regression*[2] (see Topic 53 for a discussion of these threats to internal validity). These factors are possible explanations for any changes observed from the pretest to the posttest. Of course, researchers want to determine what changes, if any, the treatment (X) caused. Thus, the interpretation of pretest to posttest change is *confounded* by multiple explanations.

Design 5 is called the **one-shot case study**. In it, one group is given a treatment (X) followed by a test (O). This is its diagram:

Design 5: *One-shot case study*

X	O

If a teacher provides instruction on a unit of material and follows it with an achievement test, he or she is using Design 5. For classroom purposes, there is nothing wrong with this design. For instance, the posttest will help the teacher to determine what grades to assign for students' achievements on the unit of instruction. However, if a teacher wants to know whether the instruction *caused* whatever achievements are seen on the test, the design is of no value because it fails to make comparisons. The teacher cannot determine whether the students achieved anything as a result of the instruction without a pretest (or a randomly selected control group). In other words, it is quite possible that the achievement the students display on the posttest is at the same level they might have displayed on a pretest if there had been one.[3]

Design 6, the **static-group comparison design**, has two groups, but participants are not assigned to the groups at random. The dashed line between the two groups indicates they are **intact groups** (i.e., previously existing groups that were not formed at random).

Design 6: *Static-group comparison design*

X	0
	0

The obvious problem with Design 6 is the threat to internal validity called **selection** (the selection of the two groups was not made in such a way that a researcher can have confidence that they are initially the same in all important respects).[4] Furthermore, without a pretest, a researcher does not have a basis for knowing whether the two groups were similar at the beginning of the experiment. For instance, the treatment might have been totally ineffective, but the experimental group might have been superior to the control group at the beginning of the experiment and may have retained the same amount of superiority throughout the experiment. This initial superiority would produce a difference in favor of the experimental group in the posttest results, which might lead to the faulty assumption that the treatment caused the difference.[5]

Because of their weaknesses, these three pre-experimental designs are of very limited value in exploring cause-and-effect relationships. However, they are sometimes useful in *preliminary pilot studies* in which a researcher's goal is to try out potential treatments and measuring tools to learn more about their acceptability and accuracy, not to obtain definitive information on causal relationships. For instance, a researcher might administer a new drug to a small group of participants in order to observe for side effects, to determine the maximum tolerable dosage, to explore different routes of administration, and so on. The results could be used in planning a subsequent true experiment on the effects of the drug, using a design that has a randomized control group (see Topic 53).

■ TOPIC REVIEW

1. Are pre-experimental designs valuable for identifying cause-and-effect relationships?
2. Suppose a researcher administered a new program to all students in a school. At the end of the school year, the researcher administered a standardized test to the students in the school as well as to students in another school who were serving as a control group. Is the comparison of the average scores for the two groups of students useful for determining the effects of the program?
3. What is the name of the pre-experimental design used in Question 2?
4. If a researcher gives a pretest on knowledge of child abuse to a group of social workers, then gives them a series of seminars on child abuse, followed by a posttest, what is the name of the pre-experimental design the researcher used?
5. Is the design used in Question 4 useful for determining cause-and-effect relationships?

■ DISCUSSION QUESTIONS

1. Suppose a researcher selected participants at random from a population and then used the one-group pretest-posttest design. Would random selection make this design good for exploring cause-and-effect relationships?

2. Have you ever used a pre-experimental design (e.g., tried doing something in a new way and observing for its effects without a control group) in any of your professional or everyday activities? If so, briefly describe it. Discuss whether your activity shed light on a cause-and-effect relationship.

■ RESEARCH PLANNING

If you will be conducting an experiment, will you be using a pre-experimental design? If yes, explain how you will conduct the study to minimize this design's serious weaknesses.

■ NOTES

1. Designs are numbered for easy reference, but do not correspond to a universal reference. Students should refer to designs by name, not number.
2. Campbell and Stanley (1963) note that this design is also subject to the *interaction of selection with history, maturation*, etc. See Campbell, D.T., & Stanley, J.C. (1963). *Experimental and Quasi-experimental Designs for Research.* Chicago, IL: Rand McNally, p37.
3. Campbell and Stanley (1963) note that this design is subject to internal threats of history, maturation, selection, and mortality.
4. Ibid.
5. As indicated in Topic 52, a pretest is not essential in a two-group design *if* the participants are assigned at random to the groups. This is because the random assignment assures that the two groups are initially the same *except for random differences*, which can be assessed with inferential statistics. See the discussion of Design 2 in Topic 52.

QUASI-EXPERIMENTAL DESIGNS

True experimental designs involve random assignment to treatment conditions and are excellent for exploring cause-and-effect relationships (see Topic 52). However, it is often not possible to assign participants at random. When this is the case, pre-experimental designs (see Topic 55) should be avoided. Instead, **quasi-experimental designs**, which are of intermediate value for exploring cause and effect, should be used.[1]

Design 7 is a widely used, quasi-experimental design that has two intact groups (not assigned at random, as indicated by the dashed line). This is the **nonequivalent control group design**.

Design 7: *Nonequivalent control group design*

$$
\begin{array}{ccc}
\hline
0 & X & 0 \\
\hdashline
0 & & 0 \\
\hline
\end{array}
$$

As indicated in Topic 53, this design is subject to the threats of *mortality*, *selection*, and *interaction of selection* with other threats such as *history*. Thus, it is far from ideal. However, it is superior to pre-experimental designs, which are not directly interpretable in terms of causal effects.

Even though participants are not assigned to groups at random in Design 7, researchers often use matching to increase the internal validity of the results. For instance, in a study that examines hospital patients' satisfaction with their experiences as it relates to hospital organizational change, a researcher might designate patients in a hospital undergoing organizational change as the experimental group, while patients in a hospital that is not undergoing organizational change are designated as the control group. To form matched groups, a researcher could select a sample of individuals from the first hospital and determine their status on relevant demographics: medical condition, age, gender, and socioeconomic status. Then, the researcher could handpick participants from the other hospital who are similar in terms of these demographics. This is better than using unmatched samples from both hospitals, but the two groups may not have been matched on all relevant variables. For instance, the researcher has not taken into account whether patients have insurance or not, and patients may have fundamentally different experiences of satisfaction on this basis. Obviously, assigning participants at random to the two conditions (using a true experimental design) would be vastly superior because the random assignment would assure the researcher that the two groups were initially the same on *all variables* except for random differences, whose effects can be assessed with inferential statistics. (Inferential statistics are covered in Part 8.)

Design 8, which is known as the **equivalent time-samples design**, has only one group (or possibly only one participant). Treatment conditions are alternated (preferably on a random basis), as indicated in the design by alternating X_1 (an experimental treatment) with X_0 (a control condition or comparison treatment).

Design 8: *Equivalent time-samples design*

$$X_0 0 \quad X_1 0 \quad X_0 0 \quad X_1 0$$

The participants in Design 8 are, in effect, serving as both the control participants (when they are receiving X_0) and the experimental participants (when they are receiving X_1). This is a major advantage because researchers know that the experimental participants and control participants (who are actually the same individuals) are identical—in fact, in all ways—at the beginning of the experiment. A major disadvantage of this design is the strong possibility of *multiple-treatment interference*. In this case, the second time the participants receive X_1, they have already been exposed to and possibly changed by the earlier exposure to X_1.

Notice that giving the treatments repeatedly in Design 8 above strengthens internal validity because it is unlikely that the threats to internal validity are operating only at the times when X_1 is given but not when X_0 is given. For instance, it is unlikely that participants mature only at X_1 and not at X_0. Similarly, it is unlikely that *history* confounds the interpretation by causing changes only when X_1 is given.

In psychology, a single-group design in which treatments are alternated is often called an ABAB design, where A and B indicate alternating treatments. Typically, when this design is used, there are multiple initial observations before any treatment is given. These initial observations constitute the **baseline**, which determines the typical variation in the behavior of participants over time before any intervention. For instance, perhaps a researcher plans to give rewards for in-seat behavior in a classroom to a hyperactive child. The researcher could measure the amount of out-of-seat behavior on a daily basis for a number of days to determine the natural amount of variation from day to day without treatment. Then, when the researcher introduces the rewards, any changes observed during treatment can be evaluated by any contrast with the natural variation before treatment. In other words, the researcher would ask: Is the decrease in out-of-seat behavior after treatment greater than the natural day-to-day decreases (and increases) observed during the baseline?

■ TOPIC REVIEW

1. What is the name of the design diagrammed immediately below?

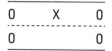

2. In the design shown in Question 1, what indicates that participants were not assigned at random to groups?

3. If a researcher uses matching to form the two groups in the design in Question 1, would the resulting experiment be superior to a true experiment?
4. What is a major advantage of the equivalent time-samples design?
5. What is a major disadvantage of the equivalent time-samples design?
6. In psychology, what is an ABAB design?

■ DISCUSSION QUESTION

1. Suppose a researcher observed two classes for baseline data on calling-out behavior (i.e., calling out in class when it is inappropriate). The researcher observed much variation in the amount of calling out in Class A, and little variation in Class B. Which class would benefit from a longer baseline? Why?

■ RESEARCH PLANNING

If you are planning to conduct a quasi-experimental design, which one will you use? Why are you using a quasi-experimental design instead of a true experimental one? What might your most critical reviewer ask you to justify about this study design? Do you have an argument to justify it?

■ NOTE

1. Only the two most widely used quasi-experimental designs are presented in this topic. For a discussion of others, see Campbell, D.T., & Stanley, J.C. (1963). *Experimental and Quasi-Experimental Designs for Research.* Chicago, IL: Rand McNally.

CONFOUNDING IN EXPERIMENTS

In experimental research, a **confound** is an extra variable that creates confusion regarding the explanation for a given difference. Suppose, for instance, a researcher gave an experimental group instruction in algebra using a new software program and, at the same time, a student teacher taught the same algebra skills to the group using manipulative devices. Furthermore, suppose the control group received no algebra instruction. If the experimental group outperformed the control group, the results would be said to be confounded because there would be no way to sort out the relative influence of the software versus the manipulatives. Unfortunately, not all sources of confounding are as obvious as the one in this example.

One important source of confounding is the **Hawthorne Effect**, which can be thought of as the *attention effect*. This effect was discovered in a series of industrial psychology studies at the Hawthorne Plant of Western Electric. In the studies, worker productivity went up when the lighting was increased. Oddly enough, productivity also went up when the lighting was decreased. The results were interpreted to mean that participants had not responded solely to the change in lighting but instead to the *attention* of being observed by the researchers. Thus, the differences observed could not be attributed to one cause (the amount of illumination or the amount of attention participants received).

To control for the Hawthorne Effect, some researchers use three groups: (1) an experimental group, (2) a control group that receives attention, and (3) a control group that receives no special attention. For instance, an experimental group could be shown a film containing aggressive behaviors to determine whether students' aggressiveness on the playground increased after they saw the film. The attention control group could be shown a film with no aggression (thus, giving attention to this control group), while the no–attention control group could be shown no film. Comparing the aggressiveness of the three groups on a playground would yield information on how much attention contributed to any changes as well as how much the film with aggressive behaviors contributed.

A related confound is the **John Henry Effect**, named for the prodigiously hardworking 19th century folk hero. This effect refers to the possibility that the control group might become aware of its "inferior" status (not being selected for the group receiving treatment) and respond by trying to outperform the experimental group. Thus, researchers should try to conceal the control group's knowledge of its status whenever possible. For ethical reasons, participants usually need to be informed that they will be participating in an experiment, but it is often sufficient to inform them that they may be in either the experimental or the control group, without revealing the group to which they were assigned.

Researchers who study the effectiveness of medications usually are concerned with the confounding **placebo effect**. The placebo effect refers to the well-established tendency of individuals to improve (or at least perceive that they are improving) simply because they know they are being treated. Suppose, for instance, a new drug was given to a group of individuals suffering from a certain condition. Because of the placebo effect, some individuals might report that they feel better (or show real improvement) even if the drug was totally ineffective.

To control for this, researchers compare results from a group receiving an experimental treatment with a control group that is given a **placebo** that resembles the treatment but is inactive. In drug studies, for instance, a placebo could be a pill that looks identical to the medication being investigated but contains only inert ingredients (e.g., a sugar pill). Because each group receives a treatment, differences between effects in the experimental group and the placebo-control group indicate how much more effective the new medication is than any placebo effect from treatment with an inactive substance.

When administering a placebo, researchers say they are using a **blind** procedure when they do not disclose to the participants whether they are receiving an active or inactive substance. (For ethical reasons, participants are told that they will be receiving *either* an active or an inactive drug.) In a **double-blind** experiment, neither the participants nor the individual dispensing the drug know which is the active drug and which is the placebo. This is done to prevent the possibility that the individual dispensing the drug will subtly communicate to the participants their status as either control or experimental participants or interpret effects differently.[1] For instance, the packaging of the drug and placebo could be color-coded; the individual who is dispensing might know only that the blue package should be dispensed to a random half while the yellow package should be dispensed to the other half, without knowing which color package contains the active drug.

Demand characteristics can also be a source of confounding. A demand characteristic is a cue that lets participants know the expected outcome of an experiment. This can be a problem if participants attempt to please the experimenter by reporting or acting in a way they believe is expected. To the extent possible, researchers should try to conceal their expectations from the participants (i.e., the researchers' hypotheses).

■ TOPIC REVIEW

1. A confound is a source of confusion regarding what?
2. What is the name of the effect that refers to the possibility that the control group might become aware of its "inferior" status and respond by trying to outperform the experimental group?
3. What is the formal name of what is characterized as the *attention effect* in this topic?
4. In addition to an experimental and a traditional control group (with no treatment), what other group can be used to control for the Hawthorne Effect?
5. The term *placebo effect* refers to what tendency?
6. In what type of experiment do neither the participants nor the individuals dispensing the drug know which is the active drug and which is the placebo?
7. A *demand characteristic* is a cue that lets participants know what?

■ DISCUSSION QUESTION

1. If you were a participant in an experiment, did you try to guess what the researcher's hypothesis was? If yes, do you think that your guess(es) influenced your behavior in the experiment? Explain.

■ RESEARCH PLANNING

If you are planning an experiment, will you take measures to minimize potential sources of confounding? What strategies could you use to do this? How will you document them in your research report?

■ NOTE

1. Note that those who dispense the drugs in these experiments might also subconsciously communicate their *expectations* (i.e., that those receiving the active drug will improve).

PART 8

Analyzing Data: Understanding Statistics

Part 8 is designed to prepare students to read and comprehend statistics. The emphasis is on understanding concepts and becoming oriented to the most common statistical tests. *No information is provided that teaches how to carry out computations in statistics.* Concepts in statistics are highly interrelated and cumulative, so students are strongly advised to read the beginning topics on descriptive statistics before reading about individual test types in order to gain the most from this part of the book. Topic 58 discusses the logic of statistics and introduces its two major branches: *descriptive statistics* and *inferential statistics*. Topics 59 through 64 cover commonly used descriptive statistics. Topics 65 and 66 transition to inferential statistics, introducing overarching concepts that are important to all specific statistical tests, including how significance is determined, how hypotheses are stated in statistical analyses, and how different scales of measure relate to the various statistical tests. Specific, commonly used statistical tests are covered next, including correlation (Topic 67), *t*-test (Topic 68), analysis of variance (ANOVA) (Topics 69 and 70), and the chi-square test (Topics 71 and 72). Regression basics (Topic 73) rounds out the discussion of statistics, followed by the final topic in the section (Topic 74), which discusses the practical significance of the results.

DESCRIPTIVE AND INFERENTIAL STATISTICS

Statistics are mathematical techniques used to analyze numerical data. Sometimes, data that began in words has been converted into numerical terms. The term *statistics* also refers to the outcome of these mathematical techniques. There are commonly used mathematical tests in statistics, and each has its own name and is associated with a specific letter or symbol when used in formulas or when reporting results. Statistics summarize data in ways that describe the data or answer questions or test hypotheses. They also test to see if the distributions of the answers form a pattern that describes associations or relationships between two or more variables.

When data is available for the entire population, the resulting values are called **parameters** instead of statistics. Statistics refers only to results that are based on the use of a **sample** drawn from a population, rather than data collected from the entire population. The important difference is that a parameter is the *actual* value of the population, whereas a statistic is an *estimate* of that value. One way to easily memorize this is to associate the matching first letters as shown here in italics: *S*amples yield *S*tatistics, and *P*opulations yield *P*arameters.

For example, a **mean** (also called an **average**, covered more in Topics 62 and 63) can be a statistic (sample) or parameter (population). It is computed the same way: a mean is found by adding all values and then dividing by the total number of values. If the mean is computed from all population values, it is a parameter and is represented with a capital letter M.[1] If it is computed from a sample, it is a statistic and represented by a lowercase letter m. For instance, the mean age of preschoolers for a single school could be calculated as a parameter by simply averaging all the students' ages. The mean age of all preschoolers in the nation could be calculated as a statistic based on a random sample from preschools in different cities and states.

There are two branches of statistics: **descriptive statistics** and **inferential statistics**. As the name suggests, descriptive statistics only attempt to *describe* the data so they can easily be comprehended. Descriptive statistics may summarize data in a number of ways, including averaging, showing the range, determining the most common answer, or looking at how the data is distributed or how far the data is spread out.

Based on how many variables are involved, descriptive statistics might be univariate, bivariate, or multivariate. For instance, a mean summarizes a single variable (e.g., age in the example above), so it is a **univariate** statistic. Other statistics look at patterns between two (bivariate) or more (multivariate) variables. Bivariate statistics measure associations between two variables. Consider sales of ice cream and the temperature. You might expect that the two are associated: as the temperature goes up, so do the number of ice creams that are purchased. A bivariate statistic describes whether an association is found between these two variables. A multivariate statistic includes at least one more variable: was the association between temperature and ice creams purchased different for men and women? Association is not enough to determine the causal relationship. Theory or order in time may allow the researcher to propose arguments about cause and effect.

A **frequency distribution** is a type of descriptive statistic. It simply lists the frequency (number of times) an answer was given by a respondent. Suppose a researcher wanted to describe the scores on a 20-point entry test received by students at the beginning of a statistics course. There were 2,000 students across all statistics courses being offered, of which the researcher took a random sample of 362 student scores. It would be difficult to see the trends in the data based on an unordered list of the 362 scores. However, a frequency distribution such as the one in Table 58.1 offers a useful summary of the scores; in this case, it shows that most students had scores from 14 through 16, with a scattering above and below these levels.

The **frequencies** in Table 58.1 are descriptive statistics because they *describe* how many students earned each score. The **percentages** in the table are also descriptive. They describe how many students *per one hundred* had each score. For instance, 3.0%, or 3 out of every 100 students, had a score of 11. It is also possible to calculate additional descriptive statistics from the frequency information, such as the mean score, which is 15.08.

Inferential statistics are used when the researcher wants to generalize the results to the population on the basis of the sample. While descriptive statistics can indicate patterns in the sample, inferential statistical tests are necessary to determine if those patterns are in fact a significant estimate of the population, or if they can be explained by sampling error. Let's return to the example in Table 58.1. If the frequency table included all 2,000 student scores, it would be a parameter and would simply represent the true frequency within the population because all members are included. But because frequencies are only reported for a sample of the population, these are statistics.

TABLE 58.1	**Frequency Distribution with Percentages**	
Score (*X*)	Frequency (*f*)	Percentage
20	5	1.4
19	9	2.5
18	24	6.6
17	35	9.7
16	61	16.9
15	99	27.3
14	68	18.8
13	29	8.0
12	21	5.8
11	11	3.0
Totals	362	100.0%

To find out if they are good *estimates* of the population of all 2,000 students, inferential statistics are needed.

Inferential statistics are based on **probability**—in other words, they estimate the likelihood that something will occur (more on probability is covered in Topic 65). In the example of an average, inferential statistics would ask: What is the likelihood that the sample average is an accurate estimate of the population average? As indicated in Part 4, random sampling produces random errors that statisticians call *sampling errors*. Inferential statistics involve the use of mathematical formulas that determine the likelihood that sampling errors occurred. In the example from Table 58.1, for instance, inferential statistics would determine whether the frequency of test scores for 362 students is a good rough estimate of the full 2,000 students. To do this, the test would determine the likely range of values within which the population parameter is likely to fall. For example, the average from the sample was 15.08. Inferential statistics estimate if the population average ranges around 15.08, as well as the number of times out of 100 that it would fall in this range—in other words, testing for significance (95% of the time, for instance). The higher likelihood that a sample statistic will fall in the range of a population parameter, the more confident the researcher is of the value. An important family of inferential statistics consists of **significance tests,** which help researchers decide whether the differences in descriptive statistics are reliable. (For a refresher on reliability, see Topic 39.) Topics 67–72 discuss tests of significance that are commonly used.

Because inferential statistics help researchers to evaluate results from samples and consider their accuracy in light of sampling errors, it follows that if researchers do *not sample*, they do *not need* inferential statistics. However, the same methods used to *describe* data and identify associations can be used.

■ TOPIC REVIEW

1. Which branch of statistics ("inferential" *or* "descriptive") helps researchers to summarize data so they can be easily comprehended?
2. By studying samples, do researchers obtain "statistics" *or* "parameters"?
3. According to Table 58.1 in this topic, how many participants had a score of 19?
4. What is the name of the statistic that describes how many participants per 100 have a certain characteristic?
5. Which branch of statistics helps researchers to estimate the effects of sampling errors on their results?
6. If a descriptive statistic involves more than two variables, what is it called?
7. What type of statistic is a frequency distribution—descriptive or inferential?
8. Are significance tests associated with "descriptive" *or* "inferential" statistics?

■ DISCUSSION QUESTION

1. What is the key difference between statistics and parameters? Discuss and formulate applications or examples that illustrate that statistics are based on probability.

■ RESEARCH PLANNING

If you are using statistics in your research, what frequency distributions might you care to
    report?

What variables are you using and what associations might you want to analyze?

■ NOTE

1. $\bar{X}$ is still sometimes used, but the most commonly used symbol for research publications is M.

SCALES OF MEASUREMENT AND STATISTICAL TESTS

As you may recall from Topic 21 on Variables in Nonexperimental Studies, there are four scales (or levels) at which variables are measured. To review, the lowest level is the **nominal** level (also called the *nominal scale*), which is thought of as the *naming* level. For instance, when researchers ask participants to name their marital status, participants will respond with *words* such as *married*, *single*, or *divorced*—not numbers. Nominal data do not put participants in any particular mathematical order. There is no logical basis for saying that one category is more or less numerically or by rank than another category.

The next level is **ordinal**. At this level, participants are placed in order from high to low, but the rank order does not correspond to a quantifiable amount, so researchers cannot be certain that the same distance exists between categories. For instance, the difference between hot, warm, neither warm nor cool, cool, and cold does not have a clear amount between choices. Traditionally, researchers would rank the values using 1 for the highest score, 2 for the next highest, and so on. However, it does not mean that the amount of difference between hot and warm is the same as between cool and cold.

To measure the *amount* of difference among participants, researchers use the next two levels of measurement. They are referred to as **continuous** variables because they correspond to a continuous number line, so the intervals between measures can be quantified. Measurements at the **interval** and **ratio** levels have measurable distances among the scores they yield.

Interval scores typically measure scales of different types, and a typical example given is reading the temperature in Celsius or Fahrenheit. While we know there is 10 degrees difference between 45 degrees and 55 degrees, or 55 degrees and 65 degrees, interval variables are not on a number scale in which zero means an absolute lack of a characteristic. Also, even though a numeric interval can be determined, the difference between 50 degrees and 100 degrees is not that it is twice as hot. By contrast, ratio variables do have a zero value that means a lack of a quality, and the numerical values do compound. For instance, when researchers say that Jill weighs 120 pounds and Sally weighs 130 pounds, they know by *how much* the two participants differ. Also, note that a 10-pound difference represents the same amount regardless of where participants are on the scale. For instance, the difference between 120 and 130 pounds is the same as the difference between 220 and 230 pounds. In addition, 100 pounds is twice as heavy as 50 pounds.

Table 59.1 offers a summary of the levels:

TABLE 59.1 **Scales of Measurement**

	Scale	Characteristic
Lowest Level	Nominal	*naming*
⇩	Ordinal	*ordering*
Highest Level	Interval	*equal interval without an absolute zero*
	Ratio	*equal interval with an absolute zero*

As another refresher from Topic 21, **dependent variables (DVs)** are the outcome or response variables. In some types of research, they are also referred to as the criterion. There is often only one dependent variable, but researchers may be investigating multiple dependent variables, and it is possible to have more than one dependent variable in some types of statistical tests (see Table 59.2 for more information). The **independent**

TABLE 59.2 **Statistical Tests by Variable Type**

Statistical test	# IVs	IV scale type	# DVs	DV scale type	Addresses question:	Associated topic #
Correlation	1	Categorical—Dichotomous* or continuous	1	Interval or ratio	Do the IV and DV have an association? How strong and in what direction is the association?	67
t-test	1	Categorical—Dichotomous*	1	Categorical, interval, or ratio	Are there differences between two groups on one DV?	68
ANOVA	≥1	Categorical	1	Interval or ratio	Are there differences between the means of two or more groups on one DV?	69 and 70
Chi-square	1	Categorical	1	Categorical	Do differences exist between groups?	71 and 72
Basic regression	1	Categorical—Dichotomous* or continuous	1	Interval or ratio	How much variance in the DV is explained by the IV?	73
Multiple regression	≥1	Categorical—Dichotomous* or continuous	1	Interval or ratio	How much variance in the DV is explained by the linear combination of the IVs?	73

*A categorical variable for which there are only two choices (e.g., male/female, yes/no, etc.).

variables (IVs) are explanatory variables. The level at which researchers measure has important implications for data analysis, so there are references to scales of measurement throughout the discussion of statistics. In statistical tests, both variable type and variable scale of measurement largely determine the appropriate statistical test to carry out. Only common, basic statistical tests are covered in Part 8. See the topics listed in Table 59.2 to learn more about each statistical test.

■ TOPIC REVIEW

1. If a researcher asks participants to name the country in which they were born, the researcher is using which scale of measurement?
2. Which two scales of measurement have equal distances between the amounts of possible responses?
3. Which scale of measurement has an absolute zero?
4. Which variable type corresponds to the outcome being measured?
5. What is one easy way to remember the order of the scales of measurement?
6. Why is it important to know the scale of measurement when using statistical tests?
7. A researcher asks if voting behavior differs based on one's race. Which of these variables is independent, and which is dependent?

■ DISCUSSION QUESTIONS

1. Name a trait that inherently lends itself to nominal measurement. Explain your answer.
2. Demonstrate an example of reducing a ratio variable to be used as a variable at a lower scale of measurement.

■ RESEARCH PLANNING

List the measures you will be using in your research, and name the scale of measurement for each one. Does this correspond to a specific type of statistical test above?

DESCRIPTIONS OF NOMINAL DATA

As indicated in the previous topic, researchers obtain *nominal data* when they classify participants according to names (words) instead of quantities. For instance, suppose a researcher asked each member of a population of 540 teachers which candidate he or she prefers for a school board vacancy and found that 258 preferred Smith and 282 preferred Jones. (Because Smith and Jones are names, the data are at the nominal level.) The 258 and 282 are *frequencies*, whose symbol is f. Researchers also may refer to them as **numbers of cases**, whose symbol is N.

The numbers of cases can be converted to *percentages* by dividing the number who prefer each candidate by the number in the population and multiplying by 100. Thus, for Smith, the calculations are:

$$258 \div 540 = 0.478 \times 100 = 47.8\%$$

When reporting percentages, it is desirable to also report the underlying numbers of cases, which is done in Table 60.1.

Table 60.1 is an example of what Topic 58 called **univariate analysis.** The researcher is analyzing how participants *vary* (thus, researchers use the root *variate*) on only *one* variable (hence, researchers use the prefix *uni–*).

Researchers can examine a relationship between two nominal variables by conducting a **bivariate analysis.** Perhaps a researcher wants to know whether there is a relationship between teachers' genders and their preferences for candidates. Table 60.2 shows the results of a bivariate analysis of these variables.

The data in Table 60.2 clearly indicate that there is a relationship between gender and the preferences for the two candidates because a larger percentage of males than females prefers Jones, but a larger percentage of females than males prefers Smith. In general, teachers' genders are predictive of their preferences. For instance, by knowing a teacher is

TABLE 60.1 Teachers' Preferences	
Candidate	**Percentage**
Jones	52.2%
	(N = 282)
Smith	47.8%
	(N = 258)
Total	100.0%
	(N = 540)

TABLE 60.2 Teachers' Preferences by Gender

Gender	Jones	Smith	Total
Male	66.4%	33.6%	100.0%
	($N = 85$)	($N = 43$)	($N = 128$)
Female	47.8%	52.2%	100.0%
	($N = 197$)	($N = 215$)	($N = 412$)

male, a researcher would predict that the teacher is more likely to vote for Jones than to vote for Smith.

In this population of teachers, there are many more female teachers than male teachers. When this is the case, examining only the numbers of cases (e.g., 85 males for Jones versus 197 females for Jones) can be misleading. For instance, in Table 60.2, a *majority* of the population of males (the smaller population) is in favor of Jones, but only a *minority* of the larger population of females is in favor of him. With percentages, legitimate comparisons of groups of unequal size are possible. This is because percentages convert numbers of cases to a common scale, with a base of 100. (The percentage of 66.4% of males for Jones indicates that *for every 100 males*, 66.4 of them are in favor of Jones, while the percentage of 47.8% of females for Jones indicates that *for every 100 females*, only 47.8 of them are in favor of Jones.)

In academic writing, some researchers report **proportions** instead of *percentages*. For instance, a percentage of 47.8% in favor of Smith in Table 60.1 corresponds to a proportion of 0.478 or 0.48. (Proportions are calculated in the same way percentages are except that the multiplication by 100 is not performed. For instance, $258 \div 540 = 0.478 = 0.48$.) Because a proportion has a base of 1, a proportion of 0.48 means that for every *one* participant, 48 hundredths of each participant favors Smith. Clearly, proportions are more difficult to comprehend than percentages. When consumers of research encounter proportions in reports, it is a good idea to convert them mentally to percentages. That is, think of the proportion of 0.48 as 48% (i.e., the percentage obtained by multiplying 0.48 by 100).

In the next topic, a method for analyzing univariate nominal data by graphing the distribution of responses is considered.

■ TOPIC REVIEW

1. If 600 individuals in a population of 1,000 are Democrats, what is the corresponding percentage of Democrats?
2. When reporting a percentage, is it a good idea to also report the underlying number of cases?
3. Do researchers use "univariate" *or* "bivariate" analyses to examine relationships between two nominal variables?
4. Percentages for different groups are expressed on a common scale with what base?
5. What is the base for a proportion?

6. Are "percentages" *or* "proportions" easier for most individuals to comprehend?
7. When consumers of research encounter proportions in research reports, it is a good idea to do what?

■ DISCUSSION QUESTION

1. Try to locate a report in the popular press in which percentages are reported. Bring a copy to class. Be prepared to discuss whether the frequencies are also reported and whether the analysis is univariate *or* bivariate.

■ RESEARCH PLANNING

Will you be measuring one or more variables at the nominal level? Explain.
Will you be reporting percentages?
Will you do a univariate analysis? A bivariate analysis? Explain.

TOPIC 61

SHAPES OF DISTRIBUTIONS

One way to describe quantitative data is to prepare a *frequency distribution*. It is easier to see the shape of a distribution if the data in a frequency distribution are used to construct a figure called a **frequency polygon**. Figure 61.1 is a frequency polygon for the data in Table 58.1 (frequency distribution of student entrance test scores).

A frequency polygon provides a better visual summary of the data, helping researchers see the distribution of data. For instance, a score of 20 (on the *y*-axis) has a frequency (*f*) of 5 (on the *x*-axis), which is why the curve is low at a score of 20. A score of 15 has a frequency of 99, which is why the curve is high at 15. The curve in Figure 61.1 is fairly symmetrical, with a high point in the middle and a drop off on the right and left. When very large samples are used, the curve often takes on an even smoother shape, such as the one shown in Figure 61.2.

FIGURE 61.1 Frequency polygon for data from Topic 58.

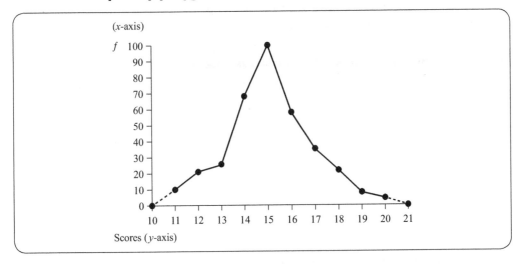

FIGURE 61.2 Normal distribution: the "bell" curve.

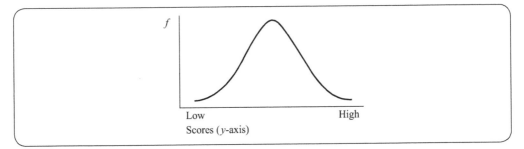

The smooth, bell–shaped curve in Figure 61.2 above has a special name: the **normal curve.** Many variables in nature are normally distributed, such as the weights of grains of sand on a beach, the heights of people, the annual amounts of rainfall, and so on. The list is almost limitless. Many social and behavioral scientists also believe that mental traits of humans are also normally distributed.[1]

Some distributions are **skewed** (i.e., they have a tail on one side and not the other). Figure 61.3 shows a distribution that is *skewed to the right* (i.e., the tail is to the right), which is called a **positive skew**. An example of a distribution with a positive skew is income. Most individuals earn relatively small amounts, so the curve is high on the left. Small numbers of rich and very rich individuals create a tail to the right.

Figure 61.4 is *skewed to the left*; it has a **negative skew**. A researcher would get a negative skew, for instance, from administering a test of basic math skills to a large sample of college seniors. Almost all would do very well and get almost perfect scores, but a small scattering would get lower scores for a variety of reasons, such as misunderstanding the directions for marking their answers, not feeling well the day the test was administered, and so on.

While there are other shapes, the figures shown here present the most common distributions. Whether a distribution is normal (or close to normal) or skewed affects how quantitative data at the interval and ratio levels are analyzed (see Topic 59 for a review of scales of measurement). The issue of analyzing skewed data is considered in the next topic about mean, median, and mode.

To make the proper associations with the names *positive skew* and *negative skew*, consider a number line on which zero is in the middle. The negative values are to the left

FIGURE 61.3 A distribution with a positive skew.

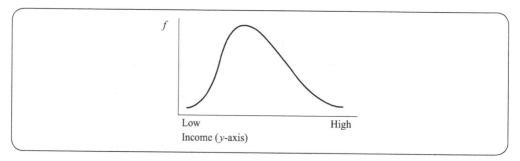

FIGURE 61.4 A distribution with a negative skew.

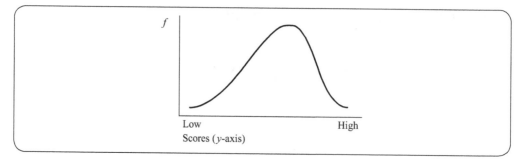

of zero. Thus, when the tail of a curve points to the left, researchers say it has a *negative skew*. Because the positive values on a number line are to the right, when the tail points to the right, researchers say the curve has a *positive skew*. Sometimes, researchers merely say "skewed to the left" to indicate a negative skew and "skewed to the right" to indicate a positive skew.

■ TOPIC REVIEW

1. According to Figure 61.1, about how many participants had a score of 16?
2. In Figure 61.1, are the frequencies on the "vertical" *or* the "horizontal" axis?
3. What is the name of the curve that is symmetrical?
4. If a distribution has some extreme scores on the right but not on the left, it is said to have what type of skew?
5. If a distribution is skewed to the left, does it have a "positive" *or* a "negative" skew?
6. In most populations, income has what type of skew?
7. Does a distribution with a tail to the right have a "positive" *or* a "negative" skew?

■ DISCUSSION QUESTION

1. Name a population and a variable you think might have a positive skew.

■ RESEARCH PLANNING

Do you anticipate that any of your distributions will be highly skewed? Explain.

■ NOTE

1. Because measures of mental traits are far from perfect, it is not possible to show conclusively that mental traits are normally distributed.

THE MEAN, MEDIAN, AND MODE

There are several ways to arrive at a descriptive statistic for the central value of a variable. The most frequently used central measure is the **mean** (or average), which is the *balance point* in a distribution. As was mentioned in Topic 58, computing a mean is simple: add up the scores and then divide by the number of scores. The most common symbols for the mean in academic journals are M (for the mean of a population) and m (for the mean of a sample). Statisticians also use $\bar{x}$, which is pronounced "X-bar."

Consider the formal definition of the mean: It is *the value around which the deviations sum to zero*. This definition is illustrated in Table 62.1, in which the mean of the scores is 4.0. When the mean is subtracted from each of the other scores, the *deviations* (whose symbol is lowercase x) are obtained. Notice that the sum of the deviations equals zero, as shown in the last column of Table 62.1.

Note that for *any set of scores*, if the steps in Table 62.1 are followed, the sum of the deviations will equal zero.[1] In other words, the mean always has this defining characteristic. If the deviations do not sum to zero, the statistic is not the mean (or a mistake was made in the computation of the mean).

Considering the formal definition, it is possible to see why the mean is also informally defined as the *balance point* in a distribution. This is because the positive and negative deviations *balance* each other out, causing the deviations to balance out to zero.

TABLE 62.1   Scores and Deviation Scores

X	minus	M	equals	x
1	–	4.0	=	−3.0
1	–	4.0	=	−3.0
1	–	4.0	=	−3.0
2	–	4.0	=	−2.0
2	–	4.0	=	−2.0
4	–	4.0	=	0.0
6	–	4.0	=	2.0
7	–	4.0	=	3.0
8	–	4.0	=	4.0
8	–	4.0	=	4.0

Sum of the deviations $(x) = 0.0$

A major drawback of the mean is that it is drawn in the direction of extreme scores (i.e., in the direction of the skew). Consider the following two sets of scores and their means.

Scores for Group A: 1, 1, 1, 2, 3, 6, 7, 8, 8
$M = 4.11$
Scores for Group B: 1, 2, 2, 3, 4, 7, 9, 25, 32
$M = 9.44$

Notice that there are nine scores in both sets of scores, and the two distributions are very similar except for the scores of 25 and 32 in Group B, which are much higher than the others and thus create a skewed distribution. (To review skewed distributions, see Topic 61.) Also, notice that the two very high scores (25 and 32) have greatly pulled up the mean for Group B. In fact, the mean for Group B is more than twice the mean for Group A just because of the two high scores. Because seven of the nine scores for Group B are 9 or less, a mean of 9.44 is not a good descriptor of the typical or center score.

While the mean is the most frequently used average, when a distribution is highly skewed, researchers use a different average: the **median.** The median is defined as the *middle score*. To get an *approximate median*, put the scores in order from low to high as they are for Groups A and B (from low on the left to high on the right), and then count to the middle. Because there are nine scores in Group A, the median (middle score) is 3 (five scores up from the bottom score of 1). For Group B, the median (middle score) is 4 (also five scores up from the bottom score of 1). For Group B, an average of 4 is more representative of the center of this skewed distribution than the mean, which is 9.44. Thus, an important use of the median is to describe the averages of skewed distributions. Another use is to describe the average of ordinal data, which will be explored in Topic 64.

A third average, the **mode,** is the *most frequently occurring score*. For Group B, there are more scores of 2 (i.e., two 2s) than any other score. Thus, 2 is the mode. The mode is sometimes used in informal reporting but is very seldom reported in formal reports of research. Note that the mode does not always have a unique value. For instance, if one individual with a score of 3 joined Group B, there would be two modes: (1) 2 because there are two 2s and (2) 3 because there would also be two 3s. Note that the mean and median, unlike the mode, always have just one value for a given set of scores (i.e., they have unique values).

Because there is more than one type of central value, it can be vague to make a statement such as "The *average* is 4.11." Average is most often associated with the mean, but is not a specific measurement term. Typically, researchers indicate a measure of central tendency by specifying whether it is a mean, median, or mode with statements such as "The *mean* is 4.11." **Measures of central tendency** is a term that is seldom used in reports of scientific research, but it is often encountered in research and statistics textbooks when describing the mean, median, and mode.

■ **TOPIC REVIEW**

1. Which average is defined as the *most frequently occurring score*?
2. Which average is defined as the *balance point* in a distribution?

3. Which average is defined as the *middle score*?
4. What is the formal definition of the mean?
5. How is the mean calculated?
6. Should the mean be used for highly skewed distributions?
7. Should the median be used for highly skewed distributions?
8. Which one of the three averages is very seldom used in formal reports of research?
9. What is a synonym for the term *averages*?

■ DISCUSSION QUESTION

1. Suppose a fellow student gave a report in class and said, "The average is 25.88." For what additional information should you ask? Why?

■ RESEARCH PLANNING

Do you anticipate calculating measures of central tendency? If so, name the one(s) you expect to report. Explain your choice(s).

■ NOTE

1. It might be slightly off from zero if a rounded mean such as 20.33 is used instead of its precise value, 20.3333333333.

THE MEAN AND STANDARD DEVIATION

Often, a set of scores is described with only two statistics: the **mean** (described in Topic 62), which describes its *average*, and the **standard deviation**, used to describe its *variability*. The term **variability** refers to the amount by which participants *vary* or differ from each other. Consider what this means by looking at the scores of three groups, all of which have the same mean but different standard deviations.

> **Group A:** 0, 5, 10, 15, 20, 25, 30
> $M = 15.00, S = 10.00$
> **Group B:** 14, 14, 14, 15, 16, 16, 16
> $M = 15.00, S = 0.93$
> **Group C:** 15, 15, 15, 15, 15, 15, 15
> $M = 15.00, S = 0.00$

Although Groups A, B, and C are the same on average, as indicated by the mean, they are very different in terms of variability. Notice that the differences among the scores of Group A (a score of 0 vs. a score of 5 vs. a score of 10 vs. a score of 15, and so on) are much greater than the differences among the scores of Group B (a score of 14 vs. a score of 14 vs. a score of 14 vs. a score of 15, and so on). At the extreme, when all the scores are the same, as in Group C, there is no variability. As a result, the standard deviation equals zero for Group C. As a rule, the smaller the variability, the smaller the standard deviation.[1]

The standard deviation (whose symbol is S or SD for a population, and s or sd for a sample) has a special relationship to the normal curve (see Topic 61). *If a distribution is normal, 68% of the participants in the distribution lie within one standard-deviation unit of the mean.*[2] For example, if a consumer of research reads in a report that $M = 70$ and $S = 10$ for a normal distribution, the consumer would know that 68% of the participants have scores between 60 and 80 (i.e., $70 - 10 = 60$ and $70 + 10 = 80$). This is illustrated in Figure 63.1.

In Figure 63.2, the mean is also 70, but the standard deviation is only 5. The smaller standard deviation in Figure 63.2 is reflected in the changes to the shape of the curve. Yet in both distributions, 68% of the cases lie within one standard deviation unit of the mean because they are both normal. Note that the middle area of Figure 63.2 is narrower *but taller* than the middle area of Figure 63.1. This additional height in Figure 63.2 makes it possible for it to have the same percentage (68%) of cases that the middle area of Figure 63.1 has.

At first, it may seem contradictory that, regardless of the value of the standard deviation, 68% of the cases lie within one standard-deviation unit of the mean in a normal curve. Actually, it is not a contradiction but a property of the normal curve. When researchers calculate the standard deviation, they are actually calculating the number of points that one

FIGURE 63.1 **Normal curve with a mean of 70 and a standard deviation of 10.**

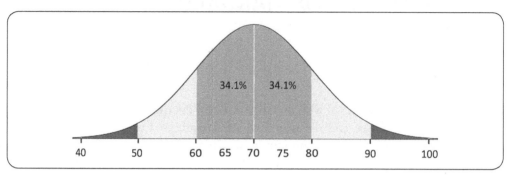

FIGURE 63.2 **Normal curve with a mean of 70 and a standard deviation of 5.**

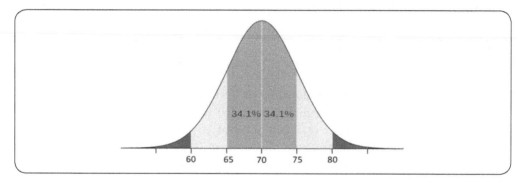

must go out from the mean to capture 68% of the cases. Perhaps more importantly, 95% of cases correspond to 1.96 standard deviations. Three units of standard deviation contains 99.73% of all cases.

Note that these rule-of-thumb percentages do *not* strictly apply if the distribution is *not* normal. The less normal it is, the less accurate the rule is. Put another way, if the middle area of a distribution does not contain approximately 68% of the cases, the distribution is not normal and standard deviation will not correspond to these proportions. The normal curve (see Topic 61) is not an invention of statisticians. Instead, it is a curve that has been observed with great frequency in nature. Statisticians derived the standard deviation in order to have a standardized method for describing the variability of normal distributions.

■ TOPIC REVIEW

1. Which average is usually reported when the standard deviation is reported?
2. What is meant by the term *variability*?
3. Is it possible for two groups to have the same mean but different standard deviations?
4. If all individuals in a group have the same score, what is the value of the standard deviation for the scores?

5. In a normal distribution, what percentage of the participants lies within one standard-deviation unit of the mean (i.e., on both sides of the mean)?

6. The middle 68% of the participants in a normal distribution have scores between what two values if the mean equals 100 and the standard deviation equals 15?

7. If the mean of a normal distribution equals 50 and the standard deviation equals 5, what percentage of the participants have scores between 45 and 50?

8. How many cases are included in 1.96 units of standard deviation?

9. If the standard deviation for Group X is 14.55, and the standard deviation for Group Y is 20.99, which group has less variability in its scores?

10. Refer to Question 9. Does Group X *or* Group Y have a narrower curve?

■ DISCUSSION QUESTION

1. Locate a journal article in which the researcher reports a mean and standard deviation. Does the researcher indicate whether the underlying distribution being described is normal in shape? Do you think the 68% rule strictly applies? Explain.

■ RESEARCH PLANNING

Will you be reporting means and standard deviations? Explain.

■ NOTES

1. Standard deviation computes how much values vary from the average. The computation is not difficult, and can also be computed using a tool such as the Standard Deviation Calculator: http://www.calculator.net/standard-deviation-calculator.html.

2. Note that *within* means on *both sides of the mean* (i.e., the mean plus/minus the standard deviation).

THE MEDIAN AND INTERQUARTILE RANGE

As indicated in Topic 62, the **median** is the *middle score* in a distribution. Being in the middle, it always has 50% of the scores above it and 50% of the scores below it. For the scores in Figure 64.1, the median is 6.5 (halfway between the middle two scores of 6 and 7).

The median is preferable to the mean when a distribution is highly skewed (see Topic 61). It also is used to describe the average when the data are *ordinal* (i.e., data that put participants in *order* from high to low) but do not have equal intervals among them (see Topic 59).[1]

When the **median** is reported as the average, it is customary to report the **range** or **interquartile range** as a measure of variability. As indicated in Topic 63, *variability* refers to the amount by which participants *vary* or differ from each other.

The *range* is simply the highest score minus the lowest score. For the scores shown above, it is 12–1 = 11. Thus, the range is 11, or a researcher might state that the scores *range from 1 to 12*. For reasons that are beyond the scope of this discussion, measurement theory indicates that the more extreme the score, the more unreliable or likely to reflect errors it is. (This is true in the natural sciences as well as the social and behavioral sciences.) Because the range is based on the two most extreme scores, it is an unreliable statistic. To get around this problem, researchers often use a modified version of the range, which is called the *interquartile range (IQR)*. The formal definition of the *interquartile range* is the *range of the middle 50% of the participants*. To calculate it, first divide the distribution into quarters, as shown in Figure 64.2 (e.g., the first quarter consists of scores 1, 1, 1, and 2).

FIGURE 64.1 Scores for Group A and their median.

1, 1, 1, 2, 3, 4, 5, 6, 7, 8, 8, 9, 10, 11, 11, 12
⇧
6.5

FIGURE 64.2 Scores for Group A divided into quarters.

1, 1, 1, 2, 3, 4, 5, 6, 7, 8, 8, 9, 10, 11, 11, 12		
⇧	⇧	⇧
2.5	6.5	9.5

FIGURE 64.3 **Scores for Group B divided into quarters.**

| 0, 5, 7, 10, 15, 22, 30, 41, 45, 57, 67, 78, 89, 92, 95, 99 |
| ⇧   ⇧   ⇧ |
| 12.5   43.0   83.5 |

TABLE 64.1   **Medians and Interquartile Range for Two Groups**

Group	Median	Interquartile range
A	6.5	7.0
B	43.0	71.0

Thus, the middle 50% of the participants are between the values of 2.5 and 9.5. *IQR* is then calculated as follows: 9.5–2.5 = 7.0.[2]

To see how the *IQR* helps to describe the variability in sets of data, compare Figure 64.2 above (for Group A) with Figure 64.3 (for Group B). In Figure 64.3, the median is 43.0 and the interquartile range is 71.0 (i.e., 83.5–12.5 = 71.0). The larger interquartile range for Group B indicates greater variability.

Thus, for Groups A and B, the findings might be presented in a research report as illustrated in Table 64.1.

Table 64.1 indicates two things. First, Group A has a lower average than Group B (as indicated by the median of 6.5 for Group A vs. the median of 43.0 for Group B). Second, Group A has less variability (as indicated by an interquartile range of 7.0 for Group A vs. 71.0 for Group B). A look at the scores in Figures 64.2 and 64.3 indicates that these results make sense. The middle score for Group A is much lower than the middle score for Group B, and the differences among the scores for Group A (1 vs. 1 vs. 1 vs. 2 vs. 3, etc.) are much smaller than the differences among the scores for Group B (0 vs. 5 vs. 7 vs. 10 vs. 15, etc.), indicating less variability in Group A than Group B.

In summary, the median describes the average (i.e., the central tendency) of a set of scores, while the interquartile range describes their variability. When the median is reported as the average (or measure of central tendency), it is customary to report the interquartile range as the measure of variability.

■ TOPIC REVIEW

1. If the median for a group of participants is 25.00, what is the percentage of participants with a score above 25.00?
2. Should the "mean" *or* the "median" be used with ordinal data?
3. How is the range of a set of scores calculated?
4. Is the "range" *or* the "interquartile range" a more reliable statistic?
5. The *interquartile range* is the range of what?

6. Suppose a researcher reported that for Group X, the median equals 55.1 and the *IQR* equals 30.0, while for Group Y, the median equals 62.9 and the *IQR* equals 25.0. Which group has the higher average score?

7. On the basis of the information in Question 6, the scores for which group are more variable?

8. Which statistics discussed in this topic are measures of variability?

9. Which two statistics mentioned in this topic are averages (i.e., measures of central tendency)?

10. When the median is reported as the measure of central tendency, it is customary to report which measure of variability?

■ DISCUSSION QUESTION

1. Name two circumstances under which the median is preferable to the mean.

■ RESEARCH PLANNING

Do you anticipate reporting medians and interquartile ranges? In what way will you use them?

■ NOTES

1. It is inappropriate to use the *mean* to describe ordinal data because the mean is the point around which the differences sum to zero. If the differences are unequal in size (as they are with ordinal data), it makes no sense to use a statistic based on the values of the differences. See Topics 59 and 62.

2. Some researchers report the value of the *semi-interquartile range*. Because *semi-* means *half*, the semi-interquartile range is half of the interquartile range. In this example, the semi-interquartile range for Group A equals half of 7.0 (i.e., 7.0/2 = 3.5).

UNDERSTANDING PROBABILITY IN INFERENTIAL STATISTICS

As discussed in Topic 58, inferential statistics are based on probability. In particular, statistics use a sample to make *inferences* about a population. To read and evaluate statistics, it is important to understand a few basic principles about how statistics use probability to make these inferences.

Two of the most commonly used examples of probability are tossing a coin or rolling a pair of six-sided dice. The probability is the chance that a person will get a specific outcome. For instance, with a coin, it is not hard to follow that one toss is one outcome for which there are two possibilities: heads or tails. One outcome out of two possible outcomes equals one-half, or a 50% chance that one will get heads and a 50% chance of getting tails. The scenario is slightly more complex with two dice. Let's take each die individually. Each will have one outcome, and there are six possible outcomes. Assuming a fair, unweighted set of dice, there is a 1 in 6 chance of rolling any of the numbers. This immediately gets more complex, when you consider rolling two dice at once, and trying to figure out the *probability* of different sum totals of the two dice. Now not every outcome has an equal chance.

For instance, there is only one possible way to get a total of 2 (roll two 1s). But there are many ways to get a total of 6, 7, or 8. The resulting pattern forms a **normal distribution** because it has a symmetrical shape in which the central values are the most frequent, and results are less frequent toward each end of the spectrum of answers, with the least frequent at either end of the possible spectrum (2 and 12). Because of its curved, symmetrical shape, normal distribution is referred to as "the bell curve." (For more on distribution shapes, see Topic 61).

The coin toss relates in an important way to inferential statistics. Consider the above probability equation, but instead of dice, let's think about samples in a research study. Let's imagine that you have drawn a random sample of 100 people that include 56 women and 44 men from an organization that employs 3,000 people and asked them to rate their satisfaction with the company. When the results come in, they look pretty much like the normal distribution from Table 65.1 and Figure 65.1. The most frequent answers are somewhere in the middle, with a few people who really love it and a few who do not rate it highly. The question now is: If everyone at the company were asked, would the results be roughly the same? And how "roughly" is within the ballpark?

Consider the mindboggling proposition of working out every combination of every sample of 100 people you could draw from a group of 3,000. Inferential statistics uses computations to address this. They indicate how unlikely it is that you could observe the numbers you did by chance. This is done using probability, also referred to as alpha (α). If the likelihood that the results could be obtained by chance is under a cutoff that the researcher sets, the results are considered to be significant. Most research uses a cutoff of 5% or .05, which is expressed as $\alpha \leq .05$. When the statistics are computed, the calculated

TABLE 65.1 **Frequency Distribution for Dice Roll Totals**

Dice total (X)	Frequency (f)	Percentage
2	1	3
3	2	6
4	3	8
5	4	11
6	5	14
7	6	17
8	5	14
9	4	11
10	3	8
11	2	6
12	1	3
Totals	36	100.0%

FIGURE 65.1 Frequencies for dice roll totals.

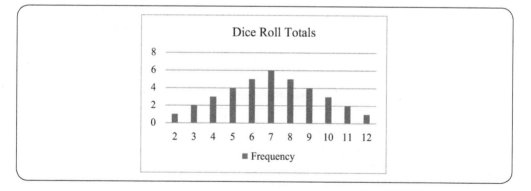

value from the sample is called the *p*-value, where "p" stands for probability. The *p*-value calculated from the data must be below the alpha set by the researcher to be "significant." In other words, if alpha is .05, the computed *p-value* must be *less than* .05 to represent statistical significance. The value means that the results are produced by chance less than 5% of the time.

Confidence levels are expressed as 100% minus alpha. This value refers to the percentage of all possible samples that could include the true population parameter within a suggested range. The range is computed statistically. Confidence levels are typically set at 95%, meaning that the true population number is within the range for 95% of the possible samples that could be drawn from the population. The range of values is called a confidence interval or **margin of error,** as the media refer to it when reporting the results of public opinion polls. For instance, a poll might find that approval of the president is at 45%, with a margin of error of ±2 (i.e., plus/minus 2) percentage points at a 95% confidence level. This indicates that readers can be highly confident that the level of approval in the population is between 43% and 47% (i.e., within two points of the 45% observed in the sample). It also indicates that for 95% of the possible samples that were selected from the population, a value between 43% and 47% would have been found.

The next topic covers how statements of the research questions in hypotheses relate to statistics.

■ TOPIC REVIEW

1. Statistics use a sample to make _____ about a population.
2. The "bell curve" is a nickname for what?
3. What is the "p" in *p*-value?
4. What is the term for the cutoff value that is commonly used in statistics to set the limit for accepting that the results from a statistical test are due to chance?
5. Which is the actual computed value from the data that determines the probability that the value was a result of chance, "p-value" or "alpha"?
6. What value is 100 minus the alpha?
7. What is another name for margin of error?

■ DISCUSSION QUESTION

1. Describe the relationship between the terms alpha, p-value, confidence level, and confidence interval. How does a researcher determine the correct confidence interval to use?

■ RESEARCH PLANNING

If you are using statistics, do you expect your data to have a normal distribution? Look up quantitative papers in your field, and flip to the visual presentation of the study's statistics. Where do you find alpha, p-value, confidence intervals, and confidence levels? How do the authors discuss them?

INTRODUCTION TO THE NULL HYPOTHESIS

Suppose a research team wanted to know if there were differences in sociability between engineers and psychologists. To answer the question, they drew random samples of engineers and psychologists, administered a self-report measure of sociability, and computed the mean (the most commonly used average) for each group. Furthermore, suppose the mean for engineers was 65.00 and the mean for psychologists was 70.00. Where did the five-point difference come from? There are three possible explanations:

1. Perhaps the population of psychologists truly *is* more sociable than the population of engineers, and the samples correctly identified the difference. (In fact, the *research hypothesis* may have been that psychologists are more sociable than engineers, which now appears to be supported by the data the researcher collected.)
2. Perhaps there was a bias in procedures. By using random sampling, the researcher has ruled out sampling bias, but other procedures, such as measurement, may be biased. For instance, maybe the psychologists were contacted during December, when many social events take place, and the engineers were contacted during a gloomy February. The only way to rule out bias as an explanation for the difference between the two means is to take *physical steps* to prevent it. In this case, the researcher would want to make sure that the sociability of both groups was measured in the same way at the same time.
3. Perhaps the populations of psychologists and engineers are the same in their sociability, but the samples are unrepresentative of the populations because of random sampling errors. For instance, the random draw may have provided a sample of psychologists who are more sociable, on average, than their population purely by chance (at random).

The name for the third explanation is the **null hypothesis**. The word *null* means "zero," "cancelled out," "empty," or "nothing." The null hypothesis can take many forms and varies from researcher to researcher depending on what they are studying, but it always proposes one thing: the results that were found are not significant. It relates directly to the probability statements from Topic 65. If the null hypothesis is found to be supported when the statistics are computed, it means that the probability (*p-value*) was higher than the alpha cutoff value. In other words, where alpha $\leq .05$ is set as a cutoff, the p-value was greater than .05, and this indicates a higher than 5% probability that the results were due to chance. Here are three versions of the null hypothesis, all of which are consistent with each other:

Version A of the null hypothesis:
The true difference between the two groups is zero.

Version B of the null hypothesis:

There is no true difference between the two groups. (The term *true difference* refers to the difference a researcher would find in a census of the two populations. That is, the *true difference* is the difference a researcher would find if there were no sampling errors.)

Version C of the null hypothesis:

The observed difference was created by sampling error. (The term *sampling error* refers only to *random errors*, not errors created by a bias.)

Significance tests (covered in the previous topic) determine the probability that the null hypothesis is supported. This sounds like a positive thing, but what it means is that the supported hypothesis is the one that says the results are not considered significant.

Suppose the researcher in the sociability study example under consideration conducted a significance test and found that the probability that the null hypothesis is a correct hypothesis is less than 5 in 100. This would be stated as $p < .05$, where p stands for *probability*. If the odds that something is true are less than 5 in 100, it seems likely that it is *not* true. Thus, the researcher would *reject the null hypothesis* and be left with only explanation 1 and 2 listed above in this topic.

There is no rule of nature that dictates at what probability level the null hypothesis should be rejected. Conventional wisdom suggests that .05 or less is reasonable, but researchers will often point out when probabilities are below .01 or .001 because these very low probabilities are also considered important cutoffs that indicate a stronger statistical significance.

When researchers fail to reject the null hypothesis because the probability is greater than .05, it is not rejected as a possible explanation. Note that the language used is that the researcher *failed to reject the null hypothesis* rather than accepting it. It is *not* possible to accept the null hypothesis as the only explanation for a difference based on inferential statistics. Failing to reject one possible explanation (the null hypothesis) does *not* mean researchers are accepting it as the only explanation. There are other possible explanations that have not been eliminated—the evidence just is not strong enough to say which explanation is correct.

An alternative way to say that a researcher has rejected the null hypothesis is to state that the difference is **statistically significant**. Thus, if a researcher states that a difference is statistically significant at the .05 level (meaning .05 or less), it is equivalent to stating that the null hypothesis has been rejected at that level.

In research reports in academic journals, the null hypothesis is seldom stated by researchers, who assume that readers know that the sole purpose of a significance test is to test the null hypothesis. Instead, researchers report which differences were tested for significance, which significance test they used, and which differences were found to be statistically significant. It is more common to find null hypotheses stated in theses and dissertations because committee members may want to make sure the students they are supervising understand the reason they have conducted a significance test. The most commonly used significance tests are described in the next topics.

■ TOPIC REVIEW

1. How many explanations were presented for the difference between psychologists and engineers in the example in this topic?
2. What is the null hypothesis in the study about the sociability of psychologists and engineers?
3. Does the term *sampling error* refer to "random errors" *or* to "bias"?
4. The null hypothesis says the true difference equals what numerical value?
5. Significance tests are designed to determine the probabilities regarding the truth of what hypothesis?
6. The expression $p < .05$ stands for what words?
7. Do researchers reject the null hypothesis when the probability of its truth is high *or* when the probability is low?
8. What do researchers do with the null hypothesis if the probability is greater than .05?
9. What is an alternative way of saying a researcher has rejected the null hypothesis?
10. What is one incorrect way of saying a researcher has failed to reject the null hypothesis?

■ DISCUSSION QUESTION

1. Work together to write out results for testing the null hypotheses for a simple hypothetical study. Where are you unsure of the correct language to use to discuss the hypotheses? Bring your questions to class.

■ RESEARCH PLANNING

Will you be testing the null hypothesis in your research? How would you state the null hypothesis for your main research question?

THE PEARSON CORRELATION COEFFICIENT (*r*)

Let's say a researcher wants to see if there is any connection between two quantitative variables (at the interval or ratio levels; see Topic 59); for instance, does the number of hours of studying have a relationship to the score on exams in a course? One common way to examine this relationship is to compute a correlation coefficient. A **correlation coefficient** is a single number that describes the degree to which the two variables show a relationship, typically by seeing if a value change in one variable results in a value change in the other variable that suggests they influence one another. It does not define the causal relationship—in other words, it does not tell you which is cause and which is effect.

The most widely used coefficient is the **Pearson product-moment correlation coefficient**, whose symbol is *r* (usually called the **Pearson** *r*). The Pearson *r* measures the degree of linear correlation between two variables. It asks: When one value of one variable increases, does the value of another variable also go up? One common example is age and height during childhood. As a child's age increases, height typically goes up. This would be considered a "positive" relationship because as one variable increases, the other one also increases. In a negative correlation, as one value increases, the other decreases: for instance, as the temperature outside goes up, sales of soup go down. The terms positive and negative are not related to any value judgment; they are related to the literal value of *r*, the correlation coefficient, which ranges from −1.00 to 1.00, where −1.00 represents a perfect negative correlation and 1.00 represents a perfect positive correlation (see Figure 67.1). A value of 0.00 indicates that there is no correlation whatsoever. Values between 0.00 and 1.00 indicate a positive correlation that gets stronger as the number gets larger, and are always a positive number whose value is less than or equal to 1. Values between −1.00 and 0.00 indicate a negative correlation.

Consider the scores in Table 67.1. In this example, the researcher has collected information about a group of employees to see if there is a relationship between performance on a self-assessment employment test and the ratings employees received from their supervisors. To find out if there is a correlation, the researcher has collected each of these scores for each employee. These are presented in Table 67.1.

Is there a correlation between employment test scores and supervisors' ratings? By looking only at the numbers in the table, we can see that employment test scores put participants

FIGURE 67.1 Values of the Pearson *r*.

INVERSE RELATIONSHIP					DIRECT RELATIONSHIP				
−1.00	−0.80	−0.60	−0.40	−0.20	0.00	0.20	0.40	0.60	0.80 ... 1.00
⇧					⇧				⇧
perfect	strong	moderate	weak		none	weak	moderate	strong	perfect

TABLE 67.1   **Direct Relationship; r = .89**

Employee	Employment test scores	Supervisors' ratings
Joe	35	9
Jane	32	10
Bob	29	8
June	27	8
Leslie	25	7
Homer	22	8
Milly	21	6
Jake	18	4
John	15	5

in *roughly* the same order as the ratings by supervisors. In other words, those who have high employment test scores (e.g., Joe and Jane) have high supervisors' ratings, *and* those who have low test scores (e.g., Jake and John) have low supervisors' ratings. This illustrates what is meant by a **direct relationship** (also called a **positive relationship**). As one number (employment test scores) goes up, supervisor ratings also go up, for the most part. We can plot this data on a graph, as shown in Figure 67.2. The x-axis is the supervisor rating and the y-axis is the employment test score. Each dot represents a person. So the left-most dot below is John, with a test score of 15 and a supervisor rating of 5. When all the data is plotted, a line is drawn that has the "best fit." You can see that the points do seem to cluster around a line, but they are not perfectly lined up along the resulting line. The correlation in Table 67.1 is not perfect. For instance, although Joe has a higher employment test score than Jane, Jane has a higher supervisors' rating than Joe. If the relationship were perfect, the value of the Pearson r would be 1.00.

When the correlation coefficient is calculated, $r = 0.89$. Based on Figure 67.1 above, a value above 0.8 is a strong correlation.

In an **inverse relationship** (also called a **negative relationship**), those who are high on one variable are low on the other. Table 67.2 provides an example. In this scenario, a researcher is conducting a study in which participants take an inventory and, based on their responses, each individual receives a score for their self-concept in which a high score means they think well of themselves and a low score means they have a poorer self-concept. Their answers are also reviewed to provide a score for their level of depression in which higher scores indicate higher levels of depression. Table 67.2 shows that individuals such as Joe and Jane are high on self-concept and low on depression, while those like Sarah and Sam are low on self-concept and high on depression. Again, the relationship is not perfect, but when we look at the numbers and plot each person's data on a graph, we can see how well the scores indicate a line (see Figure 67.3).

When the value of the Pearson r for the relationship in Table 67.2 is calculated, it is −0.85. This indicates a strong negative correlation between the two variables.

FIGURE 67.2 Table 67.1 data plotted

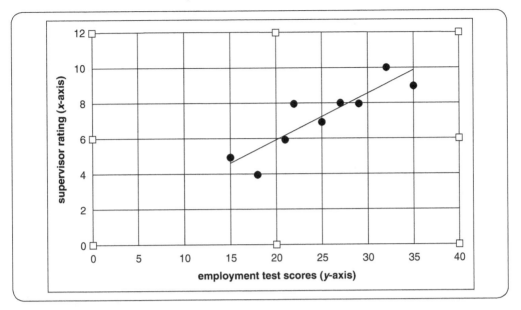

TABLE 67.2 Inverse Relationship; r = −.85

Employee	Self-concept scores	Depression scores
Joe	10	2
Jane	8	1
Bob	9	0
June	7	5
Leslie	7	6
Homer	6	8
Milly	4	8
Sarah	1	9
Sam	0	9

The relationships in Tables 67.1 and 67.2 are strong because they are near 1.00 and −1.00, but in each case, there are exceptions, which make the Pearson *r* less than 1.00 and greater than −1.00. As the number and size of the exceptions increase, the values of the Pearson *r* become closer to 0.00, indicating less and less relationship (see Figure 67.1.) Pearson *r* only measures whether there is a linear relationship between the two variables, but it is possible for variables to have other types of relationships shown by curves instead of lines.

FIGURE 67.3 **Table 67.2 data plotted.**

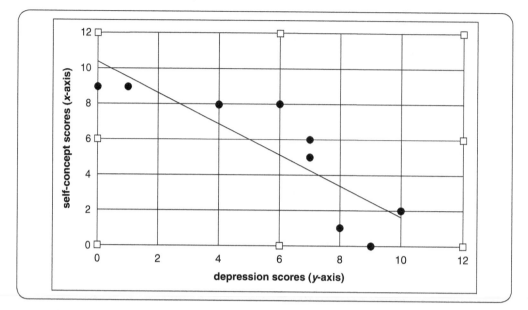

TABLE 67.3	**Selected Values of r and r^2**	
r	r^2	**Percentage better than zero***
0.90	0.81	81%
0.50	0.25	25%
0.25	0.06	6%
−0.25	0.06	6%
−0.50	0.25	25%
−0.90	0.81	81%

*Also called percentage of variance accounted for or percentage of explained variance.

It is important to note that a Pearson r is *not* a proportion and *cannot* be multiplied by 100 to get a percentage, a temptation because of its decimal values between −1.00 and 1.00. For instance, a Pearson r of .50 does not correspond to explaining 50% of the variation in the variables. To represent correlation in terms of percentages, values of Pearson r need to be converted to another statistic called the **coefficient of determination**, whose symbol is r^2, which indicates how to compute it: simply square r. Thus, for an r of 0.50, r^2 equals 0.50^2, or 0.25.[1] Multiplying .25 by 100% gives a result of 25%. What does this mean? Simply this: a Pearson r of .50 is 25% stronger than a Pearson r of 0.00. Table 67.3 shows selected values of r, r^2, and the corresponding percentages that should be considered when one is interpreting a value of r.[2]

■ TOPIC REVIEW

1. "Pearson *r*" stands for what words?
2. When the relationship between two variables is perfect and inverse, what is the value of *r*?
3. Is it possible for a negative relationship to be strong?
4. Is an *r* of −0.90 stronger than an *r* of 0.50?
5. Is an *r* of 0.75 stronger than an *r* of −0.35?
6. Is a relationship "direct" *or* "inverse" when those with high scores on one variable have high scores on the other *and* those with low scores on one variable have low scores on the other?
7. What does an *r* of 1.00 indicate?
8. For a Pearson *r* of 0.60, what is the value of the coefficient of determination?
9. What must be done in order to convert a coefficient of determination into a percentage?
10. A Pearson *r* of 0.70 is what percentage better than a Pearson *r* of 0.00?

■ DISCUSSION QUESTION

1. Name two variables between which you would expect to get a strong, positive value of *r*.

■ RESEARCH PLANNING

Will you be reporting Pearson *r* values? If so, name the two variables that will be correlated for each value of *r*.

■ NOTES

1. As a reminder, because *r* values are fractions that are less than 1, the r^2 value will always be smaller than the *r* value.
2. Note that the procedure for computing the Pearson *r* is beyond the scope of this text.

THE *t*-TEST

Suppose a researcher had a *research hypothesis* that says, "Instructors who take a short course on eLearning will have less fear of using online resources in class than those who do not take the course." The researcher tested the hypothesis by conducting an experiment in which a random sample of instructors was assigned to take the course and another random sample was designated as the control group that did not take the course.[1] At the end of the experiment, the experimental group had a mean of 16.61 on a technophobia scale, and the control group had a mean of 29.67 (where the higher the score, the greater the reluctance to use technology). These means support the research hypothesis. However, can the researcher be certain that the research hypothesis is correct? Not without testing the *null hypothesis*, which says that there is no *true* difference between the means because the values are the result of the chance errors created by random sampling, or *sampling errors*. Put another way, unrepresentative groups may have been assigned to the two conditions quite at random, creating the difference between the two means.

The *t*-test is often used to test the null hypothesis regarding the observed difference between two means.[2] For the example being considered, a series of computations, which are beyond the scope of this book, would be performed to obtain a value of *t* (in this case, 5.38) and a value of degrees of freedom (which, in this case, is $df = 179$). The values of *t* and *df* are not of any special interest to typical consumers of research because they are only substeps in the mathematical procedure used to get the *probability* (*p*) that the null hypothesis is true. In this particular case, *p* is less than .05. Thus, in a research report, the following statement could be made: The difference between the means is statistically significant ($t = 5.38$, $df = 179$, $p < .05$).[3]

As indicated in Topic 65, the term *statistically significant* indicates that the null hypothesis has been rejected. When the probability that the null hypothesis is true is .05 or less (such as .01 or .001), the null hypothesis is rejected. (When something is unlikely to be true because it has a low probability of being true, it is rejected.)

Having rejected the null hypothesis, the researcher is in a position to assert that the research hypothesis is probably true (assuming no procedural bias affected the results, such as testing the control group immediately after a change in policy made online course materials mandatory while testing the experimental group at an earlier time).

What causes a *t*-test to yield a low probability? Three interrelated factors:

1. *Sample size.* The larger the sample, the less likely that an observed difference is due to sampling errors. (As indicated in the previous topics on sampling, larger samples provide more precise data.) Thus, other things being equal, the larger the sample, the lower the value of *p*.

2. *The size of the difference between means.* The larger the difference, the less likely that the difference is due to sampling errors. Thus, other things being equal, the larger the difference between the two means, the lower the value of *p*.

3. *The amount of variation in the population.* As indicated in Topic 32, when a population is very homogeneous (has little variability), there is less potential for sampling error. Thus, other things being equal, the smaller the variability (as indicated by the standard deviations of the samples), the lower the value of p.

A special type of *t*-test is also applied to correlation coefficients. Suppose a researcher drew a random sample of 50 students and correlated their hand size with their GPAs and got an r of 0.19 on the Pearson r scale, with possible values ranging from 1.00 to −1.00. The null hypothesis says that the *true* correlation in the population is 0.00. In other words, it says that a value of 0.19 was obtained merely as the result of sampling errors. For this example, the *t*-test indicates that $p > .05$. Because the probability that the null hypothesis is true is greater than 5 in 100, the researcher would *not* reject the null hypothesis. In other words, the researcher would have a statistically insignificant correlation coefficient because the *t*-test indicated that for $n = 50$, an r of 0.19 is not significantly different from an r of 0.00. When reporting the results of the *t*-test for the significance of a correlation coefficient, it is conventional *not* to mention the value of t. Rather, researchers usually indicate only whether or not the correlation is significant at a given probability level.

■ TOPIC REVIEW

1. What does the null hypothesis say about the difference between two sample means?
2. Are the values of t and df of any special interest to typical consumers of research?
3. Suppose you read that $t = 2.000$, $df = 20$, $p > .05$ for the difference between two means. Using conventional standards, should you conclude that the null hypothesis should be rejected?
4. Suppose you read that $t = 2.859$, $df = 40$, $p < .01$ for the difference between two means. Using conventional standards, should you conclude that the null hypothesis should be rejected?
5. On the basis of the information in Question 4, should you conclude that the difference between the means is statistically significant?
6. When researchers use a large sample, are they more likely *or* less likely to reject the null hypothesis than when a researcher uses a small sample?
7. When the size of the difference between means is large, are researchers more likely *or* less likely to reject the null hypothesis than when the size of the difference is small?
8. If researchers found that for a sample of 92 participants, $r = .41$, $p < .001$, would they reject the null hypothesis?
9. Is the value of r in Question 8 statistically significant?

■ DISCUSSION QUESTION

1. Of the three factors that lead to a low probability when *t*-tests are conducted, which one is most directly under the control of a researcher?

■ **RESEARCH PLANNING**

Will you be conducting *t*-tests? Explain.

■ **NOTES**

1. Random sampling is preferred because (1) it precludes any bias in the assignment of participants to the groups, and (2) the effect of random errors produced by random sampling can be assessed with significance tests.
2. To test the null hypothesis between two *medians*, the *median test* is used. It is a specialized form of the chi-square test, which is covered in Topics 71 and 72.
3. Sometimes, researchers leave out the abbreviation *df* and present the result as $t(179) = 5.38, p < .05$.

TOPIC 69

ONE-WAY ANALYSIS OF VARIANCE (F)

Topic 68 introduced the *t*-test as a way to test the null hypothesis for the observed difference between two sample means. An alternative test for this problem is **analysis of variance** (often called **ANOVA**). Instead of *t*, it yields a statistic called F,[1] as well as degrees of freedom (*df*), sum of squares, mean square, and a *p* value, which indicates the probability that the null hypothesis is correct. As with the *t*-test, the only value of interest to the typical consumer of research is the value of *p*. By convention, when *p* equals .05 or less (such as .01 or .001), researchers reject the null hypothesis and declare the result to be *statistically significant*.

Because the *t*-test and ANOVA are based on the same theory and assumptions, when two means are compared, both tests yield exactly the same value of *p* and, hence, lead to the same conclusion regarding significance. Thus, for two means, both tests are equivalent. Note, however, that a single *t*-test can compare only two means, but a single ANOVA can compare a number of means, which is a great advantage.

Suppose, for example, a researcher administered three drugs designed to treat depression in an experiment and obtained the means in Table 69.1, in which the higher the score, the greater the depression.

The means show three observed differences:

1. Drug C is superior to Drug A.
2. Drug C is superior to Drug B.
3. Drug B is superior to Drug A.

The null hypothesis asserts that this *entire set* of three differences was created by sampling error. Through a series of computations, an ANOVA for these data was conducted with the result: $F = 10.837$, $df = 2, 15$, $p < .05$. This result might be stated in a sentence or presented in a table such as Table 69.2, which is called an ANOVA table.

While Table 69.2 contains many values, which were used to arrive at the probability in the footnote to the table, the typical consumer of research is only interested in the end result, which is the value of *p*. As indicated in previous topics, when the probability is .05 or less (as it is here), researchers reject the null hypothesis. In theory, the researcher could

TABLE 69.1 Posttest Means: Depression Scores for Three Drugs

Group X	Group Y	Group Z
Drug A	Drug B	Drug C
$M = 6.00$	$M = 5.50$	$M = 2.33$

TABLE 69.2 **ANOVA for Data in Table 69.1**

Source of variation	df	Sum of squares	Mean square	F
Between groups	2	47.445	23.722	10.837*
Within groups	15	32.833	2.189	
Total	17	80.278		

*$p < .05$

set the significance, or p-value, at any value, but the standard across disciplines is .05 as the cutoff. This means that the *entire set* of differences is statistically significant at the .05 level. The significant value varies based on the degrees of freedom, which are computed by taking the number of categories (3) and subtracting 1. Because there are three drug categories, the *df* is 2 here. ANOVA tests do *not* indicate which of the three differences are significant. It could be that only one, only two, *or* all three are significant. This needs to be explored with additional tests known as *multiple comparisons tests*. There are a number of such tests based on different assumptions, which usually yield the same result. (There is still some controversy over which multiple comparisons test is most appropriate.) For the data being considered, application of Scheffé's test (a popular multiple comparisons test) yields these probabilities:

1. for Drug C versus A, $p < .05$
2. for Drug C versus B, $p < .05$
3. for Drug B versus A, $p > .05$

Thus, the multiple comparisons test has indicated that Drug C is significantly better than Drugs A and B because the probabilities are less than .05, but Drugs B and A are not significantly different from each other because the probability is greater than .05.

In review, an ANOVA indicates whether a set of differences is significant *overall*. If so, researchers can use a multiple comparisons test to determine which individual pairs of means are significantly different from each other.

In this topic, the **one-way ANOVA** (also known as a **single-factor ANOVA**) has been considered. An ANOVA is called "one-way" when the participants have been classified in only one way. In this case, they were classified only in terms of which drug they took (A, B, or C). In the next topic, the two-way ANOVA is considered.

■ TOPIC REVIEW

1. ANOVA stands for what words?
2. If a researcher compares two means for significance, will ANOVA and the *t*-test yield the same probability?
3. If an ANOVA yields $p < .05$, should the null hypothesis be rejected?
4. If an ANOVA yields $p > .05$, is/are the difference(s) statistically significant?

5. If a researcher has four means on an achievement test for samples of students in four states, can he or she determine whether the set of differences, overall, is statistically significant by using a *t*-test? Explain.

6. For the information in Question 5, could a researcher use an ANOVA for the same purpose?

7. Should the typical consumer of research be concerned with the values of the degrees of freedom?

8. In an ANOVA table, which statistic is of greatest interest to the typical consumer of research?

9. If an overall ANOVA for three or more means is significant, it can be followed by what type of test to determine the significance of the differences among the individual pairs of means?

■ DISCUSSION QUESTIONS

1. Very briefly describe a hypothetical study in which it would be appropriate to conduct a one-way ANOVA, but it would *not* be appropriate to conduct a *t*-test.

2. If there are means for four groups (named A, B, C, and D), there are how many individual pairs of means to be compared with a multiple comparisons test?

■ RESEARCH PLANNING

Will you be conducting a one-way ANOVA? What do you anticipate comparing in this test?

■ NOTE

1. Because it yields a value of *F*, it is sometimes called an *F* test.

TWO-WAY ANALYSIS OF VARIANCE

The previous topic considered the use of analysis of variance (**ANOVA**) to test for the overall significance of a set of means when participants have been classified in only one way. Often, however, researchers use a two-way classification, such as (1) which drug was taken and (2) how long participants have been depressed. Table 70.1 shows the means for such a study in which higher depression scores indicate more depression, so a low mean is desirable.[1]

Although the participants are classified in two ways, the statistics in the table answer *three* questions. First, by comparing the column means of 6.39 and 8.38, a researcher can see that, overall, those who took Drug A are less depressed than those who took Drug B. It is important to notice that the mean of 6.39 for Drug A is based on both those who have long-term depression *and* those who have short-term depression. The same is true of the column mean of 8.38 for Drug B. Thus, by comparing the column means, a researcher is answering this question: Which drug is more effective *in general without regard to how long participants have been depressed*? In a two-way analysis of variance, this is known as a **main effect.**

Each way in which participants are classified yields a main effect in analysis of variance. Because participants were also classified in terms of their length of depression, there is a main effect for short-term versus long-term depression, which can be seen by examining the row means of 8.22 and 6.56. This main effect indicates that, overall, those with short-term depression were less depressed at the end of the experiment than those with long-term depression.

In this example, the most interesting question is one of **interaction**: Is the effectiveness of the drugs dependent, in part, on the length of depression? By examining the individual cell means (those *not* in bold in Table 70.1), it becomes clear that the answer is "yes." Drug A is more effective for short-term than for long-term depression (4.67 vs. 8.11), while Drug B is about equally effective for both types of depression (8.32 vs. 8.45). What is the practical implication of this interaction? The overall effectiveness of Drug A

TABLE 70.1 **Means for a Study of Depression: Drugs and Length of Depression Comparisons**

Length of depression	Drug A	Drug B	Row mean
Long term	$M = 8.11$	$M = 8.32$	$M = 8.22$
Short term	$M = 4.67$	$M = 8.45$	$M = 6.56$
Col. mean	$M = 6.39$	$M = 8.38$	

TABLE 70.2 Means for a Study of Depression: Drugs and Gender Comparisons

Gender	Drug C	Drug D	Row mean
Female	M = 8.00	M = 5.00	M = 6.50
Male	M = 5.00	M = 8.00	M = 6.50
Col. mean	M = 6.50	M = 6.50	

is almost entirely attributable to its effectiveness for short-term depression. In other words, if an individual has short-term depression, Drug A is indicated, but if an individual has long-term depression, either drug is likely to be about equally effective. Thus, the two classification variables *interact*: The best drug to take is dependent on the length of the depression.

For the data in Table 70.1, it turns out that $p < .05$ for both main effects and the interaction. Thus, the researcher can reject the null hypothesis, which asserts that the differences are the result of random errors. Of course, it does not always turn out this way. It is possible for one or two of the main effects to be significant but the interaction to be insignificant. It is also possible for neither main effect to be significant while the interaction is significant, which is the case for the data in Table 70.2.

In Table 70.2, notice that the column means (6.50 vs. 6.50) indicate no main effect for Drug C versus Drug D. Likewise, the row means (6.50 vs. 6.50) indicate no main effect for gender. However, there is one very interesting finding: There is an interaction of drug type and gender, which indicates that for females, Drug D is superior, while Drug C is superior for males. Note that if researchers had compared the two drugs in a one-way ANOVA without also classifying the participants according to gender (as was done here in a two-way ANOVA), they would have missed this important interaction. By examining interactions using ANOVA, researchers are one step closer to examining the effects of various traits in complex ways (not just one at a time).

■ TOPIC REVIEW

1. Suppose a researcher drew random samples of urban, suburban, and rural children, tested them for creativity, and obtained three means. Should the researcher use a "one-way" *or* a "two-way" ANOVA to test for significance? Explain.

2. Do the following means on a performance test indicate an interaction between type of reward and age?

Age level	Praise reward	Monetary reward	Row mean
Young adults	M = 50.00	M = 60.00	M = 55.00
Older adults	M = 60.00	M = 50.00	M = 55.00
Col. mean	M = 55.00	M = 55.00	

Aptitude	Method A	Method B	Row mean
High aptitude	$M = 100.00$	$M = 85.00$	$M = 92.50$
Low aptitude	$M = 100.00$	$M = 85.00$	$M = 92.50$
Col. mean	$M = 100.00$	$M = 85.00$	

3. Do the means for Question 2 indicate a main effect for type of reward?
4. Do the following means on an achievement test indicate an interaction between the method of instruction (A vs. B) and the aptitude of the students (high vs. low)?
5. Do the means for Question 4 indicate a main effect for method of instruction?
6. Do the means for Question 4 indicate a main effect for aptitude?
7. If $p > .05$ for an interaction in an analysis of variance, should the researcher reject the null hypothesis?

■ DISCUSSION QUESTION

1. Very briefly describe a hypothetical study in which it would be appropriate to conduct a two-way ANOVA but it would *not* be appropriate to conduct a one-way ANOVA.

■ RESEARCH PLANNING

Will you be conducting a two-way ANOVA? Explain.

■ NOTE

1. For instructional purposes, only two types of drugs are shown. However, ANOVA may be used when there are more than two.

INTRODUCTION TO THE CHI-SQUARE TEST (χ^2)

The chi-square (pronounced KAI, not CHAI) statistical test is named after the Greek letter chi, which is the symbol χ^2, used to represent this statistic in formulas and results. This test asks, "How likely is it that an observed distribution is due to chance (null hypothesis)?" **Chi-square** is the usual test of the null hypothesis for differences between the frequencies that are observed and the expected frequencies. Chi-square tests are used for nominal variables (see Topic 59, Table 59.2 of statistical tests).

Suppose researchers drew at random a sample of 200 members of an association of sociologists and asked them whether they were in favor of a proposed change to their bylaws. The sample size number 200 is referred to by the letter n.[1] The results in Table 71.1 show response frequencies for those who said yes and those who said no. In this survey, 60% of members are in favor of approving the bylaws change, while 40% oppose it. Note that the *observed results* are not necessarily the *true results*[2] that the researchers would have obtained if they had questioned the entire population.

The null hypothesis (see Topic 66) asserts that any observed difference was created by random sampling errors (in other words, the true difference in the population is zero). Put another way, the null hypothesis states that the observed difference ($n = 120$ vs. $n = 80$) is an *illusion* created by random errors introduced through random sampling (i.e., created by sampling errors).

After some computations for the data in Table 71.1, the results are:

$$\chi^2 = 4.00, df = 1, p < .05$$

What does this mean for a consumer of research who sees this in a report? Values of chi-square that reflect significance depend on the **degrees of freedom** (df), which sets an important parameter in the calculations and is equal to the number of categories minus 1.

TABLE 71.1 Members' Approval of a Change in Bylaws

Response	Percentage
Yes	60.0% ($n = 120$)
No	40.0% ($n = 80$)
Total	100.0% ($n = 200$)

In this case, there are two categories, yes and no, so $df = 1$ because "yes" and "no" are 2 categories, and 2–1=1. We have already covered the p-value in Topics 60 and 66, but to recap, $p < .05$ means that the calculated value of the probability that the results were due to chance is less than 5%.

Once chi-square values are calculated, they are compared to a table of values that indicate the minimum value of significance at different p-values and degrees of freedom. As an example, the minimum chi-square value that is significant with $df = 1$ and $p < .05$ is 3.841. As degrees of freedom increase (meaning that the number of categories increases), the value of significance for chi-square goes up. For 10 categories, $df = 9$. The minimum significant chi-square value at $p < .05$ is 16.919.

The chi-square value for Table 71.1 was calculated solely to obtain the probability that the null hypothesis is correct. In other words, chi-square and degrees of freedom are *not* descriptive statistics and are likely to be beyond what a typical consumer of research can interpret. Rather, they should be thought of as sub-steps in the mathematical procedure for obtaining the value of p. Thus, a consumer of research should concentrate on the fact that p is *less than* .05 in the question represented in Table 71.1.

As indicated in Topic 66, when the probability (p) that the null hypothesis is correct is .05 or less, researchers reject the null hypothesis. Rejecting the null hypotheses means that the explanation "There is no difference between 80 and 120" should be rejected. In other words, there *is* a difference and it is not explained by chance. Therefore, a researcher can say that the difference is *statistically significant* at the .05 level. At this point, the conclusion has been reached that the difference observed in the sample was *probably not* created by sampling errors. So where did the difference come from? These two possibilities remain:

1. Perhaps there was a bias in procedures, such as the interviewer leading the respondents by talking enthusiastically about the proposed change in the bylaws. Thus, the sample would no longer be representative of the population because the interviewer biased the respondents.

    If consumers of research are convinced that adequate measures were taken to prevent procedural bias, they are left with only the next possibility as a viable explanation.

2. Perhaps the population of sociologists is, in fact, in favor of the proposed change, and this fact has been correctly identified by studying the random sample.

Now, consider some results from a survey in which the null hypothesis was *not* rejected. Table 71.2 shows the numbers and percentages of participants in a random sample from a population of teachers who prefer one of three methods for teaching reading.

TABLE 71.2   Teachers' Preferences for Methods

Method A	Method B	Method C
$n = 30$	$n = 27$	$n = 22$
(37.97%)	(34.18%)	(27.85%)

In Table 71.2, there are three differences: (1) 30 preferring A versus 27 preferring B, (2) 30 preferring A versus 22 preferring C, and (3) 27 preferring B versus 22 preferring C. The null hypothesis states that this *set of three differences* was created by random sampling errors. In other words, it says that there is no true difference in the population—that a difference has been observed only because of sampling errors. The results of the chi-square test for the data in Table 71.2 are as follows:

$$\chi^2 = 1.241, df = 2, p > .05$$

Note that p is *greater than* (>) .05. According to the decision rule that p must be equal to or less than .05 for the rejection of the null hypothesis, the null hypothesis should *not* be rejected (i.e., fail to reject), which is called a *statistically insignificant* result. In other words, the null hypothesis must remain on the list as a viable explanation for the set of differences observed by studying a sample. Put another way, the probability that sampling error created the difference is too great for it to be rejected as a possible explanation for the differences.

In this topic, the use of chi-square in a *univariate analysis* (in which each participant is classified in only one way, such as which candidate each prefers) has been considered. In the next topic, the use of chi-square in a *bivariate analysis* (in which each participant is classified in two ways, such as which candidate each prefers *and* the gender of each) is considered.

■ TOPIC REVIEW

1. When researchers study a sample, are the results called the "true results" *or* the "observed results"?
2. According to the null hypothesis, what created the difference in Table 71.1?
3. What is the name of the test of the null hypothesis used in this topic?
4. What does this topic recommend the consumer of research attend to in the reported results of the chi-square test?
5. If a researcher found that a chi-square test of a difference yielded $p < .05$, what should the researcher conclude about the null hypothesis, based on conventional wisdom?
6. Does "$p < .05$" or "$p > .05$" usually lead a researcher to declare a difference statistically significant?
7. If a researcher fails to reject a null hypothesis, is the difference in question statistically significant?

■ DISCUSSION QUESTION

1. Briefly describe a hypothetical study in which it would be appropriate to conduct a chi-square test for univariate data.

■ RESEARCH PLANNING

Will you be conducting a univariate chi-square test in your research? What frequency would you be attempting to explain?

■ **NOTES**

1. *n* is the symbol used for "number" and it represents the number (or frequency) of people in each category.

2. The term *true results* stands for the results that would be obtained by conducting a census of the entire population. The results of a census are true in the sense that they are free of sampling errors.

THE BIVARIATE CHI-SQUARE TEST (χ^2) AND TYPES OF ERROR

This topic concerns the use of the chi-square test in a *bivariate analysis* (i.e., an analysis in which each participant is classified in terms of two variables in order to examine the relationship between them). Consider an example. Suppose a researcher conducted an experiment in which three methods of job training were tried with recent college graduates. Random samples of recipients were drawn for each method, and the number who obtained jobs by the end of the training sessions was determined. The resulting data are shown in Table 72.1.

Clearly, the statistics in Table 72.1 suggest there is a relationship between the method of job training and whether or not participants got jobs. Specifically, the researcher has observed that Method A is superior to Methods B and C, and that Method B is superior to Method C. A stumbling block in the interpretation of these results is the *null hypothesis*, which states there is no true difference (i.e., if all members of the population had been studied, the researcher would have found no differences among the three methods). For instance, it is possible that quite by luck of the random draw, recipients who were more employable to begin with (before treatment) were assigned to Method A, while the less employable were assigned by chance to the other two methods. A researcher can test this null hypothesis by using the chi-square test.

For the data given in Table 72.1 above, this result would be shown in a report on the experiment:

$$\chi^2 = 7.54, df = 2, p < .05$$

As indicated in Topic 66 and in other topics in this part of the book, the null hypothesis is rejected when the odds that it is true are equal to or less than .05 (i.e., $p < .05$). Thus, for these data, the researcher should reject the null hypothesis and declare the result to be significant at the .05 level. In other words, the researcher should conclude that the observed differences are too great to be attributed to random errors (i.e., sampling errors). Thus, it is unlikely that the observed relationship is merely a result of random sampling errors.

TABLE 72.1 **Training Methods and Job Placement**

Job?	Method A	Method B	Method C
Yes	$n = 20$ (66.7%)	$n = 15$ (51.7%)	$n = 9$ (31.0%)
No	$n = 10$ (33.3%)	$n = 14$ (48.3%)	$n = 20$ (69.0%)

Now consider more carefully what is meant by the term "the .05 level." When a researcher rejects the null hypothesis at exactly the .05 level (i.e., $p = .05$), there are 5 chances in 100 that the null hypothesis is correct. Thus, the researcher is taking 5 chances in 100 of being *wrong* by rejecting the null hypothesis at this level. Note that a researcher can never be certain that he or she has made the correct decision when rejecting the null hypothesis. It is always possible that the null hypothesis is true (in this case, there are 5 in 100 chances that it is true).

The possibility that a null hypothesis is rejected when it is, in fact, a correct hypothesis is called a **Type I Error**. This is when you conclude that a study supports the research hypothesis, when in reality the research hypothesis is not true. When researchers use the .05 level, the odds of making a Type I Error are 5 in 100; when they use the .01 level, the odds of making this type of error are 1 in 100; and when they use the .001 level, the odds of making it are 1 in 1,000.

When researchers fail to reject the null hypothesis, as in Topic 71 for the data in Table 71.2, they are also taking a chance of making an incorrect decision. Perhaps the null hypothesis should have been rejected, but the significance test failed to lead the researchers to the correct decision. This mistake is called a **Type II Error**. In this type of error, the researcher fails to reject the null hypothesis, which concludes that the results may be explained by chance or have no real difference. It is a Type II Error because the research hypothesis is right and the null hypothesis is not.

In review, these are the two types of errors that researchers can make:

Type I Error: Rejecting the null hypothesis when it is in fact a correct hypothesis.
Type II Error: Failing to reject the null hypothesis when it is in fact an incorrect hypothesis.

At first, this discussion of Type I and Type II errors may make significance tests such as chi-square seem weak because a researcher can be wrong, regardless of the decision made. However, the usefulness is clear in light of the full context. Specifically, once one has decided to sample at random, it is likely that random error will affect the results—at least to some extent. In light of this, researchers can never be *certain* about decisions based on the observed differences. Instead, researchers must use *probabilities* to make decisions. Researchers use probabilities in such a way as to *minimize* the likelihood that erroneous decisions are being made. To do this, researchers usually emphasize minimizing the probability of a Type I Error by using a low probability such as .05 or less. By using a low probability, researchers will infrequently be in error when rejecting the null hypothesis.

■ TOPIC REVIEW

1. Which type of analysis classifies participants in terms of two variables in order to examine the relationship between the two variables?
2. What decision should researchers make about the null hypothesis if a chi-square test leads to the conclusion that the observed differences are unlikely to be due to random errors?

3. If $p = .05$ for a chi-square test, chances are how many in 100 that the null hypothesis is true?
4. When a researcher uses the .01 level, what are the odds of making a Type I Error?
5. What is the name of the error researchers make when they fail to reject the null hypothesis when, in fact, it is an *incorrect* hypothesis?
6. What is the name of the error researchers make when they reject the null hypothesis when, in fact, it is a *correct* hypothesis?
7. Why is random sampling desirable even though it creates errors?

■ DISCUSSION QUESTIONS

1. Are both variables in Table 72.1 nominal? Explain.
2. Briefly describe a hypothetical study in which it would be appropriate to conduct a chi-square test on bivariate data.

■ RESEARCH PLANNING

Will you be using a chi-square test in a bivariate analysis? What variables will you compare? Practice how to state the research and null hypotheses with your variables.

REGRESSION BASICS

Regression is widely used as a quantitative approach to data analysis. It is a model of prediction that is both simple and flexible, leading to a long history of widespread use across disciplines. There are many different types of regression, but *multiple linear regression* is the most common and is usually the first regression technique people learn.

Multiple linear regression looks at the association between one dependent variable (or outcome) and at least one independent variable. Typically, it looks at the relationship between one dependent variable and several independent variables. This analytic tool can be used for several purposes. One use is to *explain* variation in the dependent variable as being caused by variation in the independent variable. For example, if we wanted to understand what factors affect student performance on a college entrance exam, we may be able to think of many independent variables that might help to *explain* why some students perform well and others poorly. GPA or high school quality may explain a lot, or the educational level of a student's parents. Perhaps surveying the students reveals that the amount of time each spent preparing for the exam explains differences in their scores. Each of these factors that may explain student outcomes on the exam are independent variables. In a multiple regression model, all of these factors can be evaluated *within one test*.

Another common use is to *predict* when a specific value of the dependent variable is likely to occur based on the value of the independent variable. If we take the above example, we can rearrange our question to ask: If I know the values of the independent variables—a student's GPA, school, prep time, and parent's educational level—can I correctly guess the score they will get on the college entrance exam?

Multiple regression is closely related to ANOVA tests (covered in Topics 69 and 70). ANOVA tests are appropriate when the independent variables are categorical, while multiple regression can test variables that are continuous.

Regression is also similar to correlation (Topic 67). Although the tests work differently from a mathematical point of view, both correlation and regression look at the association between variables and ask if the relationship is linear.[1] Correlation only looks at the association between two variables, but remember that it asks: As one variable's value goes up, does the other variable's value also increase? It can also test the relationship in which variables have a negative correlation; that is, as one variable value goes up, the other decreases. Regression is a model that allows a similar question as correlation but with multiple variables.

Regression also includes **control variables**. These variables are said to "control for" *demographic* characteristics. For instance, gender, age, and year in school might be control variables. A model with these control variables can be interpreted as saying, "When gender, age, and year in school are held constant, an independent variable in the model explains X amount of variation in the dependent variable." In other words, the reported effect of independent variables cannot be explained by differences based on gender, age, or year in school.

TABLE 73.1 **Student Characteristics Related to College Entrance Exam Scores**

Model		Unstandardized coefficients		Standardized coefficients		
		B	**Std. Error**	**Beta**	**t**	**Sig.**
1	(Constant)	278.86	4.83		28.768	.000
	GPA	3.752	.890	.562	1.17	.002
	Father education	17.57	4.52	.765	2.53	.046

Table 73.1 provides an example of a basic multiple regression analysis presented in the format used for journal articles in APA style.[2] The variables included in the model are listed along with their coefficients and standard errors. The significance or p-value is listed as "Sig." at the far right of the table and indicates if the relationship was statistically significant based on the cutoff value the author has determined to represent significance, usually .05. If the variable's value is positive or negative, it indicates the direction of the relationship with the dependent variable. In this case, several variables have significant positive relationships with the dependent variable.

In addition to reviewing the significance values, it is also good to review the descriptions of each variable in the test, provided within the article. It is important that variables are *independent*. In other words, it can be a concern if an independent variable measures the *same* quantity as the dependent variable, just in another form. Consider the relationship between grades received and GPA. It goes without saying that GPA is computed based on one's grades, so these two variables are not independent. GPA is completely dependent on grades, so they should not be treated within the model as separate factors where one could help to explain the other. They are simply different expressions of the same thing, so this does nothing to explain what is happening with variations in GPA. It can also be important to think about how separate independent variables may represent the same thing.

The language about the outcomes of any statistical test is exacting. Be sure to pay attention to not only the tables but also the wording the author uses to describe the results. Take care when paraphrasing that you do not change the claim that is being made. Further study of statistics can help, as can having a mentor, advisor, or stats-savvy peer look over any writing about statistical results to ensure that the specific grammar of reporting statistical results is accurate.

■ TOPIC REVIEW

1. How widely used is regression?
2. How many dependent variables are there in regression models?
3. Is it possible to use more than one independent variable in regression models?

4. Fill in the blanks: Two uses of regression models are to _____ the variation in dependent variables, or to _____ the value of dependent variables based on the values of independent variables.
5. Regression is similar to correlation because it looks for what type of relationship between variables?
6. What value indicates significance in regression models?
7. What does the sign (positive or negative) of a coefficient in a regression model indicate?
8. Beyond significance, what is one error to look for in regression models?
9. When reporting on statistical results, what is one area in which the writer should be cautious?

■ DISCUSSION QUESTION

1. Consider the implications for using a regression approach. What variables might have a *linear* relationship? Why is the relationship linear?

■ RESEARCH PLANNING

Will you be performing regression in your study? What is the dependent variable? What independent variables might be used?

■ NOTES

1. There are several types of regression, and other types are capable of testing distributions of shapes other than a straight line, but this is the most common. An example would be testing for an exponential relationship between independent variables and the dependent variable. If a variable increases exponentially for every single unit increase in the dependent variable, the shape is a curve instead of a line.
2. Note that other formats may differ slightly in formatting or labels, but will provide the same numbers.

PRACTICAL SIGNIFICANCE OF RESULTS

Statistical significance deals with the question of whether a difference is reliable in light of random errors. Assume, for instance, that a researcher assigned students at random to two groups: one that was taught a mathematics lesson with new instructional software (the experimental group) and one that was taught using a traditional lecture and textbook approach (the control group). Furthermore, assume that in comparison to the lecture and textbook approach, use of the instructional software produces a superior outcome in math achievement, but the superiority is quite small. With a very large sample, randomization should yield experimental and control groups that are very similar at the beginning of the experiment (i.e., on the pretest). Because larger samples have less sampling error than smaller ones, a significance test such as a *t*-test for the difference between the two posttest means may be able to detect the reliability of the difference, even though it is quite small, and allow the researcher to declare it to be *statistically significant* at some probability level, such as $p < .05$. This illustrates an important principle: Even a small difference can be statistically significant.[1] This is true because statistical significance determines only the likelihood that a difference is due to random errors, not whether it is a large difference.

Determining the statistical significance of a difference is the first step; determining the **practical significance** is the next step. Determining practical significance involves five considerations.

The first consideration is the cost in relation to the benefit, which is often referred to as a **cost-benefit analysis**. While there are statistical procedures that can be used to conduct such an analysis, for most purposes, common sense and good judgment can give a good answer to the question of whether the results are of practical significance in terms of cost. Consider the preceding example. Suppose all students already have access to computers for their math lessons, and the software is being donated (or is highly subsidized by a foundation). In this case, the low cost might make the small difference of practical significance. On the other hand, if expensive computers and software would need to be purchased, and the teachers would need extensive (and, therefore, expensive) training in its use, educators might forgo using the experimental method in everyday instruction because the small increase in performance would come at an unjustifiably high cost.

The example being considered illustrates that even a small difference can be of both statistical and practical significance if the cost is low. In addition, a small, statistically significant difference can be of practical significance—even if it is costly—if it is a **crucial difference** (the second consideration). A crucial difference is one that results in an increase or decrease of great importance. Consider an extreme example. Suppose an experiment in which using very expensive computerized simulations to teach physicians how to conduct a delicate form of surgery reduces the mortality rate from such surgery from 2 in 100,000 to 1.8 in 100,000. In this case, a medical school or hospital might decide that even this small difference in outcomes is worth the high cost because saving even a single life is crucial. Now consider a less extreme example: If a school needs an increase of just a few points (on the average) to cross a key threshold, such as having the average student score at or above the 50th percentile rank on a standardized math test in order to obtain substantially increased state funding for instruction, achieving this might be considered crucial by teachers, parents, and students.

The third consideration in determining practical significance is **client acceptability**. In research involving school settings, students are considered clients. If students greatly dislike a statistically superior computerized technique for improving math achievement, using the technique might cause students to develop negative attitudes toward math, even if it improves their skills. If so, the statistically significant difference might be of little practical significance because of the *negative side effect* (i.e., development of negative attitudes).

The fourth consideration is **public and political acceptability**. For instance, studies suggest that stem cell research might be fruitful in curing a number of debilitating and deadly diseases, yet some segments of the public oppose it, calling into question its practical significance as a line of research that scientists should continue to pursue.

Fifth, the **ethical and legal implications** of statistically significant results should be considered. No matter how much benefit and how low the cost, some treatments that have been shown to produce statistically superior results may violate the ethical standards of a profession or impinge on legal requirements such as the laws that govern the operation of schools and other institutions.

It should be clear that determining practical significance should not be done mechanically. If there is any question as to the practical significance of the results of a study, representative groups of potential providers of the treatments (such as teachers or psychologists, their clients, the public, and politicians) may need to be consulted. In addition, legal counsel may be needed to help in the determination of practical significance.

■ TOPIC REVIEW

1.   Is it possible for a very small difference to be statistically significant?
2.   This topic describes *how many* types of considerations for determining practical significance?
3.   If the cost is low, might a very small but statistically significant difference be of practical significance?
4.   Does a crucial difference need to be numerically large to be of practical significance?
5.   According to this topic, should client acceptability of a treatment be considered when determining practical significance?
6.   According to this topic, ethical considerations should play no role in the interpretation of the results of a study. Is this statement true *or* false?
7.   Should determining the practical significance of a study's results be a mechanical process?

■ DISCUSSION QUESTIONS

1. In addition to the two examples in this topic, name a hypothetical result that you would favor implementing, even if it were costly, because it might make a *crucial difference*.

2. Consider the last research report you read that had statistically significant results. Did the researcher who wrote the article discuss the practical significance of his or her results? Explain.

■ RESEARCH PLANNING

Can you anticipate any considerations that might limit the practical significance of the results you hope to obtain in your study? Explain.

■ NOTE

1. As indicated in Topic 68, the *t*-test is more likely to lead to significance if the difference between the two means is large. However, if there is little variation among the participants and if a large enough sample is used, even small differences can be reliably detected and declared statistically significant. Note that in some circumstances a small difference can be of great practical importance. For instance, in a national election, having only one vote more than the competing candidate out of millions of votes can lead to victory.

PART 9
Effect Size and Meta-Analysis

Part 9 covers two important supplemental topics: effect size and meta-analysis. Effect size is a statistical tool that can be used to evaluate the size of a difference, such as the difference between two means, and help to determine its significance. Topic 75 introduces the concept of effect size, and explains the most commonly used statistical measure to estimate it, Cohen's *d*. Topic 76 offers greater detail on how to evaluate the value of *d*, and Topic 77 discusses other methods for determining effect size, focusing primarily on how to use Pearson's correlation coefficient (*r*) as a measure of effect size. In Topics 78, 79, and 80, the basics of meta-analysis are explained. A meta-analysis applies statistical techniques to the empirical literature, allowing a researcher to combine and evaluate the results on a specific topic across diverse studies.

INTRODUCTION TO EFFECT SIZE (*d*)

The *magnitude* (i.e., size) of a difference when it is expressed on a standardized scale is referred to as the *effect size*. The statistic *d* is one of the most popular for describing the effect size of the difference between two means. To understand the need to consider the **effect size** of a difference, consider a practical problem in interpreting two sets of research findings that can be resolved using the statistic *d*.

Suppose that Experimenter A administered a new treatment for depression (Treatment X) to an experimental group, while the control group received a standard treatment. Furthermore, suppose that Experimenter A used a 20-item true-false depression scale (with possible raw scores from 0 to 20) and on the posttest obtained the results shown in Table 75.1.[1] Note that the difference between the two means is 5 raw-score points.

Now suppose that Experimenter B administered Treatment Y to an experimental group while treating the control group with the standard treatment. Furthermore, suppose Experimenter B used a 30-item scale with choices from "strongly agree" to "strongly disagree" (with possible scores from 0 to 120) and obtained the results in Table 75.2, which show a difference of 10 raw-score points in favor of the experimental group.

Which treatment is superior? Treatment X, which resulted in a 5-point raw-score difference between the two means, *or* Treatment Y, which resulted in a 10-point raw-score difference between the two means? The answer is not clear because the two experimenters used different measurement scales (0 to 20 versus 0 to 120).

TABLE 75.1   Statistics Obtained in Experiment A (Treatment X)

Group	m	sd
Experimental group (*n* = 50)	12.00	4.00
Control group (*n* = 50)	7.00	4.00
Difference between two means	5.00	

TABLE 75.2   Statistics Obtained in Experiment B (Treatment Y)

Group	m	sd
Experimental group (*n* = 50)	80.00	14.00
Control group (*n* = 50)	70.00	14.00
Difference between two means	10.00	

TABLE 75.3 **Differences Expressed in Raw Scores and Values of *d***		
Group	**Raw-score differences**	**Standardized differences (*d*)**
Experimenter A	5 points	1.25
Experimenter B	10 points	0.71

For the results of the two studies to be comparable, they need to be *standardized* so that both differences can be expressed on the same scale. The most straightforward way to do this is to express both differences in terms of *standard-deviation units* (instead of raw-score units).[2] In Experiment A, *one standard-deviation unit* equals 4.00 raw-score points. The formula below shows how *d* is obtained. In this formula, m_e stands for the mean of the experimental group, and m_c stands for the mean of the control group. The difference between the means (5.00) is divided by the standard-deviation unit for Experiment A (4.00 points). This yields an answer of 1.25:

$$d = \frac{m_e - m_c}{sd} = \frac{12.00 - 7.00}{4.00} = 1.25$$

The result indicates that the experimental group exceeded the control group by 1.25 standard-deviation units. For all practical purposes, there are only three standard-deviation units on each side of the mean, or the center of the normal distribution graph. Thus, *d* is expressed in standard-deviation units and has an effective range from 0.00 (no difference between the means) to 3.00.[3] For Experiment A, the experimental group is 1.25 standard deviations from the central value (0.00) on a standardized scale that ranges from 0.00 to 3.00. As you may recall, being between 1 and 2 standard deviations means that the value is not in the middle 68% but is between 68% and 95% of all values.

Using the formula for Experiment B, the difference in means (5.00) is divided by the standard deviation (10.00/14.00), yielding *d* = 0.71, which is almost three-quarters of the way above 0.00 on the three-point scale. Now we can compare the two experiments on a common (i.e., standardized) scale called *d*. Clearly, the difference in Experiment A (1.25) is greater than the difference in Experiment B (0.71).

Table 75.3 summarizes the differences. Remember that the two raw-score differences are not directly comparable because different measurement scales were used (0 to 20 points versus 0 to 120 points). By examining the standardized values of *d*, a meaningful comparison of the results of the two experiments can be made.

Within each of the two examples in this topic, the two standard deviations are equal. When they are unequal, a special averaging procedure that results in a pooled standard deviation should be used. In the next topic, the interpretation of *d* is discussed in more detail. In Topic 77, an alternative statistic for expressing effect size is described.

■ TOPIC REVIEW

1. In this topic, which experimenter had the smaller range of possible raw scores? Explain.
2. In this topic, the raw-score differences between the means (5 for Experimenter A and 10 for Experimenter B) were standardized by dividing each of them by what statistic?

3. When comparing the results of two experiments, is it possible for the experiment with the smaller raw-score difference to have a larger difference when the differences are expressed as *d*?

4. Suppose a researcher obtained a value of *d* of 2.95. Should this be characterized as representing a large difference? Explain.

5. Suppose you read that the mean for an experimental group is 20.00 and the mean for the control group is 22.00. On the basis of this information alone, can you calculate the value of *d*? Explain.

6. Suppose a researcher conducted an experiment on improving algebra achievement, and the experimental posttest raw-score mean equaled 500.00 (*sd* = 100.00), and the control group raw-score mean equaled 400.00 (*sd* = 100.00). What is the value of the effect size for the experiment?

7. What is the definition of *effect size*?

■ DISCUSSION QUESTION

1. In your own words, briefly explain why it is desirable to compute *d* when comparing the results of two experiments that use different measurement scales.

■ RESEARCH PLANNING

Do you plan to report value(s) of *d* in the Results section of your research report? How will you use it?

■ NOTES

1. Note that in the experiments in this topic, the researchers used measures that yield *higher* scores when there is *less* depression.
2. See Topic 63 to review the meaning of the standard deviation.
3. If a control group has a higher mean than the experimental group, the value of *d* will be negative.

INTERPRETATION OF EFFECT SIZE (*d*)

While there are no universally accepted standards for describing values of *d* in words, keep in mind that for most practical purposes, 3.00 (or −3.00) is the maximum value of *d* because the effective range of standard-deviation units is only three on each side of the mean, so an experimental group can rarely exceed a control group by more than 3.00.[1]

To talk about the relative size of values of *d*, many researchers use Cohen's (1992)[2] suggestions: (1) a value of *d* of about 0.20 (one-fifth of a standard deviation) is "small," (2) a value of 0.50 (one-half of a standard deviation) is "medium," and (3) a value of 0.80 (eight-tenths of a standard deviation) is "large." Extrapolating from Cohen's suggestions, a value of 1.10 might be called "very large," and a value of 1.40 or more might be called "extremely large." Values this large are rarely found in social and behavioral research.

Table 76.1 summarizes how various values of *d* are often described.

Using the labels in Table 76.1, the value of *d* of 0.71 in the previous topic would be described as being closer to large than medium, while the value of 1.25 would be described as being between very large and extremely large.

Cohen (1992), who proposed the labels for the first three values in Table 76.1, noted that he originally established them subjectively, but subsequently they have been found to be useful by other researchers in various fields of study.

The labels being discussed should not be used arbitrarily without consideration of the full context in which the values of *d* were obtained and the possible implications of the results. This leads to two principles: (1) a small effect size might represent an important result, and (2) a large effect size might represent an unimportant result.

Consider the *first principle*. Suppose that researchers have been frustrated by consistently finding values of *d* well below 0.20 when trying various treatments for solving an important problem (such as combatting a new deadly disease). If a subsequent researcher finds a treatment that results in a value of about 0.20, this might be considered a very important

TABLE 76.1 **Labels for Values of *d***

Value of *d*	Label
0.20	Small
0.50	Medium
0.80	Large
1.10	Very Large
1.40+	Extremely Large

finding. At this low level (0.20), the effect of the treatment is small, but it might be of immense importance to those ill individuals who would be helped by the treatment, however few. In addition, the results might point the scientific community in a fruitful direction for additional research.

The *second principle* is that a large value of *d*—even one above 1.40—might be of limited importance. This is most likely when the results lack practical significance in terms of cost, public and political acceptability, or ethical and legal concerns (see Topic 74 for considerations in determining the practical significance of research results).

Here are three steps for interpreting the difference between two means. First, determine whether the difference is statistically significant at an acceptable probability level, such as $p < .05$. If it is not, the difference should usually be regarded as unreliable and should be interpreted as such. Second, for a statistically significant difference, consider the value of *d*, and consider the labels in Table 76.1 for describing the magnitude of the difference. Third, consider the implications of the difference for validating any relevant theories as well as the practical significance of the results.

Before the researchers begin to follow the three steps outlined in the previous paragraph, the adequacy of the research methodology that they employed should be considered, of course. Woefully inadequate sampling (such as a very biased sample), clearly invalid measures (such as a test that measures a variable other than the one the researcher sought to study), or a very poor research design (such as a design that will not answer the research question) would each lead to very serious questions regarding the validity of the results. In such cases, consideration of values of *d* might be meaningless.

■ TOPIC REVIEW

1. Are there universally accepted standards for describing effect sizes?
2. What is the "effective range" of standard deviation units on both sides of the mean? Explain.
3. If the value of *d* for the difference between two means equals 1.00, the experimental group's mean is how many standard-deviation units higher than the control group's mean?
4. What value of *d* is associated with the label "extremely large"?
5. According to Cohen, what label should be attached to a value of *d* of 0.80?
6. Under what circumstance will a negative value of *d* be obtained?
7. Should a test of statistical significance be conducted before *or* after computing *d* and interpreting its value using labels?

■ DISCUSSION QUESTIONS

1. As noted in this topic, a small value of *d* might be associated with an important result. Name a specific problem that is currently confounding researchers and for which even a small value of *d* might indicate a result of great practical importance.
2. Is it possible for a large value of *d* to be associated with a difference that is unimportant?

■ RESEARCH PLANNING

Will you be comparing the difference between two means in your analysis? If so, do you expect to find a statistically significant difference? Do you expect to find a large value of d?

■ NOTES

1. A negative is obtained when the control group's mean is higher than the experimental group's mean. Note that less than one-half of one percent of a normal distribution lies above +3.00 and below −3.00, which means that it is technically possible—but highly unlikely—to obtain values larger than +3.00 and −3.00.
2. Cohen, J. (1992). A power primer. *Psychological Bulletin, 112*, 155–159.

EFFECT SIZE AND CORRELATION (*r*)

Cohen's *d* is so widely used as a measure of effect size that some researchers use the term *effect size* and *d* interchangeably—as though they are synonyms. However, effect size refers to any statistic that *describes the size of a difference on a standardized metric*. For instance, *d* describes the size of the difference between two means.[1] Furthermore, *d* is *standardized* because, regardless of what variables are being studied and regardless of what raw-score scale is being used to express the difference, the value of *d* is always expressed on a standard-deviation scale that almost always ranges only from −3.00 to +3.00 (see the previous topic to review *d*).[2]

In addition to *d*, a number of other measures of effect size have been proposed. One that is very widely reported is *effect-size r*, which is simply the Pearson correlation coefficient (*r*) described in Topic 67. As outlined in that topic, *r* indicates the direction and strength of a relationship between two variables expressed on a scale that ranges from −1.00 to +1.00, where 0.00 indicates no relationship. Values of *r* are interpreted by first squaring them (r^2). For instance, when $r = 0.50$, $r^2 = 0.25$ (i.e., $0.50 \times 0.50 = 0.25$). Then, the value of r^2 should be multiplied by 100 to make it a percent. Thus, $0.25 \times 100 = 25\%$. This indicates that the value of *r* of 0.50 is 25% greater than 0.00 on a scale that extends up to a maximum possible value of 1.00.

In basic studies, the choice between reporting *means* and the associated values of *d* (which can range from −3.00 to 3.00) and reporting *correlation coefficients* and the associated values of r^2 (which can range from 0.00 to 1.00)[3] is usually quite straightforward.

If a researcher wants to determine which of two groups is superior *on average*, a comparison of means using *d* is usually the preferred method of analysis.

On the other hand, if there is one group of participants with two scores per participant, and if the goal is to determine the *degree of relationship between the two sets of scores*, then *r* and r^2 should be used. For instance, if a vocabulary knowledge test and a reading comprehension test were administered to a group of students, it would not be surprising to obtain a correlation coefficient as high as 0.70, which indicates a substantial degree of relationship between two variables (i.e., there is a strong tendency for students who score high on vocabulary knowledge to score high on reading comprehension). As described in Topic 67, for interpretative purposes, 0.70 squared equals 0.49, which is equivalent to 49%. Knowing this allows a researcher to say that the relationship between the two variables is 49% higher than a relationship of 0.00.

When reviewing a body of literature on a given topic, some studies present means and values of *d* while other studies on the same topic present values of *r*, depending on the specific research purposes and research designs. When interpreting the differences in findings between studies, it can be useful to think in terms of the equivalence of *d* and *r*. Table 77.1 shows the equivalents for selected values.

TABLE 77.1 Equivalent Values of *d*, *r*, and *r*²

d	r	r^2	% for r^2
0.20	0.100	0.010	1.0%
0.50	0.243	0.059	5.9%
0.80	0.371	0.138	13.8%
1.20	0.514	0.264	26.4%
1.50	0.600	0.360	36.0%
2.00	0.707	0.500	50.0%

Consider an example that illustrates the usefulness of Table 77.1. Suppose a researcher was examining the literature on anxiety and depression and found a study in which one group was administered scales that measured the two variables, and $r = 0.37$ was obtained. Suppose that in another study, an experimental group was administered a treatment designed to induce anxiety while the control group received a neutral treatment. Then, all participants were administered a depression scale (to see whether anxiety induces depression). Further, suppose that the experimenter reported that $d = 0.80$ for the difference between the posttest means for the two groups. From Table 77.1 above, it can be seen that the effect sizes (i.e., magnitude of the differences) in the two studies are the same (i.e., for a value of *d* of 0.80 in the first column, the corresponding value of *r* in the second column is 0.371).

For values not shown in Table 77.1, it is often sufficient to locate the closest values and make approximations. More precise equivalent values of *d* and *r* require a more extensive understanding of the mathematical concepts and formulas involved in statistics. Wikiversity offers a starting point at https://en.wikiversity.org/wiki/Cohen%27s_d and includes links to online calculators for computing effect size. There are additional online resources for learning how to compute effect size statistics. Other online effect size calculators include http://www.socscistatistics.com/effectsize/Default3.aspx and http://www.uccs.edu/~lbecker/.

■ TOPIC REVIEW

1. According to this topic, what are the two measures of effect size that are very widely reported?
2. Correlation coefficients are expressed on a standard scale that always ranges from −1.00 up to what value?
3. A value of *r* should be interpreted by doing what?
4. A value of *r* equal to 0.40 is what percentage above zero?
5. If there is one group of participants, and a researcher wants to determine the strength of the relationship between two sets of test scores, which measure of effect size would typically be the more appropriate?
6. A value of *d* of 1.20 corresponds to what value of r^2?
7. A value of *r* of 0.600 corresponds to what value of *d*?

■ DISCUSSION QUESTION

1. Briefly describe a hypothetical study in which it would be more appropriate to compute a value of *d* instead of a value of *r* as a measure of effect size.

■ RESEARCH PLANNING

In this topic, there is an example of an experiment and an example of a correlational study. Will you be conducting either type of study? Explain how you might use the information in this topic in your research.

■ NOTES

1. If the means of two groups are identical, $d = 0.00$.
2. Note that it is mathematically possible for *d* to exceed 3.00 because a very small percentage of the cases lies above three standard deviations above the mean. Such values are seldom seen in the social and behavioral sciences.
3. Note that all values of r^2 are positive because squaring a negative correlation coefficient results in a positive product. Thus, the bottom of the range for values of r^2 is 0.00, not -1.00.

INTRODUCTION TO META-ANALYSIS

Meta-analysis is a set of statistical methods for combining the results of previous studies.[1] To understand its basic premise, consider the following example illustrated in Table 78.1. Suppose a researcher (named W) randomly assigned 50 students to an experimental group that received one-on-one remedial reading tutoring. The remaining 50 children were the controls. At the end of the experiment, the experimental group had a mean of 22.00, and the control group had a mean of 19.00 on a standardized reading test. Subsequently, three other experimenters (named X, Y, and Z) conducted strict replications of the first experiment using the same research methods, the same type of reading tutoring, and the same number of second-grade students drawn at random from the same pool of students (e.g., second-graders in a particular school district). The posttest means of the four experiments are shown in Table 78.1.

In Table 78.1, there are differences in the results from study to study. The differences could be caused by one or more of the following types of errors:

1. *Random sampling errors* created by assigning participants at random to the two groups, such as having more motivated students assigned (quite at random) to the experimental group in one or more of the experiments.
2. *Random errors of measurement* such as participants guessing on the multiple-choice test or some students not feeling well on test day.
3. *Known systematic errors* of which one or more of the researchers was aware, such as the unavailability of experienced tutors for one or more of the experiments.
4. *Unknown systematic errors* of which one or more of the researchers are unaware, such as tutors not following the curriculum when the researcher or researchers were not present.

All four types of errors are possible in any experiment. Hence, the results of any one experiment should be interpreted with caution. However, in this particular example, there

TABLE 78.1   Results of a Meta-analysis of Two Experiments

	Experimental group	Control group	Mean difference
Researcher W	$m = 22.00$	$m = 19.00$	$m_{difference} = 3.00$
Researcher X	$m = 20.00$	$m = 18.00$	$m_{difference} = 2.00$
Researcher Y	$m = 23.00$	$m = 17.00$	$m_{difference} = 6.00$
Researcher Z	$m = 15.00$	$m = 16.00$	$m_{difference} = -1.00$

are four experiments, which should provide more confidence in any overall conclusions than any single study could. In a *traditional, subjective narrative review of these studies*, it would be reasonable to synthesize these four experiments with a statement such as "Three of the four experiments on the tutorial instruction showed positive results, with one experiment showing a six-point difference in favor of the experimental group. However, the one negative case in which the control group exceeded the experimental group by one point reduces confidence in the effectiveness of this program."

In a *meta-analysis*, a reviewer might also make comments such as the one in the previous paragraph. However, the main thrust of the conclusions in a meta-analysis is based on a *mathematical synthesis* of the statistical results of the previous studies. To obtain the synthesis, average the results by summing the four mean differences $(3.00 + 2.00 + 6.00 - 1.00 = 10.00)$ and then dividing the sum by four because there were four studies $(10.00/4.00 = 2.50)$. Thus, in a meta-analysis, the author would state that the best estimate of the effectiveness of the program is 2.50 points.[2]

It should be clear that a meta-analysis has two important characteristics. The first one is that the statistical result (e.g., 2.50) is based on a sample, in this case, 400 students. (Note that each of the four individual studies had 50 in each group for a total of 100 in each study.) Statistics based on larger samples (such as 400 versus 100) yield more *reliable* results.

It is important to note that *reliable results* are not necessarily *valid results*. A systematic bias that skews the results (such as the experimental group having access to the answer key for the test) will yield invalid results no matter how large the sample is.

The second important characteristic of meta-analysis is that it typically synthesizes the results of studies conducted by *independent* researchers (i.e., researchers who are not working together). Thus, if one researcher makes a *systematic error* (such as using poorly trained tutors), the effects of the erroneous results will be moderated when they are averaged with the results obtained by other independent researchers who have not made the same error.

In short, the process of averaging when conducting a meta-analysis tends to decrease the effects of both the random and the systematic errors that were described in this topic.

■ TOPIC REVIEW

1. What is the meaning of the prefix *meta* as used in this topic?
2. For what purpose is a set of statistical methods called meta-analysis used?
3. Two types of random errors tend to be canceled out in the process of conducting a meta-analysis. What are the two types of random errors discussed in this topic?
4. In the report of a meta-analysis, the main thrust of the conclusions is based on what?
5. Very briefly state the second important characteristic of meta-analysis.

■ DISCUSSION QUESTION

1. On the basis of what you have learned about meta-analysis in this topic, to what extent do you think that it is a good method for advancing knowledge on an issue? Explain.

■ RESEARCH PLANNING

Some institutions (and journals) consider a meta-analysis to be a work of original research even though it is based on a re-analysis of the research results created by others. If you are planning to conduct research, would you be interested in conducting a meta-analysis as your research project (on the basis of what you know about it at this point)?

■ NOTES

1. The prefix *meta* means occurring later and/or being later and more highly organized. Meta-analysis is conducted on previous results and mathematically synthesizes them.
2. For reasons discussed in the next topic, those who conduct meta-analyses usually convert their results to one or more measures of effect size (such as d or r), which were discussed in the previous three topics.

META-ANALYSIS AND EFFECT SIZE

For instructional purposes, the example in the previous topic illustrated a meta-analysis on four studies that were as similar as possible (i.e., a study by Researcher W plus three strict replications). In practice, it is difficult to find even one perfectly strict replication of a study.

One very important way that various studies on a given topic often differ is that various researchers frequently use different measures of the same variable. To see the importance of this issue when conducting and interpreting a meta-analysis, consider the values in Table 79.1, which are based on a study in which Experimenter A used a test with possible score values from 200 to 800 (like the SAT), while Experimenter B used a test with possible score values from 0 to 50.

While the average of the mean differences can be computed ($100.00 + 2.00 = 102.00/2 = 51.00$), it lacks meaning because the results are expressed on different scales. In other words, the answer of 51.00 does *not* refer specifically to the scale that goes from 200 to 800 *nor* does it refer specifically to the scale that goes from 0 to 50. When locating additional studies on the same topic, other tests with other score-point ranges are likely to be found, making a simple average of the mean differences entirely uninterpretable.

The solution is to use a measure of *effect size*. One of the most popular is Cohen's *d*, which is expressed on a standardized scale that typically ranges from −3.00 to +3.00. (Cohen's *d* is discussed in Topics 75 and 76.) Calculating *d* for all studies to be included in a meta-analysis permits the averaging of the values of *d* to get a meaningful result.

As indicated in Topic 75, to obtain *d*, divide the difference between the means by the standard deviation. For Experiment A, $d = 100.00/200.00 = \mathbf{0.50}$. For Experiment B, $d = 2.00/3.00 = \mathbf{0.67}$. When the results of the two experiments are expressed on a common scale (*d*), it becomes clear that Experiment B (with a *d* of 0.67) had a larger effect than Experiment A (with a *d* of 0.50), which was not clear by a simple inspection of Table 79.1.

To proceed with the meta-analysis, the two values of *d* can be averaged to get a mathematical synthesis of the results $[(0.67 + 0.50)/2 = 0.58]$. Thus, **0.58** is the best estimate of

TABLE 79.1   Results Used in Conducting a Meta-analysis

	Experimental group	Control group	Mean difference
Exp. A	$m = \mathbf{500.00}$	$m = \mathbf{400.00}$	$m_{difference} = \mathbf{100.00}$
$n = 50$	$sd = 200.00$	$sd = 200.00$	
Exp. B	$m = \mathbf{24.00}$	$m = \mathbf{22.00}$	$m_{difference} = \mathbf{2.00}$
$n = 50$	$sd = 3.00$	$sd = 3.00$	

the overall effect. Referring to Table 76.1 in Topic 76, a researcher can say that the overall result of the meta-analysis is somewhat above medium in strength.

Returning to this topic's example, the standard deviations for both groups in each experiment were the same. In reality, they will almost always differ.

The two experiments in this example also had the same number of participants ($n = 50$ in each). Suppose an additional published experiment (Experiment C) is located in which 300 participants were used. A researcher would, of course, calculate d for this experiment (assume that $d = 0.90$, which is "large" according to Table 76.1 in Topic 76). By summing the three values of d and dividing by 3 (the number of studies), each study is given equal weight. In other words, the three values of d are being treated as though they were equally important, even though the value of d for Experiment C is based on a much larger sample than that of the other two experiments.

This can be addressed using statistical methods that weight the average value of d to take into account the varying numbers of participants, giving more weight to those studies with more participants in the final average. Thus, consumers of research should look to see whether a meta-analysis is based on weighted averages, which is almost always desirable.

As indicated in Topic 77, r is also a measure of effect sizes. Like d, it is expressed on a standardized scale. However, the scale for r has values that can range from −1.00 to 1.00. Like d, values of r reported in various studies can be averaged, and those averages can be weighted to take into account varying sample sizes.[1]

In this topic and the previous one, very simple examples were used to illustrate the purposes of meta-analysis and its interpretation. The simplicity of the examples may have failed to fully convey the importance of meta-analysis, so briefly consider two published meta-analytic studies. First, researchers located 162 studies that reported on the gender differences in smiling.[2] Combined, these studies contained a total of 109,654 participants. By averaging the effect sizes across the 162 studies, the researchers found that women smiled more than men, with an overall weighted mean value of d of 0.41. This value of d is close to medium in strength according to Table 76.1 in Topic 76. Note that this result is based on a large number of studies and a very large combined sample size.

In another meta-analysis, researchers reported a weighted average value of r of 0.48 for the relationship between posttraumatic stress disorder and anger, based on 29 studies involving 7,486 participants.[3] With such a large sample, the result of this meta-analysis is highly reliable.

In conclusion, meta-analysis provides a statistical method that can synthesize multiple studies on a given topic. Thus, meta-analytic studies are an important adjunct to traditional, more subjective narrative reviews of literature, which are largely non-mathematical (i.e., some particular statistics may be mentioned but the results of the studies being reviewed are not mathematically synthesized).

■ TOPIC REVIEW

1. According to this topic, is it easy to find perfectly strict replications of previous studies?
2. What is one very important way that various studies on a given topic differ?
3. Computing a mean difference across studies that used measurement scales with different possible numbers of score points is meaningless. What is suggested in this topic to overcome this problem?

4. What is usually done when the studies to be used in a meta-analysis have different sample sizes?

5. Is *d* the only standardized measure of effect size used in meta-analytic studies? Explain.

■ DISCUSSION QUESTION

1. In this topic, a meta-analytic study that reported a weighted average value of $r = 0.48$ for the relationship between posttraumatic stress disorder and anger is cited. On the basis of what you know about correlation, how would you interpret the direction and strength of this relationship?

■ RESEARCH PLANNING

Reconsider your "Research Planning" answer from Topic 78 in light of what you learned in this topic. Has your answer changed? Explain.

■ NOTES

1. The mathematics of the weighting procedure for *r* are beyond the scope of this book.
2. LaFrance, M., Hecht, M.A., & Paluck, E.L. (2003). The contingent smile: A meta-analysis of sex differences in smiling. *Psychological Bulletin, 129*, 305–334.
3. Orth, U., & Wieland, E. (2006). Anger, hostility, and posttraumatic stress disorder in trauma-exposed adults: A meta-analysis. *Journal of Consulting and Clinical Psychology, 74*, 698–706.

META-ANALYSIS: STRENGTHS AND WEAKNESSES

Meta-analysis has both strengths and weaknesses. A major strength mentioned in the previous topic is that it produces results based on large combined samples—sometimes very large samples. The previous topic cited a meta-analysis of 162 studies that produced a mathematical synthesis involving 109,654 participants, which is a lot larger than the typical number in research reports in academic journals. Such very large samples yield very reliable (although not necessarily valid) results. However, if the studies subjected to a meta-analysis have serious methodological flaws (resulting in a lack of validity), then the mathematical synthesis of their results will also lack validity.

As indicated in Topic 78, a strength of meta-analysis is that it can be used to synthesize the results of studies conducted by *independent* researchers (i.e., researchers who are not working together). Whether or not meta-analysis is used, independent confirmation of results is an important standard that is applied when one is assessing the validity of the results.

An additional strength of meta-analysis is the objectivity of its conclusions.[1] After making subjective judgments regarding how to define a topic, how to search for relevant studies, and what criteria should be used to select studies from the available pool of potential studies, the remaining steps in a meta-analysis are mathematical, leading to an objectively obtained result (such as an average value of d or r). Note that in a traditional literature review, the conclusions are expressed in words. The phrasing, emphasis, and other characteristics of written communication are used to express the conclusions. The traditional review is not objective from a mathematical point of view.

A potential weakness occurs if a researcher is not careful in the selection of studies to include in a meta-analysis. Poor selection might produce results that are difficult to interpret (at best) or meaningless (at worst). For instance, a meta-analysis involving all studies of tutoring in reading regardless of grade level (from first grade through high school) would not be very helpful in reaching conclusions that have implications for program implementation at any given grade level. This is because different types of results might be obtained at different levels (e.g., tutoring might be more helpful at the primary level than at the high school level). When combined into one grand mean, the poor effectiveness at the high school level might cancel out much of the effectiveness at the primary level (by pulling the grand mean down).

One way to handle the problem of diversity across a set of studies is to establish criteria for the inclusion of studies on a topic in a meta-analysis. For instance, a researcher might include only those that meet criteria such as employment of teachers as tutors, use of tutoring sessions that last at least 30 minutes per session, and tutoring of only primary-grade students.

Another solution to the problem of diversity is to conduct multiple meta-analyses within a single meta-analytic project. For instance, a researcher might conduct three separate analyses: one for studies involving primary-grade students, one for those involving middle-school students, and a third for high school students. Comparing results of the three analyses would provide insights into the effectiveness of the programs at different grade levels.

In a report in which separate analyses are conducted for various subgroups, the variable on which the studies were divided into subgroups (e.g., the various grade levels) is called a *moderator variable* because it may moderate the results so that the results for subgroups are different from the grand combined result. The use of moderator variables is very common in published reports of meta-analyses.

A final potential weakness of meta-analysis stems from what is known as *publication bias*. Typically, researchers are looking for significant differences (and relationships). When they fail to find them, they may be inclined *not* to write reports on such studies for submission for publication. It is also possible that some journal editors may have a bias such that they tend to reject studies with insignificant results. Hence, the body of published research available on a topic for a meta-analysis might be biased toward studies that have statistically significant results. (A researcher conducting a meta-analysis, of course, wants to include all relevant studies, whether the differences are significant or not, in order to get an *overall* estimate of effectiveness.) A partial solution to this problem is for those conducting meta-analyses to search for studies that might be reported in dissertations, convention papers, government reports, and other nonjournal sources where there might not be as much bias against studies with statistically insignificant results.

Despite the potential weaknesses, meta-analysis is an important tool for gaining mathematical perspectives on the results of the studies on a research topic. It shows what can be obtained "objectively," which can be compared and contrasted with more subjective qualitative literature reviews on the same research topic.

■ TOPIC REVIEW

1. What makes the sample size a strength in the meta-analysis of the 162 studies?
2. According to this topic, is a "meta-analysis" or a "literature review" more objective?
3. One potential weakness in meta-analysis occurs if a researcher is not careful in what aspect of designing the meta-analysis?
4. In a report in which separate analyses are conducted for various subgroups, what is the variable on which the studies were divided into subgroups called?
5. What is a second weakness of meta-analyses that is not related to the individual researcher's design choices?

■ DISCUSSION QUESTIONS

1. Is meta-analysis objective? Explain the similarities and differences between a meta-analysis and a literature review.
2. Discuss samples in meta-analysis. How is it a strength and how is it a weakness? What does it mean to say that one problem in meta-analysis is with "diversity"? What are solutions to this problem?

■ RESEARCH PLANNING

On the basis of what you know about meta-analysis, would you be interested in conducting one in the near future? At some later point in your professional career? Explain.

■ NOTE

1. Quantitative researchers value and strive for objectivity, while qualitative researchers tend to question whether objectivity is obtainable. Thus, qualitative researchers challenge the feasibility and desirability of seeking complete objectivity in scientific research.

PART 10
Preparing Research Reports

This part of the book provides an overview of how to structure a research report. Topic 81 discusses the overall structure and order in which materials are typically presented in a research report. Topics 82 through 87 then break down each section of a traditional research report, providing more detail on the typical contents that are included in parts of the research report, and how they are presented. Translating these techniques for writing typical research reports to theses and dissertations is covered in Topic 88.

THE STRUCTURE OF A RESEARCH REPORT

This topic describes the structure of a typical research report. Elements of a standard research report are Title, Abstract, Introduction, Literature Review, Method, Results, and Discussion. Reports end with a References section listing all sources that have been used within the report. Each element is covered one by one below.

The first element is the **Title**. Title wording and other items to be placed on the title page are likely to vary based on the style guide used by journals or instructions from a professor or review committee. Most likely, the title page includes the author's name and affiliation at minimum. It may also include word count, pages, or other information. Be sure to check the applicable source for any specific instructions. A typical title is concise, consisting of about 10 to 15 words, and names the major variable(s). Populations of special interest may also be mentioned in a title. This can be seen in Example 1:

Example 1

Title of a research report: The Relationship Between Political Activism and Socioeconomic Status Among Asian American Voters

The title of this study states the main variables are (1) political activism and (2) socioeconomic status, and the population consists of Asian American voters. Notice that the title in Example 1 does *not* describe the results of the research. In most cases, this is appropriate because the results of research are usually too complex to summarize in a short title. The typical parts of a research report that follow Title are shown in Table 81.1.

Most research reports begin with an **Abstract**. This is a summary designed to give readers a brief overview of all parts of the report. Abstracts for journal submissions typically have word limits between 100 and 300 words. The goal of an abstract is to help researchers and students quickly determine whether the research is of interest to them. It often includes details about who is included in the study, the basic gist of the research question, its main components, the methods used to answer it, and a mention of the most important findings. Writing abstracts is covered in more detail in the next topic.

The abstract is followed by an **Introduction**. In short reports such as journal articles and term projects, the introduction contains the **Literature Review** (see Part 2 of this book on reviewing literature).[1] Preparing introductions and literature reviews for research reports is covered in Topic 83 in this book. There is often no main heading for the introduction; it begins immediately after the abstract. In longer reports, the introduction may provide an overview of the topic and its history, and the literature review may be labeled and stand on its own. Some Literature Review sections include subheadings that indicate

TABLE 81.1	The Typical Parts of a Research Report
Title	
Abstract	
Introduction	
Literature Review	
Method	
Participants	
Measures[1]	
Procedure (optional)	
Data Analysis (optional)	
Results	
Discussion	
References	

[1]Some authors of research reports use the term instrumentation instead of measures to refer to measurement tools.

specific topics of related literature that are being reviewed. Consider the length of your publication, or if you are submitting an article for publication, and review other articles as well as the author guidelines for specific journals when deciding how to label this section of your research report.

Following the introduction/literature review is the **Method** section, which usually has its own major heading. Three areas of the methods used are typically covered here: who participated in the research, what measures were used, and either what procedure was used to carry out or analyze the research (if experiments) or how the data was analyzed (in other forms of qualitative and quantitative research). These are typically covered in this order and given subheadings. Under the subheading *Participants*, researchers state the number of participants, how they were selected, and demographics deemed relevant, such as age and gender. Depending on the nature of the research, the sample may be compared with known parameters of the population, and many writers will create summary tables to help the reader visually see the composition of participants. Writing the description of the participants is described in more detail in Topic 84.

Measures is the next subsection under Method. Here the measurement tools used in the research are described. Quantitative researchers use highly structured measures and may focus on information about those measures that establish validity and reliability. Qualitative researchers use less structured measures, which may be described in this section, including how they were formulated. Some qualitative or quantitative papers may include the full measure (survey or semi-structured interview schedule) as an appendix to offer more information and greater transparency about the research process. Describing measures in quantitative and qualitative research reports is covered in Topic 85.

Procedure is an optional subsection under the main heading of Method. This subsection follows *Measures* and may be used to describe any physical steps taken by the researcher to conduct the research. For instance, if treatments were given in an experiment, the treatments could be described in detail in this subsection.

Data Analysis may be an additional subsection under the main heading of Method, in which the steps taken to analyze the data are described. This subsection is optional in quantitative research when standard statistical techniques are used, but it is usually needed for describing more about the type of qualitative research used (e.g., describing how grounded theory or consensual qualitative research was implemented to analyze the data; see Topics 48 and 49).

Results is the next major heading. Results present the data with commentary that explains what the data says. In quantitative results, this includes tables presenting the statistics results. Qualitative results may use visual representations of data, but are more likely to present the themes and quotes that support findings. Considerations in presenting the results of research are described in Topic 86.

In the final major heading, **Discussion**,[2] researchers move away from presenting the details of the findings, now focusing on their interpretations of the outcomes of their research and its significance. See Topic 87 for guidelines on writing the discussion. The **References** conclude a research report by citing all sources used in the report (see Appendix E and F for information on citing references.)

■ TOPIC REVIEW

1. Should a title describe the results of the research?
2. The title is usually followed by what?
3. A typical title contains about how many words?
4. Is *Participants* a "major heading" *or* a "subheading"?
5. The measurement tools are described in which subsection?
6. Is *Procedure* an optional subheading?
7. Researchers present their interpretations of the outcomes of their research under which major heading?

■ DISCUSSION QUESTION

1. Consider this title for a research report: "Improving Mathematics Achievement." In your opinion, is the title adequate? Explain what might improve it.

■ RESEARCH PLANNING

Examine a research article related to the topic of your research. Does it follow the *exact* structure described in this topic? Explain. (Note: This topic describes common practices frequently followed by researchers; variations in structure are often permitted by journal editors as well as professors supervising research conducted as term projects.)

■ NOTES

1. In a traditional thesis or dissertation, Chapter 1 is an introduction to the research problem (with a limited number of citations to literature), whereas Chapter 2 is a literature review.
2. In journal articles, some researchers use headings such as "Discussion and Conclusions" and "Summary, Discussion, and Implications."

TOPIC 82
WRITING ABSTRACTS

An abstract is an important summary of the research report. More people will read your abstract than your full paper, and their decision to read your report will be based in large part on the combination of your title and abstract. For this reason, the abstract should concisely present the important characteristics of the work and also exhibit good research writing. Journals often require relatively short abstracts, frequently limiting the number of words to no more than 250. The maximum word count for abstracts used in term papers, theses, and dissertations may vary.

Brief abstracts usually cover these three essential elements:

1. Research hypotheses, purposes, or questions. These may need to be abbreviated or summarized if they are extensive.
2. Highlights of the research methods, including mention of the participants and measures.
3. Highlights of the results.

Example 1 is an abstract with these three elements. The first sentence names the purpose. The second sentence mentions the participants and measures (e.g., interviews). The final sentences summarize the results.

Example 1

The purpose of this study was to determine the opinions of parents on the Community Drug Resistance Program (CDRP). A purposive sample of 36 parents of teenagers who participated in the program was selected to be interviewed individually. Three themes emerged from the interviews. First, all the parents strongly approved of the general purposes of the program. Second, most had little knowledge of the specific program activities. Third, all supported greater parental involvement in program implementation.

Note that specific results are usually reported only sparingly, if at all, in abstracts. In Example 1, the term *most* refers to an outcome in only general terms. An abstract should tell the readers enough to decide if they want to find out more about the specific results and the methods by which those results were reached.

If space permits, consider starting the abstract with some brief background material. For instance, Example 1 could start with: "The Community Drug Resistance Program (CDRP) was first funded by the Middletown city council three years ago and has strong community support."

Space permitting, any important distinctive characteristics of the study could be mentioned in the abstract. Typically, these are characteristics that were not present in previous studies and help to establish the reasons why a reader might find this paper uniquely useful. For instance, in Example 1, the author might include as part of the background information: "None of the previous evaluations included the views of parents."

A longer abstract might end with a summary of the conclusions. For instance, Example 1 might end with: "Program directors should increase their efforts to involve parents and inform them of specific program activities."

Example 2 shows what Example 1 would look like with these additional elements.

Example 2

An abstract with five elements: The Community Drug Resistance Program (CDRP) was first funded by the Middletown city council three years ago and has strong community support. However, none of the previous evaluations included the views of parents. The purpose of this study was to determine the opinions of parents on the CDRP. A purposive sample of 36 parents of teenagers who participated in the program was selected to be interviewed individually. Three themes emerged from the interviews. First, all the parents strongly approved of the general purposes of the program. Second, most had little knowledge of the specific program activities. Third, all supported greater parental involvement in program implementation. Program directors should increase their efforts to involve parents and inform them of specific program activities.

Consider including bold subheadings to identify the various elements in the abstract. This is done in Example 3.

Example 3

An abstract with five elements identified with bold subheadings: **Background:** The Community Drug Resistance Program (CDRP) was first funded by the city council three years ago and has strong community support. However, none of the previous evaluations included the views of parents. **Purpose:** The purpose of this study was to determine the opinions of parents on the CDRP. **Method:** A purposive sample of 36 parents of teenagers who participated in the program was selected to be interviewed individually. **Results:** Three themes emerged from the interviews. First, all the parents strongly approved of the general purposes of the program. Second, most had little knowledge of the specific program activities. Third, all supported greater parental involvement in program implementation. **Conclusion:** Program directors should increase their efforts to involve parents and inform them of specific program activities.

Note that subheadings are required by some journals that publish research. In general, the longer the abstract, the more desirable it is to use subheadings. Appendix D shows five effective abstracts. Note that they may differ somewhat from the recommendations made here, which is permissible.

■ TOPIC REVIEW

1. Journals often require relatively short abstracts, often limiting the number of words to no more than how many?
2. What is the first of the three essential elements in an abstract?

3. What is the last of the three essential elements in an abstract?
4. If background material is included, should it be the first *or* last element in an abstract?
5. Is it important to include specific statistical results in abstracts?
6. Are bold subheadings always required in abstracts?

■ DISCUSSION QUESTIONS

1. Examine the abstracts in Appendix D. Note that the second one does not have bold subheadings. In your opinion, would this abstract be improved by the addition of bold subheadings? Explain.
2. Select one of the abstracts in Appendix D. Is it consistent with the suggestions made in this topic? What are its strengths and weaknesses, if any?

■ RESEARCH PLANNING

Examine the abstract for a research article related to the topic of your research. Is it consistent with the suggestions made in this topic? What are its strengths and weaknesses? Bring it to class for discussion.

INTRODUCTION AND LITERATURE REVIEW

Typically, the research report launches into the introduction of the topic and proceeds to review the literature immediately following the abstract, without a main heading. Most journals use various formatting techniques to set the abstract separately from the rest of the article, directly under the title and author information so the distinction from the body of the article is obvious.

Introductory comments are commonly integrated with the literature review. In fact, most researchers cite literature in their first paragraph.[1] In Part 2, and particularly in Topics 14 through 17, there was a discussion on how to summarize the literature, including ways to start a Review section, synthesize the findings, and connect the literature to the current study. These principles apply to the creation of the literature review at the outset of a project or for a proposal, and they can also be useful when writing a research report.

The first purpose of an integrated introduction and literature review is to identify the research problem area. The second purpose is to establish its importance. The first paragraphs of an introduction should be reasonably specific to the research problem, whether or not they are supported by citations to literature. Topic 14 provided examples for beginning the literature review, and many of the same principles apply to the introduction of a research report. As a reminder, one effective way to establish the importance of a problem is to cite statistics indicating its prevalence. However, now that you are not only reviewing literature, but are introducing your research in the context of the literature, it is important to draw attention to the main areas that your discussion of your data will speak to.

For instance, if the area of your research examines childhood obesity among 6–12 year olds in the United States, the first sentence in Example 1 is too global. An improved version is shown in Example 2.

Example 1

Beginning of a research report (too broad for the topic): Obesity is a major public health concern in all industrial nations and is an important threat to the well-being of millions. Worldwide, rates of obesity range from. . .

Example 2

Beginning of a research report (improved; more specific): Childhood obesity is a major public health concern in the United States, where rates of obesity for children 6 to 12 years of age have been estimated to range from. . .

Note that specific statistics should be cited sparingly. Cite only those that are most relevant and can be easily understood out of the context of the original research reports. Readers can consult the original sources for additional statistical details.

Another way to establish the importance of a problem is to describe the severity of its impact on individuals. For instance, a rare mental disease may affect relatively few individuals (low prevalence), yet have a devastating impact on those individuals. The severity of the impact may serve as a justification for researching a problem, even if the problem is not widespread. Again, think about how to begin by not only focusing on general facts about this issue, or what the literature says about it. Instead, you want to introduce the report so that the data of your report can respond. If, at the beginning, you describe a problem as rare but severe in its impact, your own results should also speak to this point, either by agreeing and expanding, or by contrasting what you found with what you expected to find based on the literature.

As Topic 16 explained, a literature review should not consist of a series of summaries of previously published studies. Instead, generalizations about findings (i.e., the *trends* found in the research) should be stated, with references supporting them grouped together. Example 3 illustrates how this might be done.

Example 3

Grouping references for a generalization: Several studies have indicated the weak effects of the Doe Drug Reduction Intervention Program when it is used with adolescents (Smith, 2012; Jones, 2010; Black, 2011).

Now that you have completed your research and you are ready to report your results, it is time to review that earlier work in compiling a literature review. Consider the relationship it has to your final project and its findings. It is very important to be concise in your report, and to do so, you want to present the findings as completely as possible that relate closely to your topic. You do not want to bias your report by only reporting on literature that supports your points or your findings. However, you do want to ensure that you stay focused on your topic. It is easy to wander into facts that are too general or not directly related to your particular variables or findings because they seem interesting. You will have to use judgment to review and remove facts that are interesting, but ultimately are not directly related to your topic.

It is acceptable to discuss selected studies in detail if they are closely related to your work. For instance, if your work is directly responding to another work by replicating the study, or by arguing that it is incorrect or incomplete, it might be appropriate to include in-depth coverage. In most cases, if your report is not responding directly in some way to the work, it is better to summarize.

Many research projects are designed to fill gaps in knowledge on a particular topic. When this is the case, it is important to explicitly point out those gaps in the literature review. This is illustrated in Example 4.

Example 4

Pointing out a gap in the literature (after citing literature to establish that Latino adolescents are subject to stress due to discrimination, the authors state): However, few studies have examined how Latino adolescents cope with discrimination, whether coping strategies might protect against the negative effects of perceived discrimination, and factors that promote the use of effective coping strategies.[2]

If the literature does not cover your area of research and has little of direct relevance to your study, you can describe areas of overlap, showing where they fall short in linking together the aspects you are investigating, and then emphasize the importance of your research in filling a gap.

A combined introduction/literature review should end with a statement of the specific research hypotheses, purposes, and/or questions (see Topic 24). When there are several of them, they should be numbered or lettered, as in Example 5. Note that they should flow logically from the introductory material.

Example 5

Numbered hypotheses at the conclusion of the introduction/literature review: In light of the research findings described above, these hypotheses were formulated to be tested in the current research: (1) College students who are more involved in extracurricular activities consume less alcohol, (2) have fewer friends who binge drink, (3) have. . .

Taken together, the elements you include in the introduction and literature review should concisely describe the research problem area and its importance.

■ TOPIC REVIEW

1. Does a typical research report have the main heading **Introduction**?
2. What is the first function of an integrated introduction and literature review?
3. In this topic, two ways to establish the importance of a problem are mentioned. The first is to cite statistics. What is the second way?
4. Should a literature review consist of a series of summaries of previously published studies?
5. Should statistics be cited in an introduction/literature review?
6. What should a combined introduction/literature review end with?

■ DISCUSSION QUESTION

1. Examine a research article to determine whether the introduction/literature review is consistent with the recommendations in this topic. Describe any consistencies and inconsistencies.

■ RESEARCH PLANNING

To what extent has the material in this topic helped to prepare you for writing an introduction/literature review? What are three points that are in your research findings? How does your literature review introduce the reader to these points?

Look for places where you can improve the specificity of your literature review. Where does it get too general or wander off of the topic you will discuss in the research findings?

■ NOTES

1. In a typical thesis or dissertation, Chapter 1 is an introduction, with few literature citations, while Chapter 2 is a comprehensive literature review.
2. Umaña-Taylor, A. J., Vargas-Chanes, D., Garcia, C.D., & Gonzales-Backen, M. (2008). A longitudinal examination of Latino adolescents' ethnic identity, coping with discrimination, and self-esteem. *Journal of Early Adolescence*, *28*, 16–50.

DESCRIBING PARTICIPANTS

In research reports, the subheading *Participants* appears immediately under the main heading of **Method** (see the outline in Topic 81). This section will provide information about the people who participated in the study and how they were selected.

The number of participants should be given, as well as the demographics that have been identified as relevant to the study because they played a role in the research question, the sampling strategy, or the variables that were used. In qualitative research, it may help to give an overview of the similarity and diversity of those included in the sample.

Example 1

Brief description of participants: A sample of 120 adolescents (12–16 years old, $m = 14.55$) participated in the study. There were 70 males and 50 females.

The rationale for the sample selection and the method of recruitment is typically summarized in this section (e.g., classified ads in a college newspaper or an offer of extra credit to students enrolled in a sociology course). Information should be included about the type of sample and the major decisions that informed the sampling strategy. If a *sample of convenience* (also called a *convenience sample*) is used, this should be mentioned (see Topic 25). If *informed consent* was obtained, this should also be mentioned.

Example 2 shows an expanded version of Example 1, based on the above information.

Example 2

Expanded description of participants (bold added for emphasis): All 250 students in a local middle school were **recruited** through letters mailed to their parents. Attached to the letters were **informed consent** forms for parents to sign if they agreed to allow their children to participate. Of the 250 parents, 120 returned the consent forms (a **48% response rate**), which resulted in a **convenience sample** of 120 adolescents (12–16 years old, $m = 14.55$), consisting of 70 males and 50 females.

When a large number of demographics are to be reported, researchers should consider reporting them in a statistical table. Such a table is especially important if two or more distinct groups were compared in a study. For instance, in a study comparing the academic achievement of girls attending a charter school with that of girls attending a traditional school, the demographics might be presented in a table such as the one in Example 3, where "free lunch" is an indicator of socioeconomic status because family income determines its availability. Tables are efficient for the presentation of such information, and they help readers to spot important differences. For instance, the "free lunch" difference (20% vs. 42%) stands out in the tabular presentation in Example 3 (Table 84.1).[1]

Example 3

TABLE 84.1	**Sample Demographics by Charter and Traditional School Attendance**	
	Charter	**Traditional**
Age	*m* = 8.2	*m* = 8.8
Age range	7–10	7–11
Free lunch (yes)	20%	42%
Intact family (yes)	78%	73%
Ethnicity		
Caucasian	75%	70%
African American	15%	20%
Asian	6%	5%
Other	4%	5%

The response rate, if known, should be indicated. This is important because those who respond (known as *volunteers*) may be quite different from those who do not respond (see Topic 26). If the relationship of the sample to the population is relevant to discuss, and population statistics are available for the group being researched, the researcher may provide a table comparing the demographics of the sample and population. This can help show important similarities or departures that will play a role in the discussion of results.

Quantitative researchers emphasize *random selection* of participants from populations (see Topics 26 and 27). Thus, if random selection has been used in a quantitative study, it is important to mention it.

Qualitative researchers often employ *purposive samples*. As indicated in Topic 29, researchers who use this type of sample deliberately select individuals who they think might be rich sources of information on a particular research topic. Researchers who employ purposive sampling should explain their reasoning and the steps they took to implement it (see Topic 33). Without information of this type, readers are likely to assume that a *sample of convenience* (not a purposive sample) was used.

If *saturation* was used to determine sample size in a qualitative study, this should be indicated (see Topics 29 and 33 for information on saturation). While limitations of a study due to poor sampling might be mentioned under *Participants*, researchers usually note any limitations of the study in the **Discussion** section of their research reports. The *Participants* portion of the paper should focus on the details relevant to how the sample was selected and important explanations of the participants in the sample as a group. The next sections will discuss results, and the Discussion will offer opportunity for interpretation. When in doubt, it can be very useful to find other articles that used similar methods and sampling techniques and review them as examples of the correct level of detail and types of information expected.

TOPIC REVIEW

1. The subheading *Participants* appears immediately under what main heading?
2. Should the method of recruitment be described under *Participants*?
3. Is it appropriate to mention informed consent under *Participants*?
4. When is it especially important to use a table to report demographics?
5. Are "qualitative" *or* "quantitative" researchers more likely to use purposive sampling?
6. Is saturation more likely to be mentioned in a report on "qualitative research" *or* "quantitative research"?

DISCUSSION QUESTION

1. Consider a researcher who has studied the school achievement of children who reside with their parents in a shelter for the homeless. Name two demographics that might be highly relevant and two that would be less relevant for inclusion in a research report on this topic.

RESEARCH PLANNING

Examine a research article related to the topic of your research. Is the description of the participants completely consistent with the recommendations in this topic?

NOTE

1. Note that some researchers present detailed information on demographics in the Results section.

DESCRIBING MEASURES

When a quantitative researcher uses a previously published measure, he or she should cite it and include a reference. For instance, a published achievement test would be cited and included in the reference list as a book, where the title of the test is equivalent to the title of a book (see APA guidelines in Appendix E).

Many specialized measures are published only in the sense that they were included in journal articles. When one of these has been used, the original source should be cited, as is done in Example 1.

Example 1

The Trait Forgivingness Scale (TFS; Berry, Worthington, O'Connor, Parrott, & Wade, 2005) assesses disposition to forgive. A sample item is, 'There are some things for which I could never forgive even a loved one.' Previous alphas range from .71 to .81, and construct validity has been established with constructs such as avoidance following a hurtful event.[1]

Notice in Example 1 the authors (1) name the trait the scale is designed to measure (i.e., disposition to forgive), (2) provide a sample item, and (3) indicate that reliability (i.e., alphas) and validity have been established. All three elements are desirable in the description of a measure used in quantitative research. When space permits, more detailed descriptions of these three elements might be provided.

When a measure has been widely used, this should be noted (e.g., "the measure has been widely used by other researchers in a variety of settings"). This indicates that other researchers have found the measure useful.

Quantitative researchers may also construct new measures for a particular research project. Because information on them is not available elsewhere, it is especially important for the researcher to provide detailed information on the measure in the research report. Depending on the nature of the report, the full measure may be added as an appendix to create further transparency.

Qualitative researchers usually use less structured measures than quantitative researchers, which may include interviews of different types (see Topic 46 to review), focus groups, and fieldwork in the form of participant or nonparticipant observation (see Topic 47 to review). Qualitative researchers often discuss their position in relation to the field as an entry point to discuss their method(s) of data collection. This is often accompanied with information about the types of interviews, focus groups, or observations that were used. If interviews were semi-structured or structured, or focus groups were used, they may include the scripts as an appendix to increase transparency into the process. Details about the range of interview lengths and the methods used to collect them (such as audiotaping and transcribing) are explained, as are any specific details about who was present during the interview and where it was held. If observations were used, this section also is likely to include the number of locations and relevant measures for the amount of time or number of visits during which observations took place.

Example 2 shows how researchers briefly described the semi-structured interview process used in their study of mothers learning to support children with Type 1 diabetes mellitus (T1DM):

Example 2

The in-depth, audio-recorded interviews were carried out at participants' homes and only the mother was invited. An open and accepting interview style based on phenomenology principles was used. The interview questions focused on how these mothers assisted their children's life adjustment at school, specifically with respect to T1DM. Each interview began with the question: 'What is your experience when assisting your child's life adjustment at school?' Facilitative techniques (e.g., 'Hmm' and 'Could you describe it more?') were used to obtain the most complete description possible. On average, interviews lasted approximately one hour.[2]

Notice in Example 2 the authors (1) state where the interviews were conducted and who was present, (2) describe the focus of the questions, (3) provide a sample question as well as sample prompts (e.g., "Hmm"), and (4) indicate how long the interviews lasted. All of these are desirable elements.

The authors in Example 2 might also include background information on the interviewer(s), such as whether they were women, mothers, or had children with Type 1 diabetes. When describing measures for focus groups, researchers should cover the same points as in Example 2 above. In addition, they should indicate how many focus groups were used and how many participants were included in each group. When multiple methods are used, the authors may explain their logic for doing so and include information about the order in which the different measures were collected.

In qualitative research, analysis often takes place simultaneously with the collection of data. The role of analysis may be mentioned in this section, especially if emergent categories or themes served as the impetus to adjust data collection measures or methods. However, the analytical techniques used are typically discussed in the next section, Results.

■ TOPIC REVIEW

1. Does Example 1 in this topic mention validity? If so, which type of validity is mentioned?
2. If a measure has been widely used, should this fact be mentioned?
3. When is it especially important for quantitative researchers to provide detailed information on the measures?
4. If semistructured interviews have been used, the researcher is relieved of the responsibility to describe them in detail. Is this statement true *or* false?

5. Is it appropriate to provide background information on the interviewer when semistructured interviews are used in the collection of data?

6. When focus groups are used, should the researcher indicate how many participants were in each group?

■ DISCUSSION QUESTION

1. In your opinion, how important is it for researchers to provide the sample questions from their measures?

■ RESEARCH PLANNING

Examine a research article related to the topic of your research. Is the description of the measures completely consistent with the recommendations in this topic?

■ NOTES

1. Hodgson, L.K., & Wertheim, E.H. (2007). Does good emotion management aid forgiving? Multiple dimensions of empathy, emotion management, and forgiveness of self and others. *Journal of Social and Personal Relationships, 24,* 931–949.

2. Lin, H.-P., Mu, P.-F., & Lee, Y.-J. (2008). Mothers' experience supporting life adjustment in children with T1DM. *Western Journal of Nursing Research, 30,* 96–110.

REPORTING RESEARCH RESULTS

The **Results** section is where the specific outcomes of the research project are presented. This is the place to report specific findings and summaries of data.

When research has tested a hypothesis or multiple hypotheses, these are restated and used to organize the presentation of results. It is usually best to report the results separately for each hypothesis, purpose, or question in the order in which they were introduced. For instance, if there were two hypotheses, restate the first one, and present the data for it. Then, restate the second hypothesis, and present the data for that one.

In reports of quantitative research, researchers typically do not describe the steps required to complete the statistical analyses. The researcher will simply report the means and standard deviations relating to a hypothesis without discussing computational details. The statistical tests that were used and the program in which they were analyzed may be identified here or in the Methods section. In these reports, descriptive statistics (e.g., mean, standard deviation, and percentage) are reported first, followed by the results of tests of statistical significance (e.g., chi-square, t-test, and ANOVA). This is illustrated in Example 1. Note that when there are hypotheses, the researcher should explicitly state whether each hypothesis was supported by the data.

Example 1

Beginning of the Results section in a quantitative research report: The first hypothesis was that participants who attended the extended training sessions would report more satisfaction with the program than those who attended the abbreviated sessions. The mean satisfaction score for the extended group was higher ($m = 24.00$, $sd = 1.50$) than the mean for the abbreviated group ($m = 22.00$, $sd = 1.40$). The difference between the two means is statistically significant at the .05 level ($t = 3.30$, $df = 21$). Thus, the first hypothesis was supported. The second hypothesis was that participants. . .

When there are a number of related statistics to report, it is usually best to present them in a table (instead of reporting them in sentences). Example 2 shows a table with a number of descriptive statistics. Highlights of the information displayed in statistical tables should be described in the Results section with statements such as "The means in Table 86.1 show that the supervised practice group outperformed the unsupervised practice and control groups."

In the Results section, the statistics are described and contextualized in relation to the research question or hypotheses, but the researcher will reserve for the **Discussion** section any generalizing from the data or analysis of the overall meaning of the results. The Results section is used to offer a presentation of the data and for providing context about specific results that may require elaboration.

Example 2

TABLE 86.1 **Posttest Statistics for Three Groups**			
Group	*n*	*m*	*sd*
Supervised practice	21	55.78	8.27
Unsupervised practice	20	49.02	7.66
Control group	22	46.35	9.36

In qualitative research, the Results section differs in a number of respects. First, there is usually a discussion of the steps taken to analyze the data. This may be placed under a subheading such as *Data Analysis* (see the outline in the first column of Topic 81).[1] Here, the method of analysis (such as grounded theory or consensual qualitative research) should be named and the steps taken to implement the method described (e.g., how many coders were used and how a consensus was reached).

Take as an example a qualitative study on why people continue to use complementary and alternative medicine (CAM).[2] In this study, the introduction/literature review explains that the aim of the study is to explore why CAM consumers continue or end their use of a CAM practice. It situated this question as unique and relevant. Then the Methods section explained the approach (fieldwork) where the data was collected and further defined what treatments were included in this study of CAM (homeopathy and herbalism, for instance). It provided facts about the locations for data collection that argued for their appropriateness. A subsection also covered informed consent processes that were used in the study under the subheading *Ethics*. Next, a subsection on data generation and collection provided details on the amount of time and the times of day spent in the data collection locations. That subsection also explained the research approach for collecting fieldwork and interviews, including the logic for using these data collection techniques based on the goals of the research. It outlines the number of people who were interviewed, their demographics, and the treatment they were receiving. The data analysis follows, explaining the techniques used:

Example 3

Audiotapes were transcribed verbatim (and transcriptions reviewed for accuracy) and field notes were typed up both during and immediately following the fieldwork. Atlas.ti (Scientific Software Development, GmBH, Berlin, Germany) [a qualitative data analysis program] was used to facilitate data organization, management, and analysis. The analysis began during the fieldwork when initial impressions of both potential themes and the direction of the research were noted. Following the fieldwork and a period of data immersion, the textual data were first analyzed using inductive open coding[. . . .] As the analysis progressed other techniques were also employed, including axial coding. [. . .] In the final stages of analysis, the aim was to develop process-oriented themes that answered the analytic question, "what is happening here?" Three main process-oriented themes were developed that could explain the bulk of the data and provide insights into consumers' behavior.

After the researchers in Example 3 finish describing the data analysis, the Results section goes on to present each theme and describe it in greater detail, supported with quotations that provide illustrations of the theme in the participants' words. Qualitative researchers do not present statistics but may use different tables or graphs to illustrate the primary themes or theories. The Results section of a qualitative research report typically concludes in this manner, using each theme as a subheading within the Results section with verbatim quotations from participants that illustrate its meaning. Researchers save their own overarching explanation of the meaning of their findings for the Discussion section.

■ TOPIC REVIEW

1. For research that has more than one hypothesis, purpose, or question, is it usually best to report the results for each one separately? If so, in what order?
2. In reports on *quantitative research*, do researchers typically indicate how the statistical results were computed (e.g., do they name the statistical computer program used)?
3. Should "descriptive statistics" *or* "results of tests of statistical significance" be reported first?
4. When statistical tables are included in a Results section, which of the following is true?
   A. The tables should be presented without commentary.
   B. Highlights of the contents of statistical tables should be mentioned.
5. Is a subsection titled Data Analysis more likely to appear in reports of "quantitative research" *or* "qualitative research"?
6. Are verbatim quotations more likely to appear in reports of "quantitative research" *or* "qualitative research"?
7. Do reports of "quantitative research" *or* "qualitative research" tend to have shorter Results sections?

■ DISCUSSION QUESTIONS

1. Locate a published report of quantitative research in a peer-reviewed publication within your discipline. Examine it to answer these questions: What statistics are reported and how are they organized? How does the text in the Results section address the information in the tables? Note the differences in the content covered in the Methods, Results, and Discussion portions of the paper. Did the paper include detailed information in these areas?
2. Locate a published report of qualitative research in a peer-reviewed publication within your discipline. Examine it to answer these questions: Is the Results section organized around themes? Does the Results section contain verbatim quotations from participants? Note the differences in the content covered in the Methods, Results, and Discussion portions of the paper. Did the paper include detailed information in these areas?

■ RESEARCH PLANNING

Examine research articles that use similar methods. Look for topics similar to your own, and look at different topics within journals that might interest you for publication. How is the organization of the Results section in the article similar to the organization you plan to use?

■ NOTES

1. This subsection is placed under "Method," just above the Results section. It is seldom included in reports on quantitative research when standard statistical methods have been used.
2. Bishop, F., Yardley, L., & Lewith, G.T. (2010). Why consumers maintain complementary and alternative medicine use: A qualitative study. *The Journal of Alternative and Complementary Medicine, 16*(2), 175–182.

WRITING THE DISCUSSION

The last part of the body of a research report is the **Discussion**.[1] This is the place where the researchers explain the overarching meaning of their project. The introduction and literature review began the project by framing the question, its meaning, and how it fits with prior published research. The rest of the sections leading up to the discussion provided all the necessary documentation to explain details about the questions, the approach used to answer it, the participants, the measures through which data was collected, the method of data analysis, and the meaning of variables or themes. The details of the data itself have been presented in the Results section, with explanations as needed to understand it. Now, in the Discussion section, the author does not need to account for these details but can simply describe the relevance and significance of the overall findings.

While there are many ways in which a Discussion section may be organized, certain types of information are usually included. A good way to begin is to restate the *original purposes of the research*, which may have been stated as research questions, purposes, or hypotheses. Next, indicate the extent to which the purposes were achieved as represented by the *research results*. Example 1 shows how the first two elements in a discussion might be presented. Note that specific statistics usually do not need to be presented here because a reader can refer to the Results section for them.

Example 1

Beginning of a Discussion section: The purpose of this study was to test three hypotheses regarding the relationship between stress processes and socioeconomic health disparities. The first hypothesis was that stress processes would be directly related to health disparities in a sample of U.S. adults at midlife. This hypothesis was strongly supported by the data. The second hypothesis was. . .

Notice that the researcher who wrote Example 1 indicated that the hypothesis was "strongly supported." If a researcher knows of serious methodological weaknesses in the execution of the study *or* if the effect size is small (see Topics 75–77), more tentative language should be used, such as "The data offer limited support for the first hypothesis." In qualitative studies, the Discussion section follows a similar path. Researchers may begin the discussion by restating the themes and their relation to one another and relative strength, and then describe the theory that has emerged or is supported by the themes.

At this point, it is appropriate for either qualitative or quantitative studies to briefly compare and contrast their results with those reported in the literature review (e.g., "The support for this hypothesis is consistent with the results in a prior survey by Doe [2012]"). If any results of the current study are surprising in light of the information in the literature review, this should also be pointed out. For instance, a researcher might state, "The failure of the data to support the hypothesis for young children is surprising in light of the strong support for the hypothesis in the earlier experiment by Jones (2011), in which adolescents participated. A possible explanation for this inconsistency is. . ."

When the results have practical *implications*, these should be explicitly stated, and the researcher should indicate what actions a particular person, group, or organization should perform. In Example 2, the organization is "public health agencies," and the action is "providing bilingual diabetes outreach programs."

Example 2

Practical implications in a Discussion section: The low rate of compliance by the Hispanic adults, most of whom were born in Mexico, may be due to language interference. Because many of these participants might not be fluent in English, public health agencies should consider providing bilingual diabetes outreach programs.

The Discussion section is an appropriate place to describe *limitations* (i.e., methodological weaknesses) and to indicate how the limitations might affect interpretations of the results. Although typical limitations are in sampling and measurement, a variety of other methodological problems may have affected the results and should be considered in their interpretation. Example 3 indicates the nature of the limitation in sampling *and* its potential impact on the results.

Example 3

Sampling limitation in a Discussion section: The volunteer sample for this survey consisted of disproportionately high middle- and high-socioeconomic-status individuals. Thus, the need for assistance in acquiring healthy food resources (e.g., fruits and vegetables) may have been underestimated in this study.

In the Discussion section, it is also appropriate to suggest directions for *future research*. Such suggestions should be specific because it is of little value to consumers of research to simply state that "more research is needed." Example 4 shows a discussion of future research. Notice that the suggestion is specific (i.e., use of a more limited vocabulary).

Example 4

Directions for future research in a Discussion section: Because participant feedback indicates that some participants found the questionnaire difficult to comprehend, researchers should consider using a more limited vocabulary when constructing questionnaires during future research on this topic.

If a Discussion section is long, researchers sometimes include subheadings to guide readers. On the basis of the above material, here are subheadings that might be used in the Discussion section:

Research purposes and results
Implications
Limitations
Directions for future research

The Discussion section distills the major findings and draws the deeper connections of this report's relevance to the discipline and to the part of the world under study. The entire process has led up to being able to make claims in this part of the paper. It is important to ensure that the claims are supported by the data, and the generalizations are appropriate to the data that was presented.

■ TOPIC REVIEW

1. What is the primary purpose of the Discussion portion of the report?
2. The Discussion section should begin with a reference to what?
3. Is it usually important to cite specific statistics when discussing research results in the Discussion section?
4. True or false: Discussion is the section of the report where the researcher compares and contrasts the results with studies that were reported in the literature review.
5. When discussing limitations, it is appropriate to indicate how the limitations might affect what?
6. If a Discussion section is long, researchers sometimes include what?

■ DISCUSSION QUESTION

1. Suppose a researcher only stated "More research is needed" in a discussion of future directions for research. How might they improve upon this statement?

■ RESEARCH PLANNING

In the Discussion section of your research report, do you plan to include all the elements discussed in this topic? Start with the generic outline provided at the end of the topic, and add the names of the specific items you will discuss in this section.

■ NOTE

1. In some research journals, this part is called "Conclusions." Other variations, such as "Discussion and Conclusions," may be found.

PREPARING THESES AND DISSERTATIONS

The beginning topics in this book mentioned that research involves making many decisions and documenting them. This is when that work comes to bear fruit. In many ways, the thesis or dissertation is a report that presents the research question and then formally collects and reports on the research decisions made, organizes the data that was documented, and summarizes the findings and their implications.

Theses and dissertations contain the same sections that are outlined in Topic 81 and elaborated upon in Topics 82–87. Because theses and dissertations are longer works than other ways of presenting research, more space is devoted to covering each of the topics already mentioned. Typically, this means that what would be a heading and a few paragraphs in a report comprises its own section in a thesis, or chapter in a dissertation. For this topic, we will discuss the lengthier sections as chapters even though most theses are divided into sections rather than chapters.

Longer report styles have the advantage of more space and opportunity to elaborate on the data, methods, and findings with less pressure to be ruthlessly concise. However, providing more detail and elaborating at greater length on theories, findings, and their implications can require much more work and effort.

In a thesis or dissertation, Chapter 1 is the introduction and is followed by the literature review in Chapter 2 (see Topics 12–19 and 83 for information on writing literature reviews).[1] Chapter 1 typically starts by introducing the problem area for the research and the reasons why it is important. In many cases of qualitative or mixed methods topics, it begins with a narrative that encapsulates many of the project's themes, followed by a brief explanation of how the themes are encapsulated in this narrative. Because the introduction is the researcher's overview of the topic and establishes the topic's importance, the citation of literature is only used to support statistics (e.g., "up to 59% of adults are estimated to have a plan for emergencies") and to attribute direct quotations to their sources. The vast majority of the introduction should be in the writer's own words, and direct quotations should be used sparingly to avoid interrupting the flow and voice of the writer.

Although Chapter 1 should contain few references, it may mention the literature in the Chapter 2 literature review. For instance, when establishing the importance of the problem area being defined in Chapter 1, a writer might make statements such as "As the literature review in Chapter 2 indicates, this problem is pervasive throughout populations of homeless injection-drug users in urban areas." The researcher might also mention Chapter 2 in the course of Chapter 1 to relate that gaps in the literature will be described in detail in the literature review.

Any *theories* underlying the research should be briefly described in Chapter 1. The writer should indicate clearly how the current research is related to the theory or theories (see Topic 3). Note that a detailed discussion of the literature on relevant theories should be presented in Chapter 2. Chapter 1 should end with an explicit statement of the research purposes, hypotheses, or questions. When there is more than one, they should be numbered (e.g., Hypothesis 1: Participants who. . .).

After the researcher has introduced the problem area, establishing its importance and indicating its theoretical basis, an overview of the research approach *and* the rationale for using it should be presented in Chapter 3. For instance, why was survey research selected as the approach (e.g., "to establish the incidence of binge drinking at ABC College")? Why was a qualitative research approach selected (e.g., "to gather in-depth information from the participants' perspectives, which has hitherto not been obtained")?

After the introductory chapter, the literature review, and a description of the methods used, additional chapters vary but typically consist of 2 to 4 chapters based on the results, followed by a concluding chapter that summarizes and contextualizes the meaning of the results that have been reported.

In addition to having a separate introductory chapter, theses and dissertations also differ from most other types of research reports in terms of the level of comprehensiveness and detail expected. This is because a thesis or dissertation is, in effect, a cumulative take-home examination in which students are expected to demonstrate a high level of ability to understand, organize, and present complex material.

To demonstrate an in-depth understanding of the material, writers should be highly *reflective* and *critical*. For instance, when discussing the design selected for an experiment, a researcher could reflect on the merits and limitations of the particular design employed in the study. Someone who conducted quantitative research might compare and contrast various measures (e.g., self-concept scales) and indicate the rationale for selecting one over the others for use in the thesis/dissertation research.

The typical length of theses and dissertations intimidates many students. An effective technique for managing the fear of composing a long document is to use outlines and write small sections at a time (e.g., the description of a small group of related studies for the literature review). Writing small sections, which can later be pieced together and revised for flow, makes the task manageable, while using an outline can help to create a sense of the bigger picture order of the content.

When students first become aware of the length expected in theses and dissertations, they are sometimes tempted to meet the requirement by writing a long literature review consisting of detailed summaries of previous research, with the summaries simply strung together in sequence. As indicated in Topics 17 and 83, this is inappropriate because it fails to organize the literature and to create a synthesis.

Despite the restriction on stringing together summaries of previous research, a long, detailed literature review can be created using the following technique. First, arrange studies into the smallest meaningful groups (e.g., differentiate the three studies using adolescents as participants from the two studies using adults). For each group, indicate the general nature of the findings, whether the findings are consistent from one study to the other, and any methodological flaws, especially ones that the studies in the group have in common (e.g., all studies using adults as participants used volunteer samples). Finally, select one study from each group to discuss in greater detail. The selection is usually based on which study is judged especially strong in terms of its research methodology, although the discussion will cover both its strengths and weaknesses.

There are many good resources out there on completing theses and dissertations, from organizing the writing process to avoiding writer's block. Consider resources that speak most to your style and your particular concerns. However, there is no greater teacher than to review other theses and dissertations in your field that are a part of most university libraries. Check out a few that are from your disciplinary area and that use similar methods to yours, but preferably on different topics. Review them to see how the writing is structured, paying careful attention to what order materials are covered in, the headings that are used, and the details that are included in each section. While you by no means need to replicate their decisions, it can help to have an example on hand to identify the decisions you need to make, or help to inspire you when you feel stuck. Dissertations and theses have unique characteristics. Often, students have not encountered them as readers before, so their structure is not familiar. For this reason, it can really help to see what a finished product is supposed to look like. Luckily, academic libraries offer copies either online or on the shelf of theses and dissertations that have been completed at that institution.

Lastly, be sure to check early and closely the requirements that are posted for your particular department and school. These likely include paperwork that must be filled out, fees, and specific formatting instructions for providing acceptable theses and dissertations to the school.

■ TOPIC REVIEW

1. What should the first chapter of a dissertation (or first section of a thesis) cover?
2. How often should writers use direct quotations in the first chapter of a dissertation?
3. Is it permissible in Chapter 1 to refer to the literature review in Chapter 2?
4. Which chapter should contain a detailed discussion of the literature on related theories?
5. In Chapter 1, after the researcher has introduced the problem area, establishing its importance and indicating its theoretical basis, what should be presented?
6. Is it ever appropriate in a literature review to discuss one study in greater detail than others?

■ DISCUSSION QUESTION

1. What is your opinion of the suggestion to concentrate on the composition of small sections as a way to manage the writing of a thesis or dissertation? Have you ever used this technique when writing a long paper?

■ RESEARCH PLANNING

Will you be writing a thesis or dissertation? If so, what aspect of this writing project most concerns you? What is one idea from this topic that you can use to address this concern?

■ NOTE

1. In shorter research reports, such as research articles in journals and term projects, the introductory comments are usually integrated with the literature review.

ELECTRONIC DATABASES FOR LOCATING LITERATURE

ACCESSING DATABASES

Libraries maintain license agreements with database publishers, so most access to electronic databases is freely obtained through a college or university library. This means that you can search for articles, reports, chapters, or books, identify useful sources, and download them in PDF format to read, annotate, and print. Documents can vary in the restrictions on how they can be downloaded, printed, or altered.

A few databases, such as *ERIC* and *PubMed/MEDLINE* are publicly available with full articles that are free of charge to all individuals via the Internet. To learn more about which databases are available locally or through exchange, talk to a reference librarian. Reference librarians are a greatly underutilized resource! The library's website typically offers a section on databases including tutorials and helpful resources. Often, libraries also organize their available databases in an alphabetical and a subject matter index. It is a good idea to look at the available databases in your subject area to identify those most likely to have the sources that will suit your needs.

PUBLICLY AVAILABLE RESOURCES

ERIC stands for Education Resources Information Center. The *ERIC* database contains more than 1.3 million abstracts of unpublished documents and published journal articles on educational research and practice. Hundreds of new records are added to the database daily. Visit www.eric.ed.gov for more information.

PubMed/MEDLINE is the U.S. National Library of Medicine's (NLM) premier bibliographic database covering the fields of medicine, nursing, dentistry, veterinary medicine, the health care system, and the preclinical sciences. *PubMed/MEDLINE*, the primary subset of *PubMed*, is available on the Internet through the NLM home page at www.ncbi. nlm.nih.gov/pubmed and can be searched free of charge. No registration is required. Additional *PubMed/MEDLINE* services are also provided by organizations that lease the database from NLM. Access to various *PubMed/MEDLINE* services is often available from medical libraries and many public libraries.

Google Scholar is not a database—it is a search engine that allows users to search specifically for academic and scholarly sources. Instead of going to http://google.com, *Google Scholar* can be searched by simply going to https://scholar.google.com/. The differences between a search engine and a database can be useful to know in order to use each tool well. A database subscription typically yields results that also allow access to material, although this depends on the subscription terms. Searching a database is searching an index of the items held in the database. A search engine is not a subscription and does not include access to items. It searches a broader collection of items that may be held in different databases, publishers, or other sources. *Google Scholar* can help to identify good search terms, authors, and publications as well as earmarking specific articles that fit in one's research topic. However, it may be necessary to switch to the library in order to gain free access to the sought after sources.

COMMONLY USED DATABASES IN THE SOCIAL SCIENCES, PSYCHOLOGY, AND EDUCATION

JSTOR contains the full text from more than 2,300 journals in more than 60 disciplines including social sciences, education, humanities, natural sciences, and health. Not everyone has access to all holdings in *JSTOR*: each library's subscription determines the full text that is freely available at that institution. In addition to journal articles, *JSTOR* includes over 40,000 ebooks from academic publishers.

EBSCOhost is a family of databases, which are all hosted through the *EBSCOhost* interface. The collection is multidisciplinary across many scientific, social scientific, health, and math topics and international in scope, with total holdings that includes over 12,000 full-text journals, of which over 10,000 are peer-reviewed. The *EBSCOhost* holdings also include over 60,000 videos from the Associated Press. The available resources will vary depending on the subscription held by the library.

Sociological Abstracts indexes and summarizes articles in more than 1,800 international journals and 29 broad areas of sociology from 1952 to present. *Sociological Abstracts* also summarizes books and book chapters, dissertations, conference papers, book reviews, film reviews, and game reviews.

PsycINFO indexes and abstracts journal articles from more than 2,497 journals. Books, dissertations, and university and government reports are also included. In addition, *PsycAR-TICLES* contains more than 154,000 full-text articles (not just abstracts) from 78 journals and selected chapters from books published by the American Psychological Association. Members of the public can access these databases via the Internet for a daily service fee (charged to a credit card) at www.apa.org. Consult with the reference librarian at your college or university for information on accessing these databases free of charge through your library's license agreements.

ProQuest is a platform similar to *EBSCO* in that it is an interface where many families and combinations of databases are indexed. Collection sizes vary depending on a library's subscription, but may include various business and management databases (ABI/INFORM) as well as collections in research, technology, biology, agriculture, nursing, music, and the arts.

OTHER ELECTRONIC DATABASES

There are many specialty databases that may be of use. These databases may be useful because of their focus on a single topic or area, with work that cannot be found in the larger database collections. Here are just a few examples:

ABI/INFORM (ProQuest) is a business and management database with abstracts and many full-text articles from U.S. and international publications. Topics include advertising, marketing, economics, human resources, finance, taxation, and computers.

Chicano Database identifies all types of material about Chicanos. It incorporates the *Spanish Speaking Mental Health Database*, which covers psychological, sociological, and educational literature.

Child Development and Adolescent Studies includes abstracts from professional periodicals and book reviews related to the growth and development of children from 1927 to the present.

Contemporary Women's Issues provides full-text access to journals, hard-to-find newsletters, reports, pamphlets, fact sheets, and guides on a broad array of gender-related issues published since 1992.

ProQuest Criminal Justice contains full-text articles from criminology and criminal justice journal articles on law enforcement, corrections administration, social work, drug rehabilitation, criminal and family law, industrial security, and other related fields. There are also indexes and abstracts for 425 U.S. and international journals.

Dissertation Abstracts Online is a definitive subject, title, and author guide to virtually every American dissertation accepted at an accredited institution since 1861. Selected master's theses have been included since 1962. The electronic version indexes doctoral records from July 1980 (*Dissertation Abstracts International*, Volume 41, Number 1) to the present. Abstracts are included for master's theses from spring 1988 (*Master's Abstracts*, Volume 26, Number 1) to the present. This database has very wide subject matter coverage including, but not limited to, business and economics, education, fine arts and music, geography, health sciences, political science, language and literature, library and information science, psychology, and sociology.

Family Studies Database contains citations and abstracts for journal articles, books, popular literature, conference papers, and government reports in the fields of family science, human ecology, and human development since 1970.

International Index to Black Periodicals Full Text (*IIBP Full Text*) draws its current content from more than 150 international scholarly and popular periodicals. It covers a wide array of humanities-related disciplines including art, cultural criticism, economics, education, health, history, language and literature, law, philosophy, politics, religion, and sociology, among others. All records in the current file (1998 forward) contain abstracts.

Project MUSE is a database with articles and books that covers creative arts, writing, theater, humanities, religion, social sciences, and science and technology. The database contains nearly 400,000 articles and almost a million book chapters from over 250 publishers.

Social Sciences Citation Index (*SSCI*®) and *Social SciSearch*® provide access to current and retrospective bibliographic information, author abstracts, and cited references found in more than 1,700 of the world's leading scholarly social science journals, covering more than 50 disciplines. They also cover individually selected, relevant items from approximately 3,300 of the world's leading science and technology journals. Note that the *Citation Index* lists cited authors and their works together with all authors who have discussed the cited works in their publications. This can be very helpful in conducting a literature search if a researcher starts with a classic older article that is highly relevant to the topic. By searching for all publications in which it was subsequently cited, the researcher can quickly build a collection of references that are likely to be very specific to the topic. Examining these sequentially permits the researcher to trace the history of thought on a topic or theory.

ELECTRONIC SOURCES OF STATISTICAL INFORMATION

GUIDELINE 1: WEB SOURCES ARE OFTEN MORE UP-TO-DATE THAN PROFESSIONAL JOURNALS

When writing literature reviews, writers often need up-to-date information. Because of the ease of electronic publishing, the web is more likely to have such information than conventionally printed materials. Note that it is not uncommon for a printed journal article or book to be published a year or more after it was written. Despite this delay, professional journals are usually the primary sources of detailed information on how investigators conducted their research, so they remain premier sources of information for literature reviews.

GUIDELINE 2: INFORMATION ON CURRENT ISSUES CAN OFTEN BE FOUND USING GENERAL SEARCH ENGINES

A general search engine such as Google can be used to locate information that might be included in a literature review. Consider the topic of teen pregnancy. A quick search using the search term (within quotation marks, which means it is searched together) "teen pregnancy rates" retrieved 351,000 results with related information. The first site in the list, maintained by the U.S. Department of Health & Human Services, contains the information shown in Example 1.

Example 1: Sample Topic Delimited By "Teen Pregnancy Rates"

In 2014, there were 24.2 births for every 1,000 adolescent females ages 15–19, or 249,078 babies born to females in this age group. Nearly 89 percent of these births occurred outside of marriage. The 2014 teen birth rate indicates a decline of nine percent from 2013 when the birth rate was 26.5 per 1,000 (Hamilton et al., 2015). The teen birth rate has declined almost continuously over the past 20 years. In 1991, the U.S. teen birth rate was 61.8 births for every 1,000 adolescent females, compared with 24.2 births for every 1,000 adolescent females in 2014. Still, the U.S. teen birth rate is higher than that of many other developed countries, including Canada and the United Kingdom (United Nations Statistics Division, 2015).[1]

GUIDELINE 3: FEDSTATS CONTAINS MANY IMPORTANT AND TRUSTWORTHY SOURCES OF STATISTICAL INFORMATION

Often, literature reviews begin with current statistics on how many individuals (and/or the percentage of individuals) are affected by the topic of the literature review, and up-to-date statistics are often available at https://fedstats.sites.usa.gov/.

Statistics from more than 100 federal agencies including the U.S. Census Bureau, National Center for Education Statistics (NCES), Bureau of Justice Statistics (BJS), Bureau of Labor Statistics (BLS), National Institutes of Health (NIH), and many more can be accessed here.[2] These statistics are publicly available and free to use, and sources should always be cited.

Prior to establishment of this website, individuals needed to search for statistics on an agency-by-agency basis. While the FedStats site still allows users to do this, they can also search by *topic* and the FedStats search engine will automatically search all agencies for relevant links to federal statistics. This is important for two reasons: (1) a user does not have to search each agency separately, and (2) an agency that a user is not aware of may have statistics relevant to his or her topic. FedStats contains over 400 topics that can be searched by program, subject area, agency, or alphabetically.

In addition, a site called Data.gov (https://www.data.gov/) was launched seven years ago to expand availability of U.S. government data. Datasets are publicly available to download and use in more than a dozen areas. DataUSA (http://datausa.io/) is a website created by a data science team from MIT Media Lab and Datawheel to provide visualization of demographic and economic data for open use.

GUIDELINE 4: STATE GOVERNMENT WEBSITES ARE A SOURCE OF LOCAL STATISTICS

The main web pages for various states can be accessed by using the postal service's state names' abbreviations in URL addresses, such as www.ga.gov (for Georgia) and www.ca.gov (for California). It is possible to use search engines to look up the state government and statistics, and discover data projects such as the Open Data project in California (http://data.ca.gov/SODP/index.html).

While the organization of government home pages varies greatly from state to state, they contain links that can lead to a variety of statistical information, which can be useful when local statistics are needed for a literature review. In addition, there are links to descriptions of a variety of government-funded programs. This information can be valuable for individuals who are reviewing literature on programs.

GUIDELINE 5: USE THE RAW STATISTICS FROM GOVERNMENTAL AGENCIES, NOT STATISTICS FILTERED BY SPECIAL INTERESTS

Some individuals (such as politicians) and groups (such as advocacy groups) with special interests may understandably be selective in choosing which government statistics to report and interpret on their websites. Hence, it is usually best to obtain the original government reports either in print or via the web.

GUIDELINE 6: CONSIDER CONSULTING THE LIBRARY OF CONGRESS'S VIRTUAL REFERENCE SHELF ON THE WEB

The Library of Congress maintains a website titled the Virtual Reference Shelf. It is an excellent site for general references such as dictionaries, general history, abbreviations, genealogy, and so on. This site's address is www.loc.gov/rr/askalib/virtualref.html.[3] Box 1 below shows the main links on the home page of the site at the time of this writing.

BOX 1 Links on the Home Page of the Library of Congress's Virtual Reference Shelf

Virtual Reference Shelf

Selected online resources for research:

- *Abbreviations*
- *Almanacs & Fast Facts*
- *Architecture*
- *Art*
- *Business*
- *Calculators*
- *Calendars & Time*
- *Children & Parents*
- *Consumer Information*
- *Dictionaries & Thesauri*
- *Directories*
- *Education*
- *Encyclopedias*
- *English Language & Literature*
- *Full-text Books & Periodicals*
- *Genealogy*
- *General Reference Resources*
- *Grant Resources*
- *Health/Medical*
- *History (U.S.)*
- *Images*
- *Law*
- *Libraries*
- *Maps*
- *Music & Performing Arts*
- *Politics & Government*
- *Quotations*
- *Research & Documentation*
- *Science & Technology*
- *Statistics*

GUIDELINE 7: CONSIDER ACCESSING INFORMATION POSTED ON THE WEB BY PROFESSIONAL ASSOCIATIONS

A wide variety of associations post information (and statistics) on the web. While reviewers may already be familiar with the major organizations in their respective fields, there are many specialized organizations that deal with specific issues.

To identify specialized associations, you may conduct a Google search for professional associations by using a search term specific to your major. For example, psychology majors may use the search terms "professional associations AND psychology." Examples of some of the professional associations that come up during this search include the American Psychological Association, American Board of Professional Psychology, and National Alliance of Professional Psychology Providers.

In addition to posting information and statistics on the web, associations post position papers on a variety of contemporary issues relating to their fields. The positions taken by such associations might be cited in literature reviews.

■ NOTES

1. Retrieved July 2, 2016 from www.hhs.gov/ash/oah/adolescent-health-topics/reproductive-health/teen-pregnancy/trends.html. Citations within this excerpt come from Hamilton, B.E., Martin, J.A., Osterman,

M.J.K., & Curtin, S.C. (2015). *Births: Final Data for 2014.* Hyattsville, MD: National Center for Health Statistics. Retrieved May 4, 2016 from www.cdc.gov/nchs/data/nvsr/nvsr64/nvsr64_12.pdf, and United Nations Statistics Division. (2015). *Demographic Yearbook 2013.* New York, NY: United Nations. Retrieved May 4, 2016 from http://unstats.un.org/unsd/demographic/products/dyb/dyb2013/Table10.pdf.

2. Be sure to go to https://fedstats.sites.usa.gov/ and *not* www.FedStats.*com.* The latter is *not* a government site.

3. Rather than typing long URLs, you may find it faster to perform a quick search on a major search engine such as Google using a term like "Virtual Reference Shelf." Use the quotation marks around the terms to conduct an exact phrase match.

EXCERPTS FROM LITERATURE REVIEWS

The following excerpts show the beginning paragraph(s) of literature reviews.

EXCERPT 1

Children Reading to Dogs[1]

Literacy skills have significant consequences to global health and economy. More than 796 million people in the world cannot read (approximately 15% of the population), resulting in world-wide costs of over USD $1 trillion a year, with the effects of illiteracy being very similar in developing and developed countries (Cree & Steward, 2012). Poor literacy skills have substantial health and welfare implications for society, having been associated with reduction in: health outcomes, economic growth, social participation, self-esteem and hygiene, as well as increased accidents and job absenteeism (Martinez & Fernances, 2010). It is clear that reading skills have wide-reaching implications. Likewise, in the educational environment the effects of literacy are not just relevant to performance in English lessons, but also have wider implications, determining successful academic learning in all subjects (Clark, 2011) and being associated with overall school enjoyment (Ecklund & Lamon, 2008). In the past decade there has been a worrying decline in children's enjoyment, and therefore frequency, of reading (Sainsbury & Schagen, 2004). Given that frequency of reading is directly related to reading attainment (Clark, 2011) it is essential that there are evidence-based interventions that increase children's motivation, enjoyment and frequency of reading. Despite increasing Government awareness for the necessity of improving student's motivation to read for pleasure (Department for Education, 2012) there is still no legitimised program to support this. The first high profile programme to advocate children reading to dogs was established in 1999 by Intermountain Therapy Animals, who announced Reading Education Assistance Dogs (READ). Growing interest in programmes such as READ is observed in frequent media reports and is reflected in the subsequent development of a number of initiatives around the world including (but not limited to), The Bark and Read Foundation (Kennel Club, UK), Caring Canines, Dogs Helping Kids, Read2Dogs, Classroom Canines (Delta Society, Australia), SitStayRead, Library Dogs, Tail Waggin' Tutors (Therapy Dogs International), Reading with Rover, and All Ears Reading. Proponents of READ postulate that reading to dogs helps motivate children to read by increasing relaxation and confidence, reducing blood pressure and offering a non-judgemental, safe environment in which to practice reading (Tales of JOY R.E.A.D. Program, 2012; Shaw, 2013). It is noted that READ (and similar organisations) do not supply evidence through control group comparisons to support these claims. However, in the wider literature there is evidence to suggest that improving reading motivation improves reading performance (Guthrie & Cox, 2001; Hill & Harack-iewicz, 2000; Wigfield & Guthrie, 1997), indicating that if children are more motivated to read with a dog then this could improve their reading abilities. This may be especially important for students who struggle to read, because poor reading abilities are also associ-ated with low reading motivation (Ecklund & Lamon, 2008). Also, below average readers often demonstrate increased reading anxiety; indeed, reading anxiety is a well observed form of 'classical conditioning' in the classroom environment (Jalongo & Hirsh, 2010). For example, an initially neutral stimulus (e.g., reading out-loud) is repeatedly associ-ated with a negative response (e.g., teacher judgement or peer ridicule), which results in the reader forming an association between reading and negative internal responses (e.g., anxiety, heightened emotions). Reading anxiety is common in children and is associated with physical symptoms, such as a reddening face, rapid breathing, and tension headaches (Zbornik, 2001). Evidence suggests that positive experiences can help the child to over-come negative associations and be more open to learning experiences (Amsterlaw, Lagat-tuta, & Meltzoff, 2009). READ and similar programmes postulate that reading to a dog helps to overcome these (anxiety/motivation) roadblocks to developing reading expertise in the classroom. The silent companionship of a dog as a reading partner may allow the child to work at their own pace through reading challenges without fear of being judged. However, it is unclear what evidence exists to directly support the principles of READ (i.e., improved reading abilities through increased reading motivation and reduced reading anxiety).

EXCERPT 2

Relationships of HIV/AIDS Patients with Their Families[2]

Individuals with HIV/AIDS and their caregivers in developing countries often suffer from various pressures, such as availability of adequate medical care, lack of formal support, declining resources, social isolation, stigma, and lack of community support (D'Cruz, 2003; Kelley & Eberstadt, 2005). Due to such pressures, HIV/AIDS patients and their caregivers are vulnerable to experience mental health symptoms including traumatic stress (McCaus-land & Pakenham, 2003; Owens, 2003) and depression (Land & Hudson, 2004; Wight, Beals, Miller-Martines, Murphy, & Aneshensel, 2007). The challenge of disclosing infor-mation to family members becomes another source of stress (Kalichman, Austiry Luke, & DiFonzo, 2003).

One of the major obstacles undermining the efforts to study the experience of HIV/AIDS in developing countries is the lack of access to information on the disease. Both Kel-ley and Eberstadt (2005) and Obermeyer (2006) question the accuracy of reported HIV/AIDS cases in Muslim and especially Middle Eastern countries. Most of the HIV/AIDS cases in developing countries are vulnerable to stigma and other forms of social isolation. Castle (2004) stated that negative attitudes toward people with HIV/AIDS in developing countries can be translated into harsh treatment and stigmatization by the community and, in some cases, by families of infected persons. Although stigma seems to be based on the values and attitudes of societies in developing countries, Ali (1996) noted changes in the views of people regarding HIV/AIDS. "A theology of compassion and approaches advocating harm reduction seem to be emerging in several Muslim countries, and greater acceptance of HIV positive people is justified with reference to religion" (cited by Obermeyer, 2006, p. 853).

The experience of HIV/AIDS can cause conflict within the family (Li, Jiang, Lord, & Rotheram-Borus, 2007), such as communication problems (Vangelisti, 1992) and problems in roles and family adaptation (Holmbeck, 1996). It is common to find the family is the only source of care and support for HIV/AIDS patients. That can become burdensome due to inadequate resources and assistance available for family caregivers and the unsupportive viewpoints existent in these societies (Kipp, Nkosi, Laing, & Jhangri, 2006). Therefore, it is important to explore the nature of interaction and relationship among HIV/AIDS patients and their families.

EXCERPT 3

Nurses' Medication Errors[3]

Since the Institute of Medicine (IOM) report *To Err is Human* (Kohn, Corrigan, & Donaldson, 2000), the United States has made significant efforts to improve patient safety. With regard to medication errors, numerous studies have been published identifying the epidemiology and the etiology of medication errors, and hospitals, nursing homes, and other healthcare organizations continue to evaluate evidence-based interventions and to develop safety guidelines and protocols. Despite such progress, the IOM recently estimated that at least one medication error occurs every day for every hospitalized patient, suggesting that medication errors still remain a significant problem (IOM, 2006).

Safety culture has been emphasized as a necessary condition for patient safety, which includes reducing the number of medication errors (Kohn et al., 2000). A positive safety culture exists when group members share perceptions of the importance of safety, communicate with mutual trust, and have confidence in the efficacy of preventive measures (Health and Safety Commission, 1993). The Joint Commission included an annual assessment of safety culture in 2007 patient safety goals, and many healthcare organizations have embarked on efforts to assess safety culture or, on the surface, safety climate.

Although reducing medication errors is an important goal, there is consensus that eliminating them completely is unlikely, particularly when there are high volumes of activity. It has been estimated, for example, that a 600-bed teaching hospital with 99.9% error-free drug ordering, dispensing, and administration will still experience 4,000 drug errors a year (Leape, 1994). Therefore, organizations also must improve their strategies in dealing with errors when they do occur. Unfortunately, there has been less emphasis on error management and the central feature: learning climate. The error management approach is focused on how to deal with errors when they occur. It emphasizes creating a positive learning climate, in which learning from errors is fostered in organizations. Although learning climate has been considered similar to, or incorporated into, safety climate, learning climate is focused on errors.

During the past decade, there has been increasing recognition in healthcare research of the significance of learning from errors (Berta & Baker, 2004; Edmondson, 2004; Rosen,

& Carroll, 2006). Organizations with a positive learning climate have the competence to draw the appropriate conclusions from their safety information systems and the willingness to implement major reforms where needed (Department of Health, 2000). However, little is known about how learning climate contributes to error management and, ultimately, to error reduction. In fact, the current literature on medication errors tends to be focused primarily on work conditions that are conducive to error occurrence, complex work environment, or inadequate staffing sources. Understanding the mechanism of learning in error management is therefore of importance for care organizations to achieve patient safety.

EXCERPT 4

The Effects of Being Labeled a Nerd[4]

In most schools, there seems to be a clear understanding of who is a nerd (B. B. Brown, Mory, & Kinney, 1994; Rentzsch & Schütz, 2011). According to B. B. Brown (1990), adolescents are assigned to a specific group by their peers because they have reputations and characteristics that fit with the stereotype of that crowd (see also B. B. Brown et al., 1994). The label *nerd* refers to one of the least liked crowds at school (B. B. Brown et al., 1994). It includes the following characteristics: being ambitious and intelligent, having good grades, studying a lot, displaying success publicly, being shy, having few friends, not wearing fashionable clothes, not being athletic, and not being physically attractive (Rentzsch & Schütz, 2011). The label *nerd* is feared by students who receive good grades (Pelkner & Boehnke, 2003; Pelkner, Günther, & Boehnke, 2002). Several labels are used for deprecating high-achieving students, such as *nerd* (e.g., B. B. Brown et al., 1994; Kinney, 1993), *brain* (e.g., Prinstein & LaGreca, 2002), *geek* (e.g., Tyson, Darity, & Castellino, 2005), or *teacher's pet* (e.g., Tal & Babad, 1990). The present study primarily refers to *brains* and *nerds* because of their similarity to the German label "Streber." (The German label is neither readily transferable to other derogatory terms used in school nor to the type of so-called nerds who are known for their enthusiasm about computers.) From an etymological perspective, "Streber" is a disparaging term that describes an overambitious, diligent person. Literally, it means a person who strives for success, achievement, etc.

Being labeled a nerd is not a trifle. If being labeled as such in class goes along with a lack of acceptance and being rejected, serious consequences can occur. Research shows that lack of acceptance is related to social isolation (Moulton, Moulton, Housewright, & Bailey, 1998), loneliness (Juvonen, Nishina, & Graham, 2000), reduced self-esteem (de Bruyn & van den Boom, 2005), and other forms of maladjustment (Parker & Asher, 1987). Furthermore, a 6-year longitudinal study by Prinstein and La Greca (2002) showed that students who were called *brains* by their peers exhibited increases in anxiety and loneliness as well as decreases in self-esteem over the course of time.

A potential consequence of being labeled a *nerd* is that the respective student might reduce future performance. If high-achieving students have to make a choice between doing well in school and being popular, they may try to achieve liking by decreasing success. Landsheer, Maassen, Bisschop, and Adema (1998) commented: "If high achievement in the sciences results in unpopularity, it could lead to lesser effort by better students"

(p. 188). Similarly, Pelkner et al. (2002) found that the fear of being called a nerd predicted lower achievement in mathematics. Several discussion forums on the Internet, in which parents or students describe their concerns about being labeled a nerd, provide information about the social relevance of that topic (see http://bullying.org, https://www.schueler-gegen-mobbing.de), but up to now there are no systematic studies addressing the specific effects of various factors on the social evaluation of so-called nerds. In the next section, we discuss factors that may be relevant in social evaluation and then present two studies that tested the effects of these factors.

EXCERPT 5

Nonstandard Work Schedule[5]

In the last half century, the number of women participating in the labor force in the United States has increased dramatically, with particular increases among low-income women (Blank, 2002). At the same time, the nature of work in the United States has evolved. Service and sales sectors have expanded, and the economy increasingly operates around the clock, amplifying demand for workers outside the traditional 9-to-5 workday (Presser, 2003). It is now common for individuals to work nonstandard schedules—in the evening, nights, or on weekends—leading to concerns about the effects of work scheduling on families and children. Nonstandard work is more common among lower-income individuals (Presser), and so children in low-income families are more likely to be affected by their parents' nonstandard work schedules.

Research on the effects of nonstandard work schedules on both workers and their families has generally found that nonstandard work schedules have negative effects particularly in studies of mixed- and higher-income families (Han, 2005, 2006; Han & Waldfogel, 2007; Strazdins, Clements, Korda, Broom, & D'Souza, 2006; Strazdins, Korda, Lim, Broom, & D'Souza, 2004). Studies focused on low-wage workers, however, have produced mixed results (Han, 2008; Hsueh & Yoshikawa, 2007; Joshi & Bogen, 2007; Phillips, 2002), and additional information is still needed about how mothers' nonstandard work schedules affect low-income families. Prior research has commonly compared parents categorized as working standard or nonstandard schedules, on the basis of a typical work week. That design has three limitations: unobserved selection into different schedules may bias results; "standard" and "nonstandard" categories may mask within-person variability in work schedules; and, in most studies, the "nonstandard" category includes both nights and weekends, although their consequences may differ.

EXCERPT 6

Men's Health Behaviors[6]

Approximately one third of all of the deaths in the United States might be prevented by the widespread adoption of health promotion behaviors and avoidance of health risk behaviors (Danaei et al., 2009). American men tend to engage in more than 30 controllable behaviors that increase their risk for disease, injury, and death (Courtenay, 2000a, 2000b), which may at least partly explain why American men live an average of 5.2 years less than American women (Minino, Heron, Murphy, & Kocharek, 2007). Men spend less time with their physicians; engage in fewer preventive health behaviors; consume more alcohol; use more tobacco products; have poorer diets, sleep hygiene, and weight management; and lower physical activity than women (Centers for Disease Control, 2004; Galuska, Serdula, Pamuk, Siegal, & Byers, 1996; Garfield, Isacco, & Rogers, 2008; Kandrack, Grant, & Segall, 1999; Shi, 1998).

These findings have brought men's physical and mental health to the forefront in current public health discourse (Addis et al., 2007; Baker, 2001; Bonhomme, 2007). Research on the variables that influence men's relative lack of engagement in health promotion activities and avoidance of health risk behaviors is thus of considerable importance. Masculine gender socialization is often cited as a major reason why men engage in poorer health behaviors than women (Courtenay, 2000a). Moreover, masculine gender socialization is also the major reason why men are significantly less likely than women to seek help for both mental health (Addis & Mahalik, 2003; Levant, Wimer, Williams, Smalley, & Noronha, 2009; Mahalik, Good, & Englar-Carlson, 2003) and physical health (Wyke, Hunt, & Ford, 1998). Masculine gender socialization thus appears to create a "double whammy" effect because it is associated with both poorer health behaviors *and* a reduced likelihood of using appropriate health resources when needed.

However, research on the relationships between masculine gender socialization and health behaviors is at a very early stage. Levant et al. (2009) reviewed a dozen published studies on the relationship between four measures of masculine gender socialization constructs and health behaviors and concluded that the endorsement of traditional masculinity ideology, conformity to masculine norms, masculine gender role stress, and gender role conflict are all associated with engagement in various risky health-related behaviors. Furthermore, only a handful of studies have directly compared the impact of various masculinity measures, and these studies have examined only a small subset of risky health behaviors (e.g., alcohol problems and aggression), while examining only one or two measures at a time.

■ NOTES

1. Source: Hall, S.S., Gee, N.R., & Mills, D.S. (2016). Children reading to dogs: A systematic review of the literature. *PLoS ONE*, *11*, 1–22. e0149759. doi:10.1371/journal.pone.0149759 (Excerpt from page 2.) Copyright © 2016 by Hall et al.
2. Source: Soliman, H.H., & Abd Almotgly, M.M. (2011). Psychosocial profile of people with AIDS and their caregivers in Egypt. *Psychological Reports*, *108*, 883–892. (Excerpt from pages 883–884.) Copyright © 2011 by Psychological Reports.
3. Source: Chang, Y.K., & Mark, B. (2011). Effects of learning climate and registered nurse staffing on medication errors. *Nursing Research*, *60*, 32–39. (Excerpt from pages 32–33.) Copyright © 2008 by Wolters Kluwer Health/Lippincott Williams & Wilkins.
4. Source: Rentzsch, K., Schütz, A., & Schröder-Abé, M. (2011). Being labeled *nerd*: Factors that influence the social acceptance of high-achieving students. *The Journal of Experimental Education*, *79*, 143–168. (Excerpt from pages 144–145.) Copyright © 2011 by Taylor & Francis Group, LLC.

5. Source: Gassman-Pines, A. (2011). Low-income mothers' nighttime and weekend work: Daily associations with child behavior, mother–child interactions, and mood. *Family Relations*, *60*, 15–29. (Excerpt from page 15.) Copyright © 2011 by the National Council on Family Relations.

6. Source: Levant, R.F., Wimer, D.J., & Williams, C.M. (2011). An evolution of the Health Behavior Inventory-20 (HBI-20) and its relationships to masculinity and attitudes towards seeking psychological help among college men. *Psychology of Men & Masculinity*, *12*, 26–41. (Excerpt from pages 26–27.) Copyright © 2011 by the American Psychological Association.

SAMPLE ABSTRACTS OF RESEARCH REPORTS

This appendix contains five sample abstracts. Abstracts appear at the beginning of published research reports and summarize the topic, research question, method used, and results in a short paragraph. The length is often limited by the publisher. See Topic 82 for a refresher on other characteristics of abstracts. Note that Abstracts 1, 3, and 5 use bolded subheadings, while Abstracts 2 and 4 use a paragraph style that summarizes the same types of information. This may be due to preference of the publication or author and is unrelated to the type of study that is represented.

ABSTRACT 1

Abstract of a Mixed Methods Study[1]

Objective: Universities across the country struggle with the legal and ethical dilemmas of how to respond when a student shows symptoms of serious mental illness. This mixed-method study provides information on faculty knowledge of mental health problems in students, their use of available accommodations and strategies, and their willingness to accept psychiatric advance directives (PADs) as helpful interventions for managing student crises. **Method**: Participants were 168 faculty members at a large, public, Southern university. A web-based survey was used to collect quantitative self-report data as well as qualitative data in the form of open-ended questions. Quantitative data are presented with descriptive statistics. Qualitative data were analyzed using thematic analysis. **Results**: The majority of faculty surveyed have an overall supportive stance and are willing to provide accommodations to students with a mental illness. The most common advantage faculty see in a PAD is support of student autonomy and choice, and the primary concern voiced about PADs is that students with mental illness will have poor judgment regarding the contents of the PADs they create. **Conclusions and Implications for Practice**: PADs may be effective recovery tools to help university students with mental illnesses manage crises and attain stability and academic success. For PADs to be effective, university faculty and administration will need to understand mental illnesses, the strategies students need to manage mental health crises, and how PADs can play a role in supporting students.

ABSTRACT 2

Abstract of a Survey[2]

This study assessed work-related and driver-related factors in fatigue among Finnish heavy vehicle drivers. 683 professional drivers responded to a questionnaire, 27.8%

of whom reported often feeling fatigue during their work shifts. Of the respondents, 27.5% reported having momentarily fallen asleep at the wheel while driving during the past year. Almost half (46.8%) of the fatigued drivers estimated the reasons for momentarily falling asleep were work-related. Long working shifts and short sleeps significantly increased the risk of momentarily falling asleep at the wheel. The risk of fatigue was the highest for the drivers who were unable to choose the time of their breaks.

ABSTRACT 3

Abstract of an Experiment[3]

Background: Adapting to living with chronic conditions is a lifelong psychosocial challenge.

Objective: The purpose of this study was to report the effect of a computer intervention on the psychosocial adaptation of rural women with chronic conditions.

Methods: A two-group study design was used with 309 middle-aged, rural women who had chronic conditions, randomized into either a computer-based intervention or a control group. Data were collected at baseline, at the end of the intervention, and 6 months later on the psychosocial indicators of social support, self-esteem, acceptance of illness, stress, depression, and loneliness.

Results: The impact of the computer-based intervention was statistically significant for five of six of the psychosocial outcomes measured, with a modest impact on social support. The largest benefits were seen in depression, stress, and acceptance.

Discussion: The women-to-women intervention resulted in positive psychosocial responses that have the potential to contribute to successful management of illness and adaptation. Other components of adaptation to be examined are the impact of the intervention on illness management and quality of life and the interrelationships among environmental stimuli, psychosocial response, and illness management.

ABSTRACT 4

Abstract of a Program Evaluation[4]

Public safety departments have been tasked with training staff, faculty, and students to respond to an active shooting event if it were to occur on campus. There has been an increase in student training videos and drills on college campuses, even though the impact of these programs has not been evaluated. This study takes an initial look at a training video designed to prepare students to respond to a shooter on campus, comparing it with a control video about school shootings. Students who watched either video felt more afraid that a shooting would occur on campus, in addition to feeling more prepared to respond. The training video increased feelings of preparedness over the control video, but also increased feelings of fear among female students. The implications of active shooter training on student mental health and school culture are discussed.

ABSTRACT 5

Abstract of a Qualitative Study[5]

Objective: The goal of this study was to identify factors that college students perceived as contributing to healthy and unhealthy eating patterns, physical activity (PA) levels, and weight change. **Participants**: Forty-nine 18- to 22-year-old students at a Midwestern university participated. **Methods**: Six focus groups (3 with each gender) were conducted, and data were analyzed using qualitative software to code and categorize themes and then reduce these to clusters according to commonly practiced methods of qualitative analysis. **Results**: Eating and PA behaviors appear to be determined by a complex interplay between motivations and self-regulatory skills as well as the unique social and physical environment comprising college life. Moreover, there appear to be gender differences in how these determinants impact behavior. **Conclusions**: Future research should examine these interactions in the college context in order to further our understanding of potential interventions or environmental modifications that support healthy eating and PA.

■ NOTES

1. Source: Brockelman, K., & Scheyett, A. (2015). Faculty perceptions of accommodations, strategies, and psychiatric advance directives for university students with mental illnesses. *Psychosocial Rehabilitation Journal*, *38*, 342–348. Copyright @ 2015 American Psychological Association

2. Source: Perttula, P., Ojala, T., & Kuosma, E. (2011). Factors in the fatigue of heavy vehicle drivers. *Psychological Reports*, *108*, 507–514. Copyright © 2011 by Psychological Reports.

3. Source: Weinert, C., Cudney, S., Comstock, B., & Bansal, A. (2011). Computer intervention impact on psychosocial adaptation of rural women with chronic conditions. *Nursing Research*, *60*, 82–91. Copyright © 2011 by Wolters Kluwer Health/Lippincott Williams & Wilkins.

4. Source: Peterson, J., Sackrison, E., & Polland, A. (2015). Training students to respond to shootings on campus: Is it worth it? *Journal of Threat Assessment and Management*, *2*, 127–138. Copyright © 2016 by the American Psychological Association.

5. Source: LaCaille, L. J., Dauner, K.N., Krambeer, R. J., & Pedersen, J. (2011). Psychosocial and environmental determinants of eating behaviors, physical activity, and weight change among college students: A qualitative analysis. *Journal of American College Health*, *59*, 531–538. Copyright © 2011 by Taylor & Francis Group, LLC.

AN INTRODUCTION TO APA STYLE

Topics 18 and 19 discussed the reasons that academic writing acknowledges the work of others through *citation*. This appendix provides a few basic elements of the style that is most commonly followed in psychology and related disciplines. The American Psychological Association publishes a style guide (called *Publication Manual of the American Psychological Association*) in which a comprehensive set of rules is presented. Short guides can be found for free on the association's website devoted to this topic, https://www.apastyle.org/. Most college and university libraries also offer further tutorials and helpful abbreviated guides, and guides from many different colleges and universities can be found in a quick Google search for APA style.

While different styles accomplish the task of citation differently, most citation systems work by "tagging" the text in place with some shorthand marker. This marker indicates to the reader that information in that sentence came from a source that the author is going to provide. This in-text citation may be a number or, in many cases, it is the last name of the author(s) and a year in parentheses. The latter style is called an "author–date" method and this is the style that APA uses.

The shorthand from the in-text citation can then be matched with an entry in the bibliography at the end of the paper. In the bibliography, the full information is given: name, year, title, publication, volume number, page numbers, and possibly a digital object identifier, or DOI, which is a permanent number tagged to the paper and indexed so it is easy to find in digital archives.[1] For each unique in-text citation, there should be a full bibliographic reference at the end of the manuscript. In author–date styles, it is important that the "shorthand" in the in-text citation matches the first word in the alphabetized bibliography so the reader can easily pair the two and find the indicated source.

IN-TEXT CITATIONS IN APA STYLE

In APA style, in-text citations consist of the last name and year of publication, and appear at the end of the sentence in parentheses. There is a comma between the last name and year. Example 1 shows a simple case of a single author, Doe, whose work is from 2013.

Example 1: An In-Text Citation for a Single Author

New data suggest that the influence of the mass media on social norms and customs is growing very rapidly (Doe, 2013).

Example 2 illustrates APA style for an in-text citation of a source with two authors, where an ampersand (&) is used between author names.

Example 2: An In-Text Citation of a Source with Two Authors

The influence of peer group pressure on bullying behavior by girls needs more large-scale investigations (Edwards & Jones, 2013).

When a source with one or two authors is cited multiple times in a manuscript, it is cited the same way each time. However, when there are three to five authors, the authors are all cited in the first in-text citation. Then, in subsequent citations, only the first author's last name followed by "et al." is used, as illustrated in Example 3A and 3B, where 3A is the first mention in the text and 3B is a subsequent mention of the same source.

Example 3A: First Time the Source with Three Authors Is Cited

More research is needed on the origins of gender-role socialization (Washington, Yu, & Galvan, 2013).

Example 3B: The Second and Subsequent Times the Source Is Cited

Large-scale research on gender-role socialization is relatively rare (Washington et al., 2013).

A source with six or more authors uses "et al." in all in-text citations, including the first time it is cited.

Often, two or more sources are in substantial agreement. For instance, there might be three sources with data indicating that the XYZ program is strongly supported by most parents. These three sources may be cited within a single set of parentheses, as illustrated in Example 4. Semicolons are used to separate sources, which are listed in alphabetical order.

Example 4: Three Sources Cited Within a Single Set of Parentheses

In three recent surveys, a majority of parents expressed strong support for the XYZ program (Black-stone, 2012; Brown et al., 2011; White & Bright, 2013).

When the source is a group, such as a professional organization, government agency, corporation, or similar entity, cite its authorship using the full name of the group, as shown in Example 5.

Example 5: Full Name of an Organization Cited

The origins of the theory have been traced "as far back as the 1950s" (International Association of Unlicensed Practitioners, 2012, p. 285).

When an author quotes directly from a source, the author should include the page number(s) in the in-text citation, as illustrated in Example 5 above. This is also done when an author wants to call attention to a particular part of a source. Notice how the page number is included. Details matter with citation styles. It appears at the end of the citation, after a comma separating it from the year, and after the abbreviation for page ("p."; the abbreviation for pages is "pp.").

When the authors are mentioned as a part of the sentence, it is always by last name. Their names do not need to be repeated in the in-text citation. Instead, the authors' last names become part of a sentence, which is immediately followed by the year of publication in parentheses. No ampersand is used because the names are now part of the sentence, often serving as the sentence subject as illustrated in Example 6. Note that the sentence in Example 6A and 6B contain the same information as Example 3A and 3B.

Example 6A: First Time the Source Is Cited

Washington, Yu, and Galvan (2013) claim that more research is needed on the origins of gender-role socialization.

Example 6B: The Second and Subsequent Times the Source Is Cited

Washington et al. (2013) point out that large-scale research on gender-role socialization is relatively rare.

Non-parenthetical citations emphasize the authors by making the authors' names more prominent than parenthetical citations do. Neither is right or wrong. The decision on which one to use depends on whether the writer wants to emphasize the authorship or the content.

REFERENCES IN APA STYLE

Example 7 is a reference list that illustrates how to format selected types of references in APA style. In it, the references are listed in alphabetical order, and each reference is formatted with a **hanging indent**. A paragraph with a hanging indent has its second line and all subsequent lines indented from the left margin.

Example 7: A Reference List in APA Format

References

Adams, E. S. (2014). Review of the origins of social sports theories. *Journal of Hypothetical Social Studies in Sports, 34,* 119–121.

Suresh, G., & Tewksbury, R. (2013). Locations of motor vehicle theft and recovery. *American Journal of Criminal Justice, 38,* 200–215. doi 10.1007/s12103-012-9161-7

U.S. Travel Association. (2013). *Senate Judiciary Approves Immigration Bill with Important Travel Facilitation Provisions.* Washington DC: U.S. Travel Association. Retrieved from https://www.ustravel.org/news/pressreleases/senate-judiciary-approves-immigration-billimportant -travel-facilitation-provisi

Viceroy, S. J., & Salinas, J. (2013). *The little book of big words* (2nd ed.). Any City, NC: False Hopes Press.

West, F. A., Tobble, S., & Chin, C. C. (2012). Life as observed from below. In J. Doe, M.M. Bush, and V.N. Carter (Eds.), *Observations of New York.* New York: Pretend Publishers.

The first two references in Example 7 are for journal articles. The seven elements contained in the journal article references are typically the follwing:

1. Author's name inverted. Only initials are used for first and middle names.
2. Year of publication enclosed in parentheses.
3. Title of journal article (no quotation marks).
4. Title of journal *in italics*.
5. Volume number, which is *34* in the first reference, in italics.[2]
6. Issue numbers are almost always omitted in APA style.[3]
7. Page numbers; for example, 119–121 in the first reference.[4]

The second reference in Example 7 (Suresh & Tewksbury) illustrates a listing for a journal article with two authors. Both authors' names are inverted, with the last name first and then the first name initial followed by a period. Note that instead of the word *and*, an ampersand (&) is used between the authors' names. This reference is also available on the Internet, which is indicated by the DOI number. To identify a DOI, go to www.doi.org, type in a valid DOI, and the source of the article will be identified. The DOI number can also be used in the search field of library searches to find a specific article.

The third reference (U.S. Travel Association) illustrates a document written by an organization and published on the web. It includes the date of retrieval from the Internet.

The next reference (Viceroy & Salinas) in Example 7 is for the second edition of a book, and the last reference is for a book.

See APA's *Publication Manual* or the website devoted to APA style (https://www.apastyle.org/) for additional information on formatting many other types of reference materials such as theses and dissertations as well as newspaper and magazine articles, and online sources.

■ NOTES

1. The uppercase letters *DOI* are used when discussing digital object identifiers. However, in an APA reference list, the lowercase is used.
2. Typically, Volume 1 refers to the first year of publication, Volume 2 refers to the second year of publication, and so on.
3. In the rare case in which page numbers are not consecutively numbered throughout a volume, the issue number should be included. See the *Publication Manual* for details.
4. Unlike ASA style, APA style does not use elided (abbreviated) numbers.

AN INTRODUCTION TO ASA STYLE

Topics 18 and 19 discussed the reasons that academic writing acknowledges the work of others through *citation*. This appendix provides a few basic elements of the style that is most commonly followed in sociology and related disciplines. The American Sociological Association publishes a style guide (called the *American Sociological Association Style Guide*) in which a comprehensive set of rules is presented. Short guides can be found for free on the association's website devoted to this topic, https://www.asanet.org/. Most college and university libraries also offer further tutorials and helpful abbreviated guides, and guides from many different colleges and universities can be found in a quick Google search for ASA style.

While different styles accomplish the task of citation differently, most citation systems work by "tagging" the text in place with some shorthand marker. This marker indicates to the reader that information in that sentence came from a source that the author is going to provide. This in-text citation may be a number or, in many cases, it is the last name of the author(s) and a year in parentheses. The latter style is called an "author–date" method and this is the style that ASA uses.

The shorthand from the in-text citation can then be matched with an entry in the bibliography at the end of the paper. In the bibliography, the full information is given: name, year, title, publication, volume number, page numbers, and possibly a digital object identifier, or DOI, which is a permanent number tagged to the paper and indexed so it is easy to find in digital archives.[1] For each unique in-text citation, there should be a full bibliographic reference at the end of the manuscript. In author–date styles, it is important that the "shorthand" in the in-text citation matches the first word in the alphabetized bibliography so the reader can easily pair the two and find the indicated source.

IN-TEXT CITATION IN ASA STYLE

Example 1 illustrates an *in-text citation*, in which the last name of the author being cited and the year of publication are placed in parentheses at the end of a sentence in the text. It differs from APA style in that there is no comma between name and year.

Example 1: An In-Text Citation for a Single Author

New data suggest that the influence of the mass media on social norms and customs is growing very rapidly (Doe 2013).

Example 2 illustrates ASA style for an in-text citation of a source with two authors.

Example 2: An In-Text Citation of a Source with Two Authors

The influence of peer group pressure on bullying behavior by girls needs more large-scale investigations (Edwards and Jones 2013).

If a source with **one or two authors** is cited more than once in a given manuscript, it should be cited in the same way each time. However, when there are **three authors** of a given source, the first time the authors are cited, all names are used. Then, in subsequent citations, only the first author's last name followed by "et al." is used, as illustrated in Example 3A and 3B.

Example 3A: First Time the Source with Three Authors Is Cited

More research is needed on the origins of gender-role socialization (Washington, Yu, and Galvan 2013).

Example 3B: The Second and Subsequent Times the Source Is Cited

Large-scale research on gender-role socialization is relatively rare (Washington et al. 2013).

When a source being cited has **four or more** authors, use "et al." the first and all subsequent times the source is cited. Often, two or more sources are in substantial agreement. For instance, there might be three sources with data indicating that the XYZ program is strongly supported by most parents. These three sources may be cited within a single set of parentheses, as illustrated in Example 4. Note that semicolons are used to separate sources and that the sources are listed in alphabetical order.

Example 4: Three Sources Cited Within a Single Set of Parentheses

In three recent surveys, a majority of parents expressed strong support for the XYZ program (Black 2012; Brown et al. 2011; White and Bright 2013).

When the source is a group such as a professional organization, government agency, corporation, or similar entity, cite its authorship using the full name of the group, as shown in Example 5.

Example 5: Full Name of an Organization Cited

The origins of the BEST program have been traced "as far back as the 1920s" (Association for Hypothetical Studies 2012:7–8).

When an author quotes directly from a source, the author should include the page number(s) in the in-text citation. Illustrated in Example 5 above, the page numbers (7–8) appear immediately after the colon without a space and without an abbreviation for the word *page*. This is also done when an author wants to call attention to a particular part of a source.

At times, the authors' last names become part of a sentence, while the year of publication remains parenthetical. Typically, the authors' last names become the subject of a sentence as illustrated in Example 6A and 6B, which contains the same information as Example 3A and 3B.

Example 6A: First Time the Source Is Cited

Washington, Yu, and Galvan (2013) claim that more research is needed on the origins of gender-role socialization.

Example 6B: The Second and Subsequent Times the Source Is Cited

Washington et al. (2013) point out that large-scale research on gender-role socialization is relatively rare.

You can see non-parenthetical citations emphasize the authorship by making the authors' names more prominent than parenthetical citations do. Neither is right or wrong. The decision on which one to use depends on whether the writer wants to emphasize the authorship or the content.

REFERENCES IN ASA STYLE

Example 7 is a reference list that illustrates how to format selected types of references in ASA style. In it, the references are listed in alphabetical order, and each reference is formatted with a **hanging indent**. A paragraph with a hanging indent has its second line and all subsequent lines indented from the left margin.

Example 7: A Reference List in APA format

References

Adams, Eric S. 2014. "Review of the Origins of Social Sports Theories." *Journal of Hypothetical Social Studies in Sports*, 34(2):119–21.

Suresh, Geetha and Richard Tewksbury. 2013. "Locations of Motor Vehicle Theft and Recovery." *American Journal of Criminal Justice*, 38(2):200–15. doi 10.1007/ s12103-012-9161-7.

U.S. Travel Association. 2013. "Senate Judiciary Approves Immigration Bill with Important Travel Facilitation Provisions." Washington DC: U.S. Travel Association. Retrieved June 11, 2013 (https://www.ustravel.org/news/press-releases/ senate-judiciary-approves-immigration-bill-important-travel-facilitation-provisi).

Viceroy, Steven J. and José Salinas. 2013. *The Little Book of Big Words*. 2nd ed. Any City, NC: False Hopes Press.

West, Fred A., Steve Tobble, and Catherine C. Chin. 2012. "Life as Observed from Below." Pp. 12–20 in *Motivations of Successful Professors*, edited by J. Doe, M.M. Bush, and V.N. Carter. New York: Pretend Publishers.

The first two sources in Example 7 are for journal articles. The first one (Adams) illustrates a reference for a journal article with only one author. The seven elements included in the journal reference are:

1. Author's name inverted.
2. Year of publication.
3. Title of journal article in "quotation marks."

4. Title of journal in *italics*.
5. Volume number, which is 34 in the first reference. (Typically, Volume 1 refers to the first year of publication; Volume 2 refers to the second year of publication; and so on.)
6. Issue number in parentheses immediately followed by a colon (typically, there are 4 to 12 issues per year). In the first reference, the issue number is 2, which indicates it is the second issue of the year.
7. Page numbers (119–21 in the first reference), which are elided (contain an abbreviation). The "21" stands for 121.

The second reference in Example 7 (Suresh and Tewksbury) illustrates a listing for a journal article with two authors. Only the name of the first author (Suresh) is inverted. Also the word *and* is used between the authors' names.[2] In addition to being published in a journal, the second reference is also available on the web, which is indicated by a DOI number. It is possible to go to www.doi.org, type in a valid DOI, and the source of the article will be identified. The DOI number can also be used in the search field of library searches to find a specific article.

The third reference (U.S. Travel Association) illustrates a document written by an organization and published on the web. It includes the date of retrieval from the web.

The next reference (Viceroy and Salinas) in Example 7 is for the second edition of a book, and the last reference, which has three authors, is also for a book.

See the *ASA Style Guide* for additional information on other types of reference materials. Check out the PDF short guide to ASA style provided by the American Sociological Association at https://www.asanet.org/sites/default/files/savvy/documents/teaching/pdfs/Quick_Tips_for_ASA_Style.pdf, search Google for ASA style resources, check out your library resources, or ask a reference librarian.

■ NOTES

1. The uppercase letters *DOI* are used when discussing digital object identifiers. However, in an ASA reference list, the lowercase is used.
2. APA uses the symbol *&* instead of the word *and*.

INDEX

Note: Page numbers in italic indicate a figure or table on the corresponding page.